The Hitchhiker's Guide to VMS

An Unsupported-Undocumented-Can-Go-Away-At-Any-Time Feature of VMS

By Bruce Ellis

The software described in this book is subject to change at any time and should not be construed as a commitment by the author, Professional Press, or Digital Equipment Corporation. Although all code is tested before publication, the publisher and the author are not liable for any damage that the utilities might do to your system.

The characters and events described in this book are purely fictional. Any likeness to actual individuals or events is purely coincidental.

Printed in the United States of America.

Cover design by Tom Owen.
Illustrations by Jim Serfass.

Library of Congress Cataloging-in-Publication Data

Ellis, Bruce, 1956-
The hitchhiker's guide to VMS : an unsupported-undocumented-can-go-away-at-any-time feature of VMS / by Bruce Ellis
p. cm.
ISBN 1-878956-00-0
1. VAX/VMS (Computer operating system) I. Title.
QA76.76.063E48 1990
005.4'44—dc20 90-47783
CIP

Please address comments and questions to the publisher:
Professional Press Books
101 Witmer Road
Horsham, PA 19044
(215) 957-1500 FAX (215) 957-1050

Table of Contents

Figures

Preface

About seven years ago, I was teaching a VMS Internals course and, after covering one topic, I asked for questions. When there were none, I pleaded for any questions on any subject. Someone blurted out, "The meaning of life?" Before I could respond, out came the response from a couple of students, "Forty-two." This was my introduction to Douglas Adams and his famous *The Hitchhiker's Guide to the Galaxy*.

I later read the series and thoroughly enjoyed the four-part "trilogy." As an educator, the notion of a book with all the answers to all possible questions was intriguing. I mulled over the idea of writing a book, based on an electronic book that had all the answers to all possible questions on VAX/VMS. I discussed the idea with Rex Jaeschke (Dr. C), and he convinced me that it was a possibility.

Over time, I connected with Karen Detwiler and *VAX PROFESSIONAL*. After another year of playing around with ideas, the first episode of "The Hitchhiker's Guide to VMS" appeared in the June, 1989 issue of *VAX PROFESSIONAL*. A year after the first article was published, I finished writing the series.

The intent of the *Guide* is to entertain, educate, and inform. It is not intended to replace *VMS Internals and Data Structures* by Kenah, Goldenberg, and Bate, but rather to complement it as a tool. Although the *Guide* is less complete, hopefully it is more directed and fun and easy to read.

Over the years, I have often been asked how I got to know so much about VMS. I still have much to learn, but my current knowledge is based on two major activities: researching the many questions posed by my students, and "doing" things with VMS.

The book places the main character, Billy Bitsenbites, in the role of student and the *Guide* in the role of an electronic Socrates. Billy asks questions as a student might. Although Billy appears to take a few quantum leaps, his questions develop as his knowledge grows.

Most importantly, Billy "does" VMS. He writes code and solves VMS problems. This book contains more than 15 complete programs. The programs are intended as learning tools, not as products. You will find that additional refinement can be done on all of them. But they do work and illustrate several different system programming techniques.

The code has been tested through Version 5.3 of VMS. Future releases may cause specific pieces of the code to break, but if the *Guide* has served its purpose, you, like Billy does in Episode 3, will be able to make any required corrections. In fact, the ZAPPER.MAR program (see Figure 32) was originally written under version 3 of VMS and has undergone only minor changes since its original version.

Note that the first two articles have pre-version 5.2 restrictions. They were included because they are fundamentally sound, regardless of version, and illustrate the evolutionary process of system programming.

The topics were spread as evenly as possible over the three major subsystems of VMS. You will find three or four episodes addressing the memory management, process and scheduling, and I/O subsystems. Some of the episodes span several subsystems.

The programs illustrate many concepts and techniques for VMS system programming, including synchronization, queueing ASTs, allocating pool, user-written system services, and the change mode to kernel system service. The table of contents lists the technical concepts described in each episode.

Issues of security are bound to come up with regard to activities described in the book. The first and last episodes deal with taking privileges needed to perform required tasks. Have we opened the proverbial Pandora's Box? Perhaps.

It is important to note that both of these "break-ins" could have been prevented. The first break-in required physical access to the console. The second break-in was based on the abuse of a user-written system service that could have been better designed. Each break-in teaches valuable system programming and security lessons.

Note that the author does not promote the hacking of computer systems. Hopefully, by informing the community of the potential dangers of careless system management, we can all prevent future break-ins.

Finally, the path to a thorough knowledge of VMS requires research and working with the system. I hope this book helps you along that path.

Bruce Ellis
July 1990

Acknowledgments

Thanks to:

All the students, instructors, members of the DECUS community, and members of VMS engineering who have helped in furthering my knowledge of VMS.

Douglas Adams for providing *The Hitchhiker's Guide to the Galaxy*.

Bob Dylan, Joan Armitrading, Lou Reed, the Talking Heads, Pink Floyd, Neal Young, Tom Waits, and Jimi Hendrix for providing the music that made it possible to type through the many nights.

Dave Miller and Kevin Kennelly for keeping the systems going.

The *VAX PROFESSIONAL* Review Board members (Kevin Barkes, Bob Curley, Bill Law, Dave MacArthur, Bob McCaskey, John McGlinchey, and Phil Naecker) for the comments, corrections, and recommendations that helped form the book.

My, VASTEK partners Dave MacArthur and Dennis O'Brien for lending an ear and lots of support.

Special thanks to:

Rex Jaeschke for getting the project rolling.

Tracy Schreiber for her thorough technical analysis and recommendations on improving each episode of the *Guide*.

Karen Detwiler for her cooperation, understanding, and guidance through the editing process.

My brother, Jim Ellis, for shooting the photo for the back cover.

Sarah, Kellie, Jamey, and Jessica for their love and support through the demands of completing this book.

This book is dedicated to

my wife Sarah,

my children Kellie, Jamey, and Jessica

and to the memory of my uncle H.K. “Corky” Ellis.

"If it's a good idea, go ahead and do it. It's much easier to apologize than it is to get permission."

Grace Hopper

Episode 1

Stealth Mode

It was late one evening as Billy Bitsenbites stared at his terminal, examining the characters on his screen. Every time the program ran, the call to SYS$QIO printed out a few nonsense characters. He used the debugger and played games with the string but could not get the format correct.

"If I were given sufficient training, I would have been able to get this done a long time ago," he thought to himself. "That Dennis Cutlery! He impresses management, and they give him all the training so he can do a terrible job managing the system. In the meantime, I have unrealistic deadlines and get no training, and ramp-up time on this project is slowing everything down."

He banged the keyboard awhile and realized that the string should have been passed by reference instead of by descriptor.

"Real consistent, guys! Ninety percent of the services need descriptors, and this darn QIO wants a stupid string address."

He was reasonably satisfied that his program worked and reasonably ticked off at Dennis Cutlery for not helping with this earlier in the day. Cutlery was responsible for helping the users and managing the system. He was, at best, mediocre at both of these activities. Bitsenbites lay his head down on his desk, thinking of how nice it would be to get even with Cutlery for getting in his way. But his last thought, before nodding off, was that he did not know enough about VMS to really get even. That, of course, was before he was introduced to a book (of sorts) called *The Hitchhiker's Guide to VMS*.

Billy fell into a deep sleep, from sheer exhaustion. After a few hours, he awoke upset that he had been snoozing at work on his time. He started to pack his things to head home, when he saw a ghost-like figure, wearing a natty brown leisure suit, walking toward him. The man was on the taller side, bald, with a broad face. He walked up to Billy, handing him what appeared to be a book, and said, "Are you looking for this?"

The man walked off, saying, "Remember, our primary goal is not quantity. It's quality, and with quality, quantity will come."

"Wha-?" thought Billy. "Who was that guy? He seemed to be a ghost." Billy could not have been closer to the truth. He looked down at the book. The cover read *The Hitchhiker's Guide to VMS*.

Billy picked up the gray tome and examined the blue print. At the bottom of the cover was etched the following, not-so-reassuring, statement: "An unsupported, undocumented, can-go-away-at-any-time feature of VMS." He opened the book and heard a whirring noise, as an LCD display lighted on the inner cover of the book and a microcassette tape spun in the lower righthand corner of the encasement. The tape was a

boot media called TM42, son of TK70, grandson of TK50, great grandson of TU58 and great great grandson of DECtape. Some things never change, much.

After the bootstrap procedure had completed, the book both printed and spoke the following introduction, "*Welcome to* The Hitchhiker's Guide to VMS, *a tool for system friendly users. Please enter any questions at the lower keyboard. We are here to serve and protect.*"

An interesting aspect to the *Guide* was that although it was developed with the ability to speak, it could not listen to the human voice, a trait indigenous to the typical Digital sales representative. Some, however, believe that Digital came across a shipment of HP calculator keyboards and not knowing what to do with them, built them into the book to relieve surplus inventory, a trait indigenous to components of the console subsystems on the VAX.

Billy tried to think up a clever question for the book to answer. Instead he entered, "Who are you?"

The book responded, "*The Hitchhiker's Guide to VMS* has the following entry on *The Hitchhiker's Guide to VMS: The VMS operating system is becoming a more complex beast as time passes. This is evident in the fact that fewer people seem to know what is going on underneath the surface. In fact, rumor has it that some of the developers no longer understand what is happening within the subsystems that they are working on.*

"When things get this complicated, people invent myths to make sense of their uncertainty. The myths can be difficult to prove valid. Through time, some of the myths are no longer challenged and become generally accepted as fact. As no reference guide historically existed that would answer all questions a user might have, the user went to many sources for answers. He commonly accepted as valid the answer that made the symptoms of his problem go away, without deeper investigation.

"The Guide *was developed by computer hitchhikers (sometimes referred to as hackers), who would work their way in and out of systems, as the singular definitive source to the VMS operating system. Entries made to the* Guide *by these hitchhikers are all facts. The* Guide *makes the claim that any behavior proven to be myth will be patched into the executive so as to indeed become factual.*

"The book itself was designed within the hardware architecture of the DECbook 9370. The 70 comes from the seven CPUs tied together in a symmetric multiprocessing version of VMS. Nobody seems to quite know where the 93 comes from. (Although with proper understanding of the

Guide, *in the wrong hands, it could be the true VAXkiller.)*

"The backplane of the 9370 is the fast bus interconnect (FBI). The FBI is a proprietary bus that operates at either 24 or 42 megabytes per second. (No one knows for sure which is the real speed, because the dyslexic technical writer entered both speeds in different places in the specification.) Mass storage is contained on writable CDs, so that the book can automatically correct any errors or changes in the content.

"Are you interested in the software interface?"

"Later," Billy entered. "How do I get ..."

"Even?" the *Guide* asked.

Had Billy asked about the software, he would have found out that the *Guide* supported an intuitional database. Based on the user's personality, the book would guess what he would type next. The advantage of doing this from a performance standpoint was that processes on all other CPUs could be busy gathering and formatting the response before the question was entered completely. This gave the user instantaneous response, if the *Guide*'s intuition was correct. The *Guide* boasted a 95 percent hit rate, which probably says more about the programmer's personality than the intuitive capabilities of the *Guide*.

Astounded by the guess, Billy entered, "Yes."

"Getting even is an easy and trivial task," responded the book. "However, getting even and not getting caught requires a little more work as well as a better general understanding of the system. You could bury your code within the heart of the operating system, but, prior to this, you must be able to operate in privileged mode without your process being easily detected. In other words, your process must operate in stealth mode."

These were a lot of concepts for Billy to pick up in one blast. "Whoa!" he entered. "Before we go too far, what exactly ..."

"Is a process?" the *Guide* finished. Billy hit <Return> in acknowledgment.

"In two words, it is a scheduling entity."

Upset by the terse reply, Billy entered, "Turn this ..."

"It is off."

He followed with, "How about a little more than two words?"

"The process is a scheduling entity that supports the execution of images, or more generally called programs. Three contexts form a process, including hardware context, software context and memory management context.

"The hardware context is a description of the process to the VAX. It includes the 16 general purpose registers (i.e., RO- R11, AP, FP, PC and four stack pointers consisting of one for kernel, executive, supervisor and user access mode), the processor status longword (PSL), the memory management registers (P0 and P1 base and length registers) and the asynchronous system trap (AST) level register, which describes the mode at which ASTs are deliverable. This information is stored in a data structure called the hardware process control block (PCB) when the process is not in the current (CUR) state. It is in the CPU registers when the process is current.

"The memory management context of the process comprises two virtual address spaces, i.e., P0 and P1 space. These are the process' private address spaces. Data and code that must be shared by multiple processes typically is stored in system (S0) space.

"P0 space is the program region and stays around for the life of the current image. When the image runs down, P0 space goes away and will be remapped during the execution of the next image. The first page of P0 space is inaccessible to guard against addressing mode and argument passing problems. In fact, when the program attempts to touch these locations, an access violation fault is generated.

"Also mapped to P0 space are any shareable images (typically run-time libraries) against which the image is linked, plus the debugger and the traceback handler. The debugger and traceback handler are mapped into P0 space, unless the image has been linked with the /NOTRACE qualifier. The traceback handler is the guy who gives you those nice pretty error messages that include the line number and call sequence of that error. Although this information is nice for debugging, unless you are using secretaries to debug your programs, generally you do not want to release a piece of code for production use until it has been debugged fully and linked /NOTRACE.

"P1 space is the program region and stays around for the life of the process. The initial P1 space is built at process creation time. P1 space contains plenty of information, including:

1. The four per process stacks (user, supervisor, executive and kernel).
2. Record management services (RMS) buffers and data structures.
3. The command language interpreter (CLI). Digital supplies three of these: Digital command language (DCL), the monitor confusion (just kidding, actually console) routines (MCR), and the Bourne (again) shell.

4. A table of channel control blocks (CCBs) that are created at channel assignment time and used to locate device specific data structures.
5. The process allocation region, which is used to store process logicals, an image list and windowing context. This region is sized by the SYSGEN parameter CTLPAGES.
6. The CLI symbol table, which is sized by the parameter CLISYMTBL.
7. The per process common area, which can be used to pass information from one program run to the next using the run-time library procedure LIB$GET_COMMON.

"P1 space includes other context areas as well.

"The process' virtual address space is described by a data structure called the process header (PHD). The PHD contains the P0 and P1 page tables that map the respective address spaces, the working set list that maps the virtual addresses that are currently valid (i.e., that you can touch without a page fault) for the process, and the process section table that describes the disk location of pages in the image file.

"The PHDs are allocated out of the balance slot area of S0 space, which is limited to BALSETCNT (a SYSGEN parameter) of memory resident PHDs. If more processes exist on the system than BALSETCNT + 2, because of process entry slots for the null and swapper process (yes Virginia, the trappings for the null still exist), then we must swap to free up balance slots. You also might note that the hardware PCB, containing the hardware context when not current, is stored in the PHD.

"The software context of the process is a description of the process to VMS. This description includes the process name, user name, account name, process ID, user identification code (UIC), privilege mask, current and base scheduling priorities, quotas, event flags, terminal name, and so on. The primary process software context is stored in a data structure called the software process control block (PCB). (By the way, the acronym PCB refers to the software PCB. The hardware PCB always will be prefaced with *hardware*.) The software PCB is the heart of a process and from it, you can locate all other process data structures. Some software context also is stored in the PHD, in particular, accounting information.

"A detached process is a process with no owner, i.e., one that can stay around even after the creator has been deleted. A subprocess is an owned process that shares pooled and deductible quotas and allocated devices with the creator. Subprocesses are forced to die when the creator is killed. The combination of a detached process and all owned subprocesses is called a job.

"A data structure called the job information block (JIB) contains job-related software context information. This information includes the user and account names, the pooled and deductible quotas, a list of structures called mount list entries that describe privately mounted volumes, and a mask describing the primary/secondary hours and days, so we can terminate any jerk logged in after these specified times."

Bitsenbites thought about what makes up a process. A process, it seems, is made up of three data structures: the PCB making up the process portion of the software context, the JIB making up the job portion of the process context, and the PHD forming the memory management context while also containing another data structure called the hardware PCB that stores the hardware context of a process when the process is not current. He suddenly realized that something was missing.

"What is a data structure?" he queried the *Guide*.

"A data structure is an array of contiguous bytes that describes some operating system entity, such as a process, an I/O request, a lock request, and so forth. The array of bytes is broken into fields that describe some aspect of the process, the event flag to set on completion of an I/O request, the lock ID of the lock request, and so on. The data structures are allocated dynamically and must be located through some sort of pointer.

"The fields are located at a specific position relative to the beginning of the data structure. For example, many of the data structures are maintained in a doubly linked list, in which case, the first field, 0 bytes from the beginning of the data structure, would be a forward link pointer to the next data structure in the list or pointing back to the listhead for the last item in the list.

"Because addresses are a longword (i.e., four bytes) in size, the next available field would be four bytes into the data structure. In a doubly linked structure, this would be the backlink pointer, pointing to the previous structure in the list, or, in the case of the first item, pointing back to the listhead.

"The next field would be eight bytes into the structure. This field, typically, contains the size or the amount of dynamic memory used to hold the data structure. We need this information so that we can properly return the structure back to the pool (or ocean, as the case may be) of dynamic memory when we no longer need to describe the process or I/O request, and so on. The size field is one word (i.e., two bytes) in size, so the next available field would be 10 bytes into the data structure.

"This field is normally the type field, describing the type of data structure occupying the memory. This is used as a sanity check, to guarantee that we can detect when some hoser places an I/O request packet on a scheduling queue, before we get into big trouble. The next available field would be 11 bytes into the structure, because the size field is a byte in size."

After pondering this response, Billy asked the *Guide*, "Okay, let me see if I'm getting this straight. To operate in stealth mode, I am going to have to figure out the data structures used by the SHOW commands to locate and identify my process, and somehow change those structures so they do not see me in quite the same way. Is that the general idea?"

"Very good. You may officially place the propeller back on your beanie," the *Guide* responded.

"Some day, I am going to meet the jerks who programmed you and get even," Billy blasted back. "Now, how about some insight as to what to poke and how to do it?"

"To do this will require some MACRO coding. Do you know MACRO?"

"Kinda."

"The first piece of a program that you would need would be what?"

"An entry mask," Billy responded, "like:"

```
.ENTRY NO_USER,^m<>
```

"Good. And the last piece?"

"An .END statement, like .END NO_USER, to tell the assembler where to stop and where the program starts," Billy proudly replied.

"We're cooking," the *Guide* cheered. "Now to be able to massage the data structures, we are going to have to get into kernel mode. To do that, we will use the $CMKRNL system service. This service supports two arguments, for now the most important being the ROUTIN argument that defines the subroutine that you want to call in kernel mode."

"To call the system service I could use the _S or _G form of call, if I remember correctly." Billy added, "How about $CMKRNL_S ROUTIN=BLAST_IT?"

"Add a RET at the end, and you are finished with the main program and only have to write the subroutine," the *Guide* chimed in.

"Well, I have the entry mask and the return statement, and from the PCB, I can find out all about the process. But how do I find the PCB?"

"The beauty of the $CMKRNL system service is that R4 points to the PCB upon entry."

"Okay, I have that, but where do I go from there?"

"Well, the $SHOW USERS command knows that you are a user, because you have a terminal associated with your process."

"How do I determine where in the PCB the terminal field is located?" Billy asked.

"The VMS developers used a symbolic naming convention to describe offsets into data structures. To define the offsets into the PCB, there is a macro $PCBDEF; for other structures, there would be a $xyzDEF macro, where xyz would be the data structure type. These macros are defined in the library SYS$LIBRARY:LIB.MLB. You can include the library with the statement:

```
.LIBRARY   /SYS$LIBRARY:LIB.MLB/
```

"You can find a textual description of the fields in the file SYS$LIBRARY:LIB.REQ. For now, note that the terminal field is stored as an ASCII counted string at PCB$T_TERMINAL. The T after the $ is designating that this is a text string."

"So I could use:

```
CLRB PCB$T_TERMINAL(R4)
```

to say that there is no terminal associated with my process?"

"Yes," replied the *Guide*.

"What about the interactive job count, though?" asked Billy.

"Very good insight. The interactive job count is stored in the global memory location SYS$GW_IJOBCNT. The GW is telling you that this is a global word location and, to be able to reference this location, you must link with the system symbol table, SYS$SYSTEM:SYS.STB. You can use the .LINK directive to include this automatically at link time.

"You also must signal the process deletion sequence not to decrement this count at log out time. You can clear the interactive bit in the status field of the PCB to do this.

"The interactive bit can be accessed using the symbol PCB$M_INTER if you are going to use a mask-oriented instruction like BICL, or PCB$V_INTER if you are using a variable bit instruction like BBCC. The status longword is located at PCB$L_STS."

"What about the accounting record?" Billy asked.

"Are you sure you need me?" asked the *Guide*. "To bypass an accounting record, you also will want to set the PCB$M_NOACNT bit in the status field. You might want to see whether you are a subprocess by checking the owner field, i.e., PCB$L_OWNER. If the field contains a 0, no process owns your current process."

Billy created the file STEALTH.MAR, assembled and linked it (see Figure 1). He tried to run the program and got the error message, "No privilege for attempted operation."

"Hey, Book," Billy entered, "how do I get CMKRNL privilege?"

"Are you in the computer room?" the *Guide* asked.

"Yes," replied Billy.

"Then go up to the console and enter:

```
^p
HALT
B/1
```

"Got it," typed Billy. "What do I do at the SYSBOOT prompt?"

"Enter:

```
SET UAFALTERNATE 1
CONTINUE
```

"Assuming that there is no SYSUAFALT file or logical name, you should be able to log in at the console with any username and password and be fully privileged."

"It worked." Billy pounded on the keyboard. He ran his program and did the $SHOW USERS. Voilà, he saw no users and an interactive job count of 0 (see Figure 2). He then did a $SHOW SYSTEM and saw he was still there.

"Hey, I am still showing up in $SHOW SYSTEM," Billy banged into the *Guide*.

"Take it easy," replied the *Guide*. "Change your process name to something inconspicuous, like SYMBIONT_0042."

"All right," concluded Billy.

WHAT HAPPENS next? Will Billy get even? What new and wonderful things will Billy learn about VMS in the process? Will his code stand up to the vigors of version 5.2?

Process Control Block

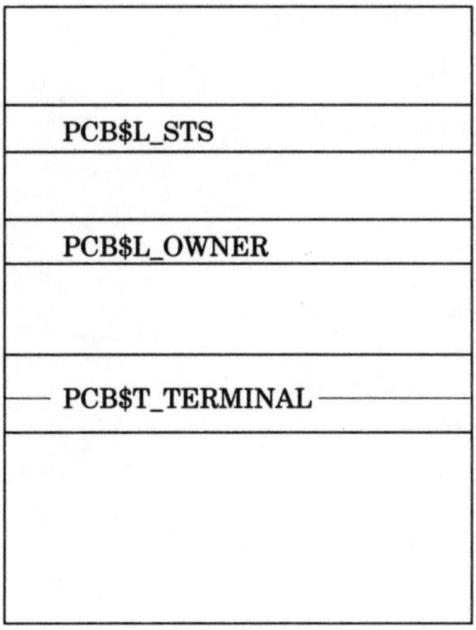

PCB$L_STS
PCB$L_OWNER
PCB$T_TERMINAL

Fields affected in process control block by STEALTH.MAR

Figure 1.

```
$ typ stealth.mar
;*****************************************************************************
;       Program stealth
;       Function: Remove our process from show users display
;       Author: Billy Bitsenbites (Bruce Ellis)
;*****************************************************************************

        .library        /sys$library:lib.mlb/
        .link   /sys$system:sys.stb/
        $pcbdef

        .entry  no_user,^m<>
;*****************************************************************************
;       Get into kernel mode and have fun
;*****************************************************************************
        $cmkrnl_s       routin=blast_it
        ret
        .entry  blast_it,^m<>
        tstl    pcb$l_owner(r4)                 ;Subprocess?
        bneq    outta_here                      ;if so, scram
        bbcc    #pbc$v_inter,pcb$l_sts(r4),-    ;Have we been here before?
                 outta_here                     ; if so, scram. Otherwise,
                                                ; we clear the interactive
                                                ; bit so interactive count is
                                                ; not decremented on logout
        ctrb    pcb$t_terminal(r4)              ;Else clear terminal string
                                                ; count, thus removing from
                                                ; $SHOW USERS
        decw    g^sys$gw_ijobcnt                ;Decrement the interactive
                                                ; job count so show users does
                                                ; not look funny
        bisl    #pcb$m_noacnt,pcb$l_sts(r4)     ;No account process
outta_here:
        movl    #ss$_normal,r0
        ret
        .end    no_user
$ mac stealth
$
$ link stealth
$
```

Figure 2. Output from running STEALTH.MAR.

```
$sh us

                     VAX/VMS Interactive Users
                      30-MAR-1989 22:02:34.95
              Total number of interactive users = 1

Username         Process Name     PIB          Terminal
BITS             Bitsenbites      23200846     VTA450          LTA51
$
$
$ r stealth
$
$
$ sh users

                     VAX/VMS Interactive Users
                      30-MAR-1989 22:02:51.76
              Total number of interactive users = 0
$
$
$ lo
  BITS           logged out at 30-MAR-1989 22:03:11.32
Local -011- Session 1 disconnected from VAXCLUSTER
$acco/since="30-MAR-1989-20:03"/user=bits
Date/Time                Type      Subtype          Username     ID
30-MAR-1989 21:51:13     PROCESS   INTERACTIVE      BITS         232008A4

Source  Status
VTA448  1000000001
```

Episode 2

Fun with Pool and ASTs

Billy Bitsenbites sat in awe of the power that lay before his fingertips. The portals to the universe of VMS were open, and the system was exposed in a way that he had never before dreamt.

He had change mode to kernel (CMKRNL) privilege. He was virtually invisible. But something was missing. He should be able to do something useful.

He thought about how poorly Dennis Cutlery managed the system. Cutlery was not that sharp, illustrated by how slowly the system responded. Billy had seen many idle processes sitting around with large working sets. As the load on the system increased, it eventually ran out of memory and the performance dragged.

He wondered if there was some way of freeing up memory before the processes ran out. The thought came to him that he might be able to force some of the idle processes to be swapped out to disk.

Billy picked up *The Hitchhiker's Guide to VMS*. The electronic tome whirred and clicked as he opened it. He entered the following question:

"Hey *Guide*, how do I force a process to be swapped out on a VMS system?"

"You don't," responded the *Guide*.

"What do you mean, you don't?" queried Billy.

"Well, if you really wanted to do this, you could rewrite the swapper or possibly play games with SYSGEN parameters."

"Why would I not want to do this?" Billy wondered.

"Paging is generally a more effective solution for response time oriented tuning. In fact, if you look at the version 3 release of VMS, you'll see that the development team introduced the notion of secondary trimming of process working sets down to the SYSGEN parameter SWPOUTPGCNT pages in size. This was because on slower machines with slower disks, swapping becomes very costly. In fact, the VAX 11/730 was introduced at the release of version 3, and swapping on it was roughly equivalent to death."

"Okay, let me explain the problem. I have a bunch of idle processes sitting around, tying up memory and eventually causing us to run out. I would like to get some of this memory back before we run out and the swapper goes nuts. Can you help me out on this?"

"Let me get this straight. You want to grab back some memory from an idle process?"

"Right."

The *Guide* continued, "Do you want to do this manually or continually?"

"For now, which would be easiest?"

"Manually," the *Guide* responded. "Have you thought of shrinking his working set and leaving him something to go on when he becomes active again?"

"What would be the advantage of doing this, over just swapping the guy out?"

"The pages that are swapped include only pages in the process' working set. The main body of the pages are swapped in the first phase of swapping. This first phase of swapping is not exceptionally costly, and there might be somewhat of a gain from a throughput viewpoint. The advantage is that the I/O operations here will tend to be grouped as a single large, virtually contiguous I/O. This will minimize the effects of rotational latency and seeking on the drive.

"The problems with this approach tend to show up when we go to the second phase of swapping. The process header (PHD) is the data structure that supports the memory management structures including the process page tables, the working set list, and the process section table. The process header is allocated out of a pageable portion of system space, called the balance slot area. It is charged against the process' working set list and is not swapped with the main process body.

"The PHDs are the first candidates for swapping, if they describe swapped process bodies. If they are swapped, any memory references to pages on the free or modified page lists would be divorced, and a hard fault (i.e., one requiring I/O) would have to be performed to reclaim any of these pages, because the page table entries could no longer track these pages in memory. If you were to swap more than one process at a time, processes would be generating both paging and swapping I/Os. This would soon lead to abysmal performance characteristics."

Billy thought about this for a little bit. After making sense of what the book was saying, he said, "I get the message that an occasional swap probably is not going to kill the system, but this is not optimal ongoing behavior. I still would like to get the pages back from idle processes."

"Two system services allow for the reduction of a process working set. They are purge working set ($PURGWS) and the adjust working set list ($ADJWSL) system services."

"Thanks," Billy responded.

Billy grabbed a *System Services Reference Manual* and started digging for descriptions of the services. He read the descriptions and checked the arguments. Suddenly, a perplexed look came over his face.

"Hey, Book," he would have shouted if you could shout into a keyboard. "There are no arguments to specify the process whose working set you want to change. How do you do that?"

"You don't," answered the *Guide*. "The services only allow the adjustment of your own working set."

"Why did you send me on this wild goose chase?" Billy demanded.

"If you execute the service in the context of the other process, you can get him to adjust his own working set."

"Hold it. My code is going to execute in his context? I am going to become him?" Billy typed with astonishment.

"Right," the *Guide* chimed in. " 'Where ego, I go too,' Peter Gabriel once said."

Billy sat and contemplated this thought as a smile started to curl around his lips. He then banged in, "I kind of like this idea. How do I go about becoming him?"

"Do you know what an AST is?" the *Guide* asked.

"Sure, it's an asynchronous system trap," Billy proudly replied.

"That is similar to saying that a mutex is a mutual exclusion semaphore," the book countered, unamused. "Do you know what an asynchronous system trap is?"

"It's a subroutine that VMS will call when an asynchronous system service, like $QIO, completes."

"Pretty good," the *Guide* responded. "A little more generically, it's a subroutine that VMS calls asynchronously upon completion of an event. VMS also uses ASTs to get from one process context to another.

"Services like $GETJPI use ASTs to get into another process context to be able to access that process' private virtual address space, like P1 space. The name of the image that the process is currently running is stored in P1 space, and $GETJPI uses ASTs to obtain this information.

"Another example of VMS' use of ASTs is illustrated in the delete process system service ($DELPRC). In VMS, you can't really kill a process. You have to tap him on the shoulder and ask him to commit suicide. The reason for this technique is to guarantee that the process cleans up after itself, i.e., closes files, deassigns channels, and so on. The AST provides the tap on the shoulder.

"VMS also uses ASTs to get from system context back to process context. This is required when timers expire and I/O completes.

"ASTs come in two varieties:

1. Normal, which are called, run at interrupt priority level (IPL) 0 and can be delivered in any list access mode.
2. Special kernel ASTs, jumped to through a jump to subroutine (JSB) instruction, run at IPL 2."

"Air brakes, please. What is IPL?"

"IPL is a processor priority, used to block activities at that IPL and all lower IPLs. The VAX supports 32 IPLs. These IPLs are associated with interrupts. An interrupt is used to block the system and allow a piece of code, located through the system control block (SCB), to service the request corresponding to the interrupt. To keep track of where the system was running prior to the interrupt, the program counter (PC) and processor status longword (PSL) are saved on the stack for later restoration by the return from interrupt (REI) instruction, which will be used to dismiss the current interrupt.

"The IPLs are divided into two categories, that is, hardware requested, which ranges from IPL 16 to 31, and software requested, which ranges from IPL 0 to 15. Specific IPLs are associated with specific events. For instance, IPL 24 is used for clock interrupts (except on a MicroVAX, which uses IPL 22), IPL 20 to 23 are reserved for device interrupts, IPL 8 to 11 are used for fork processing, IPL 2 is used for AST delivery, and so on."

"Thanks, now back to ASTs. How do I go about queueing an AST?"

"First, you will have to allocate and fill in an AST control block (ACB). The ACB is laid out with the following fields:

```
ACB$L_ASTQFL      ;AST queue forward link
ACB$L_ASTQBL      ;AST queue backward link
ACB$W_SIZE        ;Amount of non-paged pool used to
                  ; store the ACB
ACB$B_TYPE        ;The dynamic structure type
```

```
ACB$B_RMOD        ;Request mode field. Bits <1:0>
                  ; define the mode. 0=Kernel, 1=Exec,
                  ; 2=Super, 3=User Bit 7 if set defines
                  ; this as a special kernel AST. Bit 6 if
                  ; set defines that quota has been charged.
                  ; Bit 5 if set says not to deallocate the
                  ; ACB. Bit 4 defines a piggyback special
                  ; kernel AST.
ACB$L_PID         ;The Process-Id of the process to receive
                  ; the AST.
ACB$L_AST         ;Address of the normal AST to call when the
                  ; AST is delivered.
ACB$L_ASTPRM      ;AST parameter to pass as the first argument
                  ; to the routine.
ACB$L_KAST        ;Address of the special kernel AST routine
                  ; to JSB to if the KAST bit is set in the
                  ; RMOD field.
```

"After the ACB has been filled in, all you have to do is stick the address of it in R5, stuff a boost class in R2, and JSB to SCH$QAST."

"Whoa," Billy entered quickly. "I have a few questions here. For starters, what is this boost class that you are talking about?"

"VMS provides boosts to processes that have had events reported. The events usually are related to some response time related issues, and the boosts allow the processes with more pressing events to run more quickly and float toward their base priority, currently, whenever they are rescheduled.

"Reportable events include process creation and terminal input completion which receive boosts of six added to the base priority of the process, terminal output which receives a boost of four, and non-terminal buffered I/O and direct I/O completion which receive boosts of two. There are other activities that will receive boosts of two or three.

"The macro $PRIDEF defines constants for boost classes. For instance, if you wanted the guy to run as quickly as possible, you might slam PRI$_TICOM into R2, and he would get the largest possible boost of six."

"I like that. Run my code and run it quick. Do you think I could get a priority boost delivered to my sales representative? Just kidding. If I remember correctly, my P0 and P1 space will be different from his, so to get VMS to locate my code, and for that matter the ACB, I must get them into system space. Any recommendations on how to go about doing that?"

"Two options are available in version 5 for getting code into system space. The more traditional approach would be to use non-paged dynamic memory, or as it is more commonly called, non-paged pool. Data structures that you need to keep around for awhile are allocated out of non-paged pool. When you are finished using the structure, it is deallocated and returned to the pool.

"The need for non-pageable pool is necessitated by code that runs at IPL 3 or greater. Page faults are process context activities. VMS assumes that a page fault occurring at an IPL greater than 2 was made in system context and issues a bug check. Non-paged pool prevents this behavior.

"VMS also traditionally loaded code that was contingent on your configuration into non-paged pool. Device drivers, CPU dependent code, the connection manager, and the distributed lock manager are all examples of code that is loaded into pool. In fact, in version 4 systems, the pool requirements went up substantially for VAXcluster support.

"At Spit Brook Road in Nashua, New Hampshire, there is a pond outside the VMS development building and a sign, saying NON-PAGED POOL, points to it. With the pool requirements since V4.0, they might have to set up a sign pointing about 50 miles to the east, stating NON-PAGED OCEAN. The modular executive might minimize the need for this sign.

“V5.0 supports the modular executive for maintainability. You could write an executive loadable image that would be loaded automatically at bootstrap time. This technique might be the way to go for a long-term solution, because the AST code could be accessible from modes other than executive and kernel. The space for the code also need not be allocated and deallocated. This is a more involved effort, so we will hold off on this technique and opt for the more traditional technique of allocating non-paged pool.

“To allocate a chunk of non-paged pool, you would JSB to the routine EXE$ALONONPAGED. The input to this routine requires that R1 contains the size of pool to be allocated. The process also should be running at least at IPL 2 to block process deletion. The output has R2 containing the address of the allocated pool.”

“So now all I have to do is convert the process ID (PID) that I get from $SHOW SYSTEM to binary, and I am in business. Right?”

“Wrong. The PID that you get from the $SHOW SYSTEM display is the extended PID, and the PID that you need is the internal PID.”

“What is the difference between the internal and extended PID?”

“When VMS boots, two tables are allocated from non-paged pool. The size of these tables is defined by the SYSGEN parameter MAXPROCESSCNT. One is an array of longwords, and the other is an array of words. The array of longwords is called the process control block (PCB) vector table. It is pointed to by the longword location SCH$GL_PCBVEC. The array of words is called the sequence vector table and is pointed to by the location SCH$GL_SEQVEC.

“The first longword in the PCB vector table is initialized to point to the null process’ PCB. The null’s PCB can be located through SCH$AR_NULLPCB. The second entry is initialized to point to the swapper’s PCB. The swapper’s PCB also can be located through SCH$AR_SWPPCB. All subsequent entries are initialized to point to the null’s PCB, indicating that they are free slots in the table.

“When a process is created, a free slot is located in the table and is set to point to the newly created process’ PCB. The index into the table forms the low word of the internal PID. With the index, you can locate the PCB of any given process.

“If we were to use only the index, you might run into synchronization problems. Let us say that you were trying to delete a process and before you typed in the index, the process whose index you were entering had gone away. The slot might be reused by a new process, maybe your boss’.

If you only used the index, you accidentally might delete the wrong process and possibly be looking for a new job.

"To guarantee uniqueness of the internal PID, the sequence vector table tracks how many times a slot in the PCB vector table has been used. The same index that was used in the PCB vector table is used as a word index in the sequence vector table. The slot in the sequence vector table tracks the number of times a slot in the PCB vector table has been used. The sequence number forms the high word of the internal PID. This combination guarantees a unique PID for the process systemwide.

"With the advent of VAXclusters in V4.0 of VMS, processes now maintain information in locking data structures on other systems in a VAXcluster. This change requires that PIDs be unique clusterwide.

"The connection manager maintains a cluster system ID (CSID) that uniquely identifies a node in a VAXcluster. This CSID is stored in the location SCH$GW_LOCALNODE for the local node. This is dumped into the high bits of the extended PID, the sequence number is sandwiched into the middle bits, and the index forms the low bits. The number of bits required to describe the index is defined by the maximum process index (stored in SCH$GL_MAXPIX), which is one less than the SYSGEN parameter MAXPROCESSCNT.

"To perform the conversion from extended PID to internal PID, a couple of routines can be used, namely, EXE$EPID_TO_IPID and EXE$NAMPID. EXE$NAMPID is probably the most effective one to use and is used by most VMS process control services."

"How do you guarantee the process does not go away while you are building the ACB?" Billy questioned.

"To guarantee synchronization prior to V5.0, the system used IPL. IPL 8 was used to synchronize with the scheduling subsystem. After V5.0, a new technique was needed, because IPL is meaningful only on a single CPU, and V5.0 supports symmetric multiprocessing (SMP), which allows kernel mode code to run concurrently on multiple CPUs.

"To support synchronization in an SMP environment, VMS uses spinlocks. A spinlock is a structure with one very important bit. This bit identifies whether a CPU currently is accessing a spinlock protected subsystem. If the bit is set, the CPU spins or loops, waiting for the bit to become clear. When the bit is clear, the CPU sets the bit, marking the subsystem as being in use.

"Spinlocks combined with IPL are used to guarantee synchronization in an SMP environment. Static spinlocks are assigned to specific subsystems, so that any CPU requesting a spinlock synchronizes properly with all other CPUs. To prevent deadlocks, spinlocks are assigned ranks and must be taken out in proper ranking order. Otherwise, with full checking multiprocessing as defined by the SYSGEN parameter MULTI-PROCESSING, the system will crash. For more information on spinlock ranking, check the *VMS Device Support Manual* in the VMS documentation set.

"One of the nice features of the EXE$NAMPID routine is that it takes out a spinlock on the scheduling subsystem, if it returns successfully. All you have to do is make sure you release the spinlock before you leave your code. This can be done using the following macro:

```
UNLOCK LOCKNAME=SCHED, NEWIPL=#0
```

"The inputs to EXE$NAMPID are:

1. 4(ap) — Contains the address of the PID of the target process.
2. 8(ap) — Contains the address of a descriptor for the process name.
3. R4 — Contains your PCB address.

"The outputs are:

1. R0 — Contains completion status.
2. R1 — Contains the internal PID of the target process.
3. R4 — Contains the PCB address of the target process.
4. 4(ap) — Has the EPID of the target written to location.
5. IPL/spinlocks — IPL=8 and owns SCHED spinlock if successful; on failure, IPL=2 and no spinlocks are owned.

"Now you should be ready."

"I can read in the PID, using LIB$GET_INPUT and convert from ASCII to binary using OTS$CVT_TZ_L," Billy said. "I can call the $CMKRNL system service to call my routine in kernel mode. If I pass an argument list with 4(ap) pointing to the PID, I am all set up for the JSB to EXE$NAMPID. Does this sound good so far?"

"A good start," responded the *Guide*. "But you might want to lock the code area that is going to be running at elevated IPL into your working set, using the lock working set system service ($LKWSET). The required argument is INADR; it contains the address of a quadword that holds the starting and ending addresses of what you want locked. This will prevent crashes caused by your P0 code generating page faults at IPL greater than two."

"I'll add that," Billy entered. "But how do I raise my IPL before allocating non-paged pool?"

"Good insight. You could write to the processor register PR$_IPL using the move to process register (MTPR) instruction, or you could use the standard macro SETIPL as follows:

```
SETIPL        #IPL$_ASTDEL"
```

"What if I allocated one chunk of pool to hold both the ACB and the code?"

"Good thought. That would be more efficient and probably easier to code," the *Guide* proudly replied to its star pupil.

"I can JSB to EXE$ALONONPAGED to grab my chunk of pool and copy the ACB and code, using a MOVC3 instruction. I can fill in the size field, and set the type field to be DYN$C_ACB. How would I compute the address of the AST routine in pool?"

"Let's say that the start of the ACB that you are copying into pool is located at BLASTER_AST, and the code starts at BLASTER_AST_CODE," the *Guide* proposed. "You could subtract the start of the ACB from the start of the code and, using displacement mode, offset from the beginning of pool. The code would look like this:

```
MOVAL  <BLASTER_AST_CODE-BLASTER_AST>(R2),ACB$L_KAST(R2)"
```

"Which type of AST should I use?" Billy entered.

"Because the code is in pool and pool is kernel writable and executive readable, you are limited somewhat. A special kernel AST would be the way to go to guarantee that the other process does not get deleted until you return the pool holding the ACB and code."

"I can clear the field ACB$B_RMOD and set the bit ACB$M_KAST. All that leaves is converting the EPID to internal PID, doing a JSB to EXE$NAMPID and copying R1 into ACB$L_PID to initialize the ACB. Copy the address of the ACB into R5, give him a big boost by placing PRI$_TICOM in R2, and jump off to SCH$QAST to blast the AST across."

"Make sure you give up the spinlock and add some error handling code, and you are finished with the main code. After you write the AST routine, you are done," the *Guide* added.

"Which routine should I use, $PURGWS or $ADJWSL?" Billy asked.

"$PURGWS will kick out all non-locked pages and leave the working set list alone. This might be optimal, but $PURGWS leaves at IPL 0, which would defeat the purpose of the special kernel AST. $ADJWSL returns at IPL 2, so this would be the proper service to use now," replied the *Guide*.

"I can figure out the working set adjustment. Now, what about deallocating the pool?"

"If this had been a normal kernel AST, the pool would be gone before you executed your code and so would your code, leading to an unpleasant crash. Because it is a special kernel AST, you are presented with a dilemma.

"To deallocate your pool, you normally would JSB to EXE$DEANONPAGED with the address of the ACB copied from R5 to R0. Note that AST delivery leaves the address of the ACB in R5 for a special kernel AST. However, there is nowhere to return to, because you just deallocated yourself. If you were to use a jump (JMP) instead of a JSB, you would disappear with the deallocation routine returning back to the AST delivery code."

"Slick. I like it."

Billy assembled and linked the code (see Figure 3). He found a process using ALL-IN-1. The process was sitting idle for awhile and tying up large amounts of memory.

The Hitchhiker's Guide to VMS has this entry on the need for larger working sets:

"The working set list minimizes memory use by a single process. One of the major factors affecting working set requirements is the notion of locality. Locality is the grouping of code or data in close proximity in virtual memory while it is being accessed. The better the locality, the smaller a working set can be."

The Hitchhiker's Guide to VMS has this entry on locality in an ALL-IN-1 application: *"ALL-IN-1 (sometimes called ALL-IN- FUN or ALL-IN-NONE, just kidding) has given new meaning to the notion of locality. Apparently, any code residing in the same galaxy has been coded with acceptable locality."*

Billy blasted the process and found that the working set did indeed shrink (see Figure 4).

"Hey, Book, this is getting fun," Billy concluded.

WILL THIS STUFF stay fun? Has Billy seen Ghandi one too many times and given up the idea of getting even? Where into VMS will he venture next?

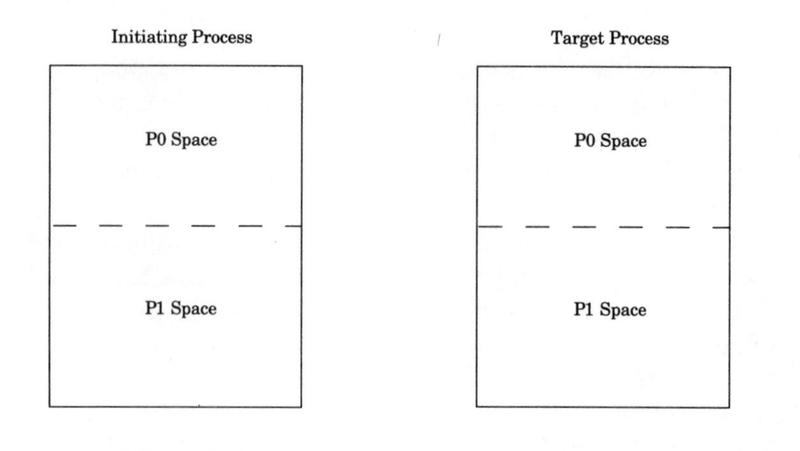
Initiating Process
P0 Space
P1 Space
Target Process
P0 Space
P1 Space

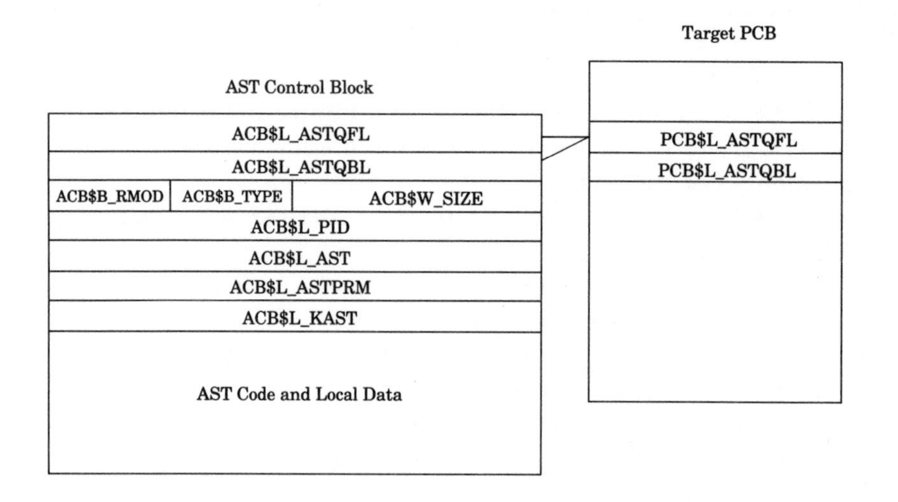
S0 Space
Target PCB
AST Control Block
ACB$L_ASTQFL
ACB$L_ASTQBL
ACB$B_RMOD
ACB$B_TYPE
ACB$W_SIZE
ACB$L_PID
ACB$L_AST
ACB$L_ASTPRM
ACB$L_KAST
AST Code and Local Data
PCB$L_ASTQFL
PCB$L_ASTQBL

AST flow for WSBLASTER.MAR

Figure 3.

```
;^^^^^^^^^^^^^^^^^^^^^^^^^^^^^^^^^^^^^^^^^^^^^^^^^^^^^^^^^^^^^^^^^^
;       Program:        wsblaster
;       Author:         Billy Bitsenbites (Bruce Ellis)
;       Date written: 9/28/87
;       Synopsis:       This program takes a Process Id as input
;                       and adjusts the associated process working
;                       set down to 250 pages.
;^^^^^^^^^^^^^^^^^^^^^^^^^^^^^^^^^^^^^^^^^^^^^^^^^^^^^^^^^^^^^^^^^^

;Include the system macro library
        .library        /sys$library:lib.mlb/
;Link against the system symbol table
        .link           /sys$system:sys.stb/
;^^^^^^^^^^^^^^^^^^^^^^^
;Include definitions
;^^^^^^^^^^^^^^^^^^^^^^^
        $pcbdef                 ;Process control block
        $dyndef                 ;Dynamic memory types
        $ipldef                 ;Interrupt Priority Level
        $acbdef                 ;AST Control block
        $pridef                 ;Priority boost classes
        $spldef                 ;Spinlock

        .macro check  ?1
        blbs   r0,1
        $exit_s         r0
1:
        .endm  check
pid_a:  .long  8        ;ASCII descriptor for PID storage
        .address        10$
10$:    .blkb  8
pid:    .blkl  1        ;Storage for binary representation of PID
pmt:    .ascid /pid> /
pid_arg:                ;argument list for exe$nampid
        .long  1
        .address        pid
        .long  0
lock_adr:
        .address        lock_start
        .address        lock_end
;^^^^^^^^^^^^^^^^^^^^^^^^^^^^^^^^^^^^^^^^^^^^^^^^^^^^^^^^^^^^^^^^^^
;       User mode code

;^^^^^^^^^^^^^^^^^^^^^^^^^^^^^^^^^^^^^^^^^^^^^^^^^^^^^^^^^^^^^^^^^^
        .entry blaster,^m<>
        pushal pid_a  ;Read in pid
        pushal pmt    ;  with prompt
        pushal pid_a
        calls  #3,g^lib$get_input
        check
        pushal pid    ;Convert pid from Hex ASCII to
        pushal pid_a  ;  a longword binary value
        calls  #2,g^ots$cvt_tz_l
        check
;^^^^^^^^^^^^
; Lock down code and data accessed at elevated IPL
;^^^^^^^^^^^^
        $lkwset_s       inadr=lock_adr
        check
;^^^^^^^^^^^^^^^^^^^^^^^^^^^^^^^^^^^^^^^^^^^^^^^^^^^^^^^^^^^^^^^^^^
;       Get into kernel mode and blast him
;^^^^^^^^^^^^^^^^^^^^^^^^^^^^^^^^^^^^^^^^^^^^^^^^^^^^^^^^^^^^^^^^^^
        $cmkrnl_s       routin=negate_him,arglst=pid_arg
        ret
;^^^^^^^^^^^^^^^^^^^^^^^^^^^^^^^^^^^^^^^^^^^^^^^^^^^^^^^^^^^^^^^^^^
;       Kernel mode code
;       description:
;               1)      Checks the pid and converts to PCB address
;                       and obtains IPID
;               2)      Allocates pool for an ACB, including the
;                       code for the special kernel ast
;               3)      Queues a special kernel AST to the process
;
```

Figure 3 contd.

```
;^;^^^^^^^^^^^^^^^^^^^^^^^^^^^^^^^^^^^^^^^^^^^^^^^^^^^^^^^^^^^^^^^^^^^^
     .entry negate_him,^m<r2,r3,r4,r5>
       setipl #ipl$_astdel          ;Don't delete me
       movl   #blaster_ast_size,r1  ;Allocate the pool for the
       jsb    g^exe$alononpaged     ; ACB+code
       blbc   r0,scram              ;no pool then leave
;^^^^^^^^^^^^^
;Copy the code into pool
;^^^^^^^^^^^^^
       pushr  #^m<r0,r1,r2,r3,r4,r5>
       movc3  #blaster_ast_size,blaster_ast,(r2)
       popr   #^m<r0,r1,r2,r3,r4,r5>
       movw   R1,acb$w_size(r2)     ;Fill in size for later deallocation
       movb   #dyn$c_acb,acb$b_type(r2)    ;set type as ACB
;^^^^^^^^^^^^^
;Fill in the address of the KAST routine
;^^^^^^^^^^^^^
       moval  <blaster_ast_code-blaster_ast>(r2),acb$l_kast(r2)
       clrb   acb$b_rmod(r2)        ;Clear request mode bits

       bisb   #acb$m_kast,acb$b_rmod(r2)   ;Mark as special kernel AST
       pushl  r2                           ;NAMPID hoses R2, thanks a lot guys
lock_start:
       jsb    g^exe$nampid                 ;find him
       popl   r2                           ;restore R2
       blbc   r0,cleanup                   ;on error deallocate the pool
       movl   r1,acb$l_pid(r2)             ;copy in his IPID
       movl   r2,r5                        ;R5 must point to ACB for SCH$QAST
       movl   #pri$_ticom,r2               ;give him a big boost
       jsb    g^sch$qast                   ;Queue the AST
       unlock lockname=SCHED,newipl=#0     ;Give up SCHED spinlock
                                           ;that nampid took out
       movl   #ss$_normal,r0               ;success
outta_here:
       ret                                 ;sayonara
scram: setipl #0                           ;reset IPL
       brb    outta_here                   ;return error status
cleanup:
       pushl  r0                           ;save error status
       movl   r2,r0                        ;deallocate the pool
       jsb    g^exe$deanonpaged
       popl   r0                           ;restore error status
       brb    scram                        ;beat it

;^^^^^^^^^^^^^^^^^^^^^^^^^^^^^^^^^^^^^^^^^^^^^^^^^^^^^^^^^^^^^^^^^^^
;      ACB with code following
;^^^^^^^^^^^^^^^^^^^^^^^^^^^^^^^^^^^^^^^^^^^^^^^^^^^^^^^^^^^^^^^^^^^
blaster_ast:
acb:   .blkb  acb$k_length                 ;Allocate storage for ACB
old_ws:       .blkl  1                     ;saved working set size
blaster_ast_code:
       $adjwsl_s     wsetlm=old_ws         ;get current working set size
       blbc   r0,escape                    ;on error scram
       pushl  r3                           ;save r3
       subl3  #250,old_ws,r3               ;compute the difference between
                                           ;the current working set size
                                           ;and the new size of 250 pages
       blss   escape                       ;if he is already under get out
       mnegl  r3,r3                        ;negate the difference
       $adjwsl_s     pagcnt=r3             ;Adjust down to 250 pages
escape:       movl   r5,r0                 ;set up for deallocation
       popl   r3                           ;restore r3
       jmp    g^exe$deanonpaged            ;give up the pool and disappear
       blaster_ast_size=.-blaster_ast
lock_end:
       .end   blaster
```

Figure 4. ***Output showing that memory was recaptured from idle processes.***

```
$ mac wsblaster
$ link wsblaster
$
$ sh sys
VAX/VMS V5.1-1  on node LABDOG 16-JUL-1989 03:48:50.49   Uptime    0 00:15:59
  Pid     Process Name        State  Pri      I/O        CPU       Page flts Ph.Mem
00000021  SWAPPER            HIB     16        0   0 00:00:01.53         0      0
00000024  ERRFMT             HIB      8       59   0 00:00:00.60        75     99
00000025  OPCOM              HIB      8       34   0 00:00:00.68       195     74
00000026  JOB_CONTROL        HIB      8      209   0 00:00:01.99       182    353
00000027  NETACP             HIB     10       47   0 00:00:01.32       190    362
00000028  EVL                HIB      6       74   0 00:00:02.07       545     47  N
00000029  REMACP             HIB      9       24   0 00:00:00.27        77     45
0000002B  SYMBIONT_0002      HIB      4       26   0 00:00:01.34       376    147
0000002C  MULTINET_SERVER    HIB      4      120   0 00:00:02.45       298     74
0000002D  SMTP_SYMBIONT      HIB      4       24   0 00:00:01.50       349     42
0000002F  ELLISB             CUR      4      307   0 00:00:32.60      5805    233
$
$ r wsblaster
pid> 26
%SYSTEM-F-NOPRIV, no privilege for attempted operation
$ set proc/priv=all
$
$ r wsblaster
pid> 26
$ sh sys
VAX/VMS V5.1-1  on node LABDOG 16-JUL-1989 03:49:29.43   Uptime    0 00:16:38
  Pid     Process Name        State  Pri      I/O        CPU       Page flts Ph.Mem
00000021  SWAPPER            HIB     16        0   0 00:00:01.53         0      0
00000024  ERRFMT             HIB      8       59   0 00:00:00.60        75     99
00000025  OPCOM              HIB      8       34   0 00:00:00.68       195     74
00000026  JOB_CONTROL        HIB     12      209   0 00:00:02.01       184    250
00000027  NETACP             HIB     10       47   0 00:00:01.35       190    362
00000028  EVL                HIB      6       74   0 00:00:02.07       545     47  N
00000029  REMACP             HIB      9       24   0 00:00:00.27        77     45
0000002B  SYMBIONT_0002      HIB      4       26   0 00:00:01.34       376    147
0000002C  MULTINET_SERVER    HIB      4      120   0 00:00:02.45       298     74
0000002D  SMTP_SYMBIONT      HIB      4       24   0 00:00:01.50       349     42
0000002F  ELLISB             CUR      4      346   0 00:00:33.67      6190    150
$
$ r wsblaster
pid> 27
$
$ sh sys
VAX/VMS V5.1-1  on node LABDOG 16-JUL-1989 03:49:52.70   Uptime    0 00:17:01
  Pid     Process Name        State  Pri      I/O        CPU       Page flts Ph.Mem
00000021  SWAPPER            HIB     16        0   0 00:00:01.53         0      0
00000024  ERRFMT             HIB      8       59   0 00:00:00.60        75     99
00000025  OPCOM              HIB      8       34   0 00:00:00.68       195     74
00000026  JOB_CONTROL        HIB     12      209   0 00:00:02.01       184    250
00000027  NETACP             HIB     12       47   0 00:00:01.39       190    250
00000028  EVL                HIB      6       74   0 00:00:02.08       564     35  N
00000029  REMACP             HIB      9       24   0 00:00:00.27        77     45
0000002B  SYMBIONT_0002      HIB      4       26   0 00:00:01.34       376    147
0000002C  MULTINET_SERVER    HIB      4      120   0 00:00:02.45       298     74
0000002D  SMTP_SYMBIONT      HIB      4       24   0 00:00:01.50       349     42
0000002F  ELLISB             CUR      5      377   0 00:00:34.27      6370    151
$
$ r wsblaster
pid> 28
$ sh sys
VAX/VMS V5.1-1  on node LABDOG 16-JUL-1989 03:50:17.98   Uptime    0 00:17:26
  Pid     Process Name        State  Pri      I/O        CPU       Page flts Ph.Mem
00000021  SWAPPER            HIB     16        0   0 00:00:01.53         0      0
00000024  ERRFMT             HIB      8       59   0 00:00:00.60        75     99
00000025  OPCOM              HIB      8       34   0 00:00:00.68       195     74
00000026  JOB_CONTROL        HIB     12      209   0 00:00:02.01       184    250
00000027  NETACP             HIB     10       47   0 00:00:01.40       193    250
00000028  EVL                HIB      9       74   0 00:00:02.09       565     36  N
00000029  REMACP             HIB      9       24   0 00:00:00.27        77     45
0000002B  SYMBIONT_0002      HIB      4       26   0 00:00:01.34       376    147
```

Figure 4 contd.

```
0000002C  MULTINET_SERVER     HIB      4      120   0 00:00:02.45      298     74
0000002D  SMTP_SYMBIONT       HIB      4       24   0 00:00:01.50      349     42
0000002F  ELLISB              CUR      4      404   0 00:00:34.85     6551    159
$ r wsblaster
pid> 2f
$
```

Episode 3

Billy Learns That Things Break

Bitsenbites ran wildly about the computer room, tearing off the console listings and madly typing at his terminal.

"That stupid *Guide*. I never should have let him get me into this mess," Billy thought aloud.

He opened the gray tome marked *The Hitchhiker's Guide to VMS*. After a brief period of whirring and clicking, he started typing.

"Hey *Guide*," he slammed into the keyboard.

"What's your problem?" responded the *Guide*.

The keys on the *Guide* were pressure sensitive. If too much pressure were applied, the *Guide* received error status in the keyboard interrupt service routine. This status, when returned to the *Guide*'s software, enabled an abusive mode of response. If this continued, the *Guide* was programmed to become quite belligerent.

Taken aback at the *Guide*'s response, Billy entered, "My code is falling apart."

"Could you be a little more specific?" countered the *Guide*.

"Well, first I ran the STEALTH program, and I still showed up in the $SHOW USERS display. Then, I ran the WSBLASTER program, and not only did it not work, but it crashed the system!" (See Figures 1 and 3).

"I tested that code thoroughly," Billy continued. "I tried it with full-checking multiprocessing enabled, and it worked. I tried it on an outswapped process, and it worked. I tried it on a VAXcluster, and it worked. All these tests worked fine. Now suddenly it crashes."

"What version of VMS are you running?" queried the *Guide*.

"Version 5.2," Billy answered.

"What is different in version 5.2?"

"The big thing is the clusterwide process services." Then Billy wondered, "Wait a minute. Hey *Guide*, you're supposed to be answering my questions. I'm not supposed to be answering yours. Have you taken a crash course in Digital Equipment Corporation software support?"

"Look, number 1, I have not been fed the version 5.2 release notes. Number 2, have you tried to get a copy of the version 5.2 source listings lately? DECdirect doesn't have a part number, and the *Guide*'s salesperson thinks that the source listings magically appear on the printer," the *Guide* snapped back.

The Hitchhiker's Guide to VMS has the following entry on the timeliness of VMS internals material distribution:

"Although Digital has become more responsive with the distribution of VMS internals updates, the source listings (traditionally referred to as the fiche) have become more difficult and expensive to obtain. This is a classic example of the law of diminishing returns. Perhaps the reason for this is that even though the statement 'Digital has it now' never held up, they can, at least, say 'Digital had it before the customers.' "

"Gee, and I just read a glowing report on the wonders of version 5.2 in an article titled "Version 5.2: A Major League Effort" in the October 1989 *VAX PROFESSIONAL*. The guy who wrote it must be some kind of a jerk," Billy reflected. He continued, "A 'dot' release shouldn't have caused my previously linked code to crash the system, should it?"

"With the loadable executive, which was introduced in version 5.0 of VMS, the developers enabled the ability to make functional changes to system code without requiring a major relinking of privileged code. If modification of code linked against the executive images were required, a major and minor identification check should have caused the code to abort prior to entering a privileged mode. Evidently, the developer made assumptions that your code didn't," the *Guide* answered.

"Look, Book, I wanted to work on code to track open files and I need your help, but I have to get these programs working first. Can you help me?" Billy pleaded.

"One program at a time," the *Guide* responded. "Because the WSBLASTER program crashed the system, we'll have to find where and why. First, analyze the crash dump, and to do that, you'll probably want to run in stealth mode. So let's attack the STEALTH program first," proposed the *Guide*. "What's different about the $SHOW USERS display in a version 5.2 system?"

"It prints out clusterwide process information. It also displays the number of interactive, batch and subprocesses running under a given username."

"What happens when you run the old version of the STEALTH code?"

"The old version clears the terminal name, but the count of interactive users does not decrease," Billy replied. "My process still shows up in the display, even after the STEALTH code has been run. The field SYS$GW_IJOBCNT seems to contain some nonsensical value."

"To support the clusterwide $SHOW USERS command, the developers probably modified it to use the SYS$GETJPI system service, which was designed to work clusterwide. This system service call probably is the reason they rewrote the utility. In the process of rewriting, they added a new criterion for what connotes a user process. The other field that describes the interactive nature of a process is the job type field, which is stored in the job information block (JIB) in the field JIB$B_JOBTYPE. Try clearing that field," the *Guide* offered.

"How would I locate the JIB?" Billy queried.

"Through the offset PCB$L_JIB in the PCB," the *Guide* replied.

"I can skip the subprocess and interactive bit checks, because I don't want to change the interactive job count field. Let me try it out," Billy responded (see Figure 5).

A little later, an elated Billy Bitsenbites entered into the *Guide*, "Hey, it works!" (See Figure 6). "Now how do we attack WSBLASTER?"

"First, we must analyze the crash dump," the *Guide* answered.

"Okay. To begin to analyze the crash, I need to issue the following command:

```
ANALYZE/CRASH SYS$SYSTEM
```

Billy entered the SDA commands shown in Figure 7 to analyze the crash.

He continued, "SDA states that the reason for the crash is:

```
CWSERR, Error detected while processing clusterwide service request
```

"So, now I need to locate the signal and mechanism arrays to find the program counter (PC) at the time of the crash."

"Hold on," the *Guide* interrupted. "You want to locate the signal and mechanism arrays only when the reason for the crash was either:

```
INVEXCPTN, Exception while above ASTDEL or on interrupt stack
```

or

```
SSRVEXCEPT, Unexpected system service exception
```

"The message you received in the dump was an indication of an inconsistency detected by VMS code. Check the PC to determine where the problem was detected. Before you do this, you should issue a READ/EXECUTIVE command in SDA to read the executive symbol tables."

"I issued an EXAMINE/INSTRUCTION @PC to determine the location of the BUG_CHECK macro, and I don't see it," Billy asserted.

"This exception is a trap, so the PC points after the trapping instruction. You want to back up a little bit to locate the BUG_CHECK macro. Try the following SDA command:

```
EXAMINE/INSTRUCTION .-10;20
```

"It will back up through the location pointed to by the PC."

"I backed up and examined the instructions just before the PC and found the BUG_CHECK macro," Billy said. "It has a BUG_CHECK code of 06A4."

"The 4 in the low three bits marks this code as a severe bugcheck. It would force a crash regardless of whether the BUGCHECKFATAL parameter were set to 1 or 0.

"The 06A0 is the bugcheck code. If you issue a SHOW/SYMBOL BUG$/ALL command, you should see a symbol BUG$_CWSERR that is equal to the value 06A0."

"I did that, and you are right on," Billy acknowledged.

"Now examine the instructions that caused the bugcheck, and you'll be able to determine the code that needs to be changed," the *Guide* continued.

"At the location EXE$NAMPID, there's the following instruction stream:

```
MFPR       #12,-(SP)
CMPL       #0,(SP)+
BGEQU      EXE$NAMPID+0000c
BUG_CHECK  #06A4
```

"What's going on here?" Billy demanded.

The *Guide* answered, "The MFPR instruction is a move from processor register instruction. The instruction is saving the contents of the process register 12 on the stack. Processor register 12 is the interrupt priority level (IPL) register, which contains the IPL at which the processor is currently running."

"Oh," Billy interrupted, "and the CMPL instruction is checking to see whether the IPL was less than or equal to zero when EXE$NAMPID was jumped to. But why would this code care whether the IPL was equal to zero? And how could the IPL be less than zero? I noticed in the SHOW CRASH SDA command that the processor was running at IPL 2. But once again, why should this be a problem in version 5.2, when it was no problem in earlier versions of VMS?"

"If the EXE$NAMPID routine is the location of support for the clusterwide process services," explained the *Guide*, "we would need to force the requesting process into a wait state while the services sent a message to the remote node, to determine the existence of the process. After the information is obtained, the services we need reactivate the requesting process. The services probably use the same technique that we used to get from one process context to another."

"That technique was the method of queueing an asynchronous system trap (AST)," Billy interrupted. "I get it now. ASTs are delivered via an IPL 2 interrupt, and if we were waiting at IPL 2, we'd be blocking the reactivation AST."

"Now you should determine how you got to EXE$NAMPID. This could be done simply, because you wrote the code. However, because you're in SDA, let's examine the stack by issuing a SHOW STACK command. At the top of the stack, you should be able to locate the return PC from the JSB instruction that got you into EXE$NAMPID."

"I did that, and the return PC is 2D8," Billy entered. "Now, if I back up and go forward, I see that the code executed a MTPR #2,#12 instruction. This instruction raises the IPL to 2. I did this because I later was allocating non-paged pool. What if I rearranged the JSB to EXE$NAMPID with the allocation of non-paged pool?"

"That rearrangement will solve the problem of the sanity check. However, the checking of an IPL greater than 0 was done for a reason. You should check the EXE$NAMPID code to determine if there's a chance this code ships your request to another node that has no idea why you're calling EXE$NAMPID. There is a chance that your code could crash later in the routine if EXE$NAMPID were modified to accept any additional inputs. This is probably not the case, but you may want to check," the *Guide* responded.

Billy examined the string of instructions starting at EXE$NAMPID and then entered into the *Guide*, "The code examines the location CLU$GL_CLUB and then branches off if this value is non-zero. I assume this field has something to do with determining whether you're operating in a VAXcluster or not."

"Very good," responded the *Guide*. "If you want to join the cluster, you have to be described in the CLUB. It's an exclusive CLUB, and not everybody is admitted. Just kidding. Seriously, the cluster block (CLUB) is used by the connection manager to describe an overall view of the VAXcluster, including the total vote count, the quorum, the expected votes, the characteristics of the quorum disk, if there is a quorum disk, and so on.

"This cluster block is pointed to by the location CLU$GL_CLUB, if we're operating in a VAXcluster. If we're not, the location contains a zero."

"As I painstakingly follow the code paths without the assistance of all symbols and comments" (not shown in Figure 7) Billy pointed out, "I end up at a location that calls CWPS$PARSE_PRCNAM. This guy eventually issues JSB instructions to the routines, CWPS$ALLOCATE_SRV and CWPS$SSND_PCNTRL_RQST. There are loads of instructions between the initial call, through BSBW instruction, and the point where these routines are called, so I'm not sure of the conditions they're called under.

"Even if they were called, I can't figure out exactly what they do, because the locations contain a JMP @#EXE$LOAD_ERROR instruction, which I assume implies they're not loaded (although I feel like getting loaded), because the system we crashed isn't a VAXcluster."

"These routines simply may determine whether the process exists on the remote node," explained the *Guide*. "Presumably, to prevent any other code that called EXE$NAMPID from breaking, they could return a status code that the system services which operate remotely could check. With this status code, the services would know to initiate the remote request.

"In a worst case scenario, they could send a message to the remote node telling it to do something, which it wouldn't understand."

"There's a system service status code SS$_REMOTE_PROC that returns an error status," Billy said.

"It would seem sufficient to check for error status when returning from EXE$NAMPID and ignoring the request if this error status were returned," the *Guide* suggested.

"What if this technique did not work as you recommended? Then it could crash one or more cluster nodes," the fearful Billy questioned.

"No pain, no gain."

"That's easy for you to say. I'm a little nervous about crashes. Let's say that until I can test this code on a crashable node in a VAXcluster or examine the version 5.2 source listings, you help me guarantee that the process I'm blasting is located on my local node," Billy proposed.

"If you're going to be a coward about this, there are a couple of solutions. We could chain through the process control block (PCB) vector table, just as EXE$NAMPID did prior to version 5.2. This requires several sanity checks.

"Or we could add a sanity check just prior to the JSB to EXE$NAMPID. Because the code operates as before on the local node, this sanity check should guarantee that the process is operating on the local node by checking the extended process identification (EPID). If the specified process isn't operating on the local node, you could return the SS$_REMOTE_PROC error status. The only problem with this technique is you might give the requestor misleading information that the remote process exists."

"I can live with that a lot easier than an unexpected crash. I promise that when I get a chance to test the code in a VAXcluster, I'll remove the possible unnecessary checks. But for now, how do we know which node the EPID represents?" Billy pleaded.

"The EPID contains the index into the PCB vector table, used to locate the process control block of the target process. The middle bits contain a sequence number, which is used to provide a level of uniqueness when using the index.

"The high bits of the EPID contain a cluster system identification (CSID) that's generated by the connection manager to uniquely identify a node in a VAXcluster. To determine whether we're on the local node, all we have to do is extract these bits from the EPID and compare the value to the contents of the location SCH$GW_LOCALNODE, which contains the compressed CSID of the local node."

"Also easy for you to say. How do we extract the correct bits?" Billy queried.

The *Guide* responded, "The bit position PCB$V_EPID_NODE_IDX identifies where the CSID bits start in the EPID. The symbol PCB$S_EPID_NODE_IDX defines the size of the node index bit field, and PCB$S_EPID_NODE_SEQ identifies the size of the node sequence number bit field. The sum of the two size fields would equal the size of the CSID. By using an extract and zero variable bit field (EXTZV) instruction, we could yank out the bits and make a comparison to the local node's CSID."

"Now, let me get this straight," Billy said with a grin. "I could add the following instructions to check for whether I am following instructions to make the check for whether I am operating on the local node:

```
MOVL    @4(AP),R6                   ;Get the EPID
EXTZV   #PCB$V_EPID_NODE_IDX,-      ;extract the CSID
        #CSID_WID+1,-               ;and wildcard bit where
        R6,R6                       ;csid_wid=
                                    ;pcb$s_epid_node_idx+
                                    ; pcb$s_epid_node_seq
CMPW    G^SCH$GW_LOCALNODE,R6       ;Same node?
BNEQ    ERROR                       ; if not, scram
```

"Will this do it?"

"Yes," answered the *Guide*. "However, you are making assumptions about the adjacency of the node index and node sequence number that should be checked using the ASSUME macro. This macro is documented in the *VMS Internals and Data Structures* manual written by Kenah, Goldenberg and Bate, or Goldenberg and Kenah, depending on version. This macro allows you to detect any changes to these fields, when a future release of VMS modifies these values, by receiving error status at assembly time of the sources.

"You must also make sure that the code at the end of the program is locked into your working set as the movc3 is now touching this code at IPL 8."

"Okay, I'll move the label lock_end to the end of the program. Let me try it out," Billy responded (see Figure 8).

A little later, Billy returned to the *Guide* and entered, "It works." (See Figure 9.) "Thanks a lot. Now, about determining which files are open for a given process ... ."

WHAT NEW CODE will Billy write next? Is he serious about determining the files open to a process? Will he need to analyze a crash again? Has he given up the idea of getting even? What happened to Dennis Cutlery? Are there no women in Billy's life? Does Billy have a life?

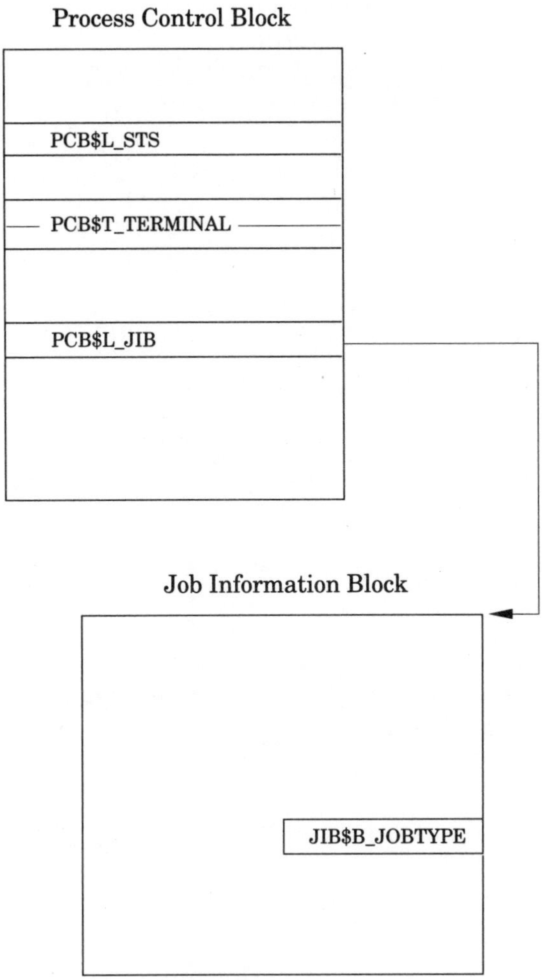

Process Control Block

PCB$L_STS

PCB$T_TERMINAL

PCB$L_JIB

Job Information Block

JIB$B_JOBTYPE

Fields affected by updated version of STEALTH.

Figure 5.

```
$ typ stealth_too.mar
;^^^^^^^^^^^^^^^^^^^^^^^^^^^^^^^^^^^^^^^^^^^^^^^^^^^^
;       Program stealth
;       Author: Billy Bitsenbites (Bruce Ellis)
;       Function: Remove our process from the $SHOW USER display
;       Modifications:  11/11/89  BAE  Added the clearing of the
;       jobtype field in the JIB and removed the decrementing
;       of the interactive job type code to remove version 5.2
;       obstacles.  Also removed the subprocess check as it
;       is currently unnecessary.
;^^^^^^^^^^^^^^^^^^^^^^^^^^^^^^^^^^^^^^^^^^^^^^^^^^^^

        .library            /sys$library:lib.mlb/
        .link       /sys$system:sys.stb/
        $pcbdef
        $jibdef
        .entry    no_user,^m<>
        $cmkrnl_s           routin=zap
        ret
;^^^^^^^^^^^^^^^^^^^^^^^^^^^^^^^^^^^^^^^^^^^^^^^^^^^^
;    Get into kernel mode and have fun
;^^^^^^^^^^^^^^^^^^^^^^^^^^^^^^^^^^^^^^^^^^^^^^^^^^^^
     .entry  zap,^m<>
     bicl    #pcb$M_inter,pcb$l_sts(r4)         ;clear the interactive bit
     clrb    pcb$t_terminal(r4)                 ;clear the terminal count
     movl    pcb$l_jib(r4),r5                   ;get the jib address
     clrb    jib$b_jobtype(r5)                  ;nail the job count
     bisl    #pcb$m_noacnt,pcb$l_sts(r4)        ;no account process
     movl    #ss$_normal,r0                     ;success
     ret
     .end    no_user
$
$ mac stealth_too
$ link stealth_too
$
```

Figure 6. *Using the SHOW USER command to show the results of running STEALTH_TOO.*

```
        VAX/VMS User Processes at 16-NOV-1989 05:39:40.91
     Total number of users = 1,  number of processes = 1

 Username     Interactive  Subprocess   Batch
 ELLISB            1
$ r  stealth_too
%SYSTEM-F-NOPRIV, no privilege for attempted operation
$ set proc/priv=cmkrnl
$ r stealth_too
$
$ sh us
        VAX/VMS User Processes at 16-NOV-1989 05:39:57.91
     Total number of users = 0,  number of processes = 0
$
```

Figure 7. *Example of SDA commands used to analyze the crash.*

```
ellis>ana/crash sys$system:


VAX/VMS System dump analyzer

Dump taken on 13-NOV-1989 23:37:16.87
CWSERR, Error detected while processing cluster-wide service request

SDA> sh crash

System crash information
------------------------
```

Figure 7 contd.

```
Time of system crash: 13-NOV-1989 23:37:16.87


Version of system: VAX/VMS VERSION V5.2

System Version Major ID/Minor ID: 1/0


System type: MicroVAX II

Crash CPU ID/Primary CPU ID:  00/00

Bitmask of CPUs active/available:  00000001/00000001


CPU bugcheck codes:
        CPU 00 — CWSERR, Error detected while processing cluster-wide service request


CPU 00 Processor crash information
---------------



CPU 00 reason for Bugcheck: CWSERR, Error detected while processing
                               cluster-wide service request


Process currently executing on this CPU: ELLISB


Current image file: DUB1:[USERS.ELLISB]WSBLASTER.EXE;2


Current IPL: 2  (decimal)


CPU database address:  813C4000


CPU 00 Processor crash information
---------------
General registers:

       R0  = 00000001   R1 = 00000056   R2  = 813A1880   R3  = 7FF8D552
       R4  = 8123AD00   R5 = 7FFE5EFC   R6  = 7FFED188   R7  = 7FFED188
       R8  = 7FFECA50   R9 = 7FFECC58   R10 = 7FFED7D4   R11 = 7FFE2BDC
       AP  = 00000221   FP = 7FFE77C0   SP  = 7FFE77B8   PC  = 8118DE1B
       PSL = 00C20009




CPU 00 Processor crash information
---------------
Processor registers:


       P0BR   = 813EF400    SBR     = 008D0E00    ASTLVL = 00000004
       P0LR   = 000000C9    SLR     = 0000B900    SISR   = 00000000
       P1BR   = 80C09200    PCBB    = 004B1A20    ICCS   = 00000040
       P1LR   = 001FF9AB    SCBB    = 008CD200    SID    = 08000000

       TODR   = B33DED0B    SYSTYPE = 01010000


       ISP    = 813C6600
       KSP    = 7FFE77B8
       ESP    = 7FFE9800
       SSP    = 7FFECA4C
       USP    = 7FF37D5C
```

Figure 7 contd.

```
CPU 00 Processor crash information
---------------------------------

                No spinlocks currently owned by CPU 00
SDA> read/exec
%SDA-I-READSYM,  reading symbol table SYS$COMMON:[SYS$LDR]SYSLDR_DYN.EXE;1
%SDA-I-READSYM,  reading symbol table SYS$COMMON:[SYS$LDR]DDIF$RMS_EXTENSION.EXE;1
%SDA-I-READSYM,  reading symbol table SYS$COMMON:[SYS$LDR]RECOVERY_UNIT_SERVICES.EXE;1
%SDA-I-READSYM,  reading symbol table SYS$COMMON:[SYS$LDR]RMS.EXE;2
%SDA-I-READSYM,  reading symbol table SYS$COMMON:[SYS$LDR]SYS$NETWORK_SERVICES.EXE;1
%SDA-I-READSYM,  reading symbol table SYS$COMMON:[SYS$LDR]SYS$TRANSACTION_SERVICES.EXE;1
%SDA-I-READSYM,  reading symbol table SYS$COMMON:[SYS$LDR]CPULOA.EXE;1
%SDA-I-READSYM,  reading symbol table SYS$COMMON:[SYS$LDR]LMF$GROUP_TABLE.EXE;1
%SDA-I-READSYM,  reading symbol table SYS$COMMON:[SYS$LDR]SYSLICENSE.EXE;1
%SDA-I-READSYM,  reading symbol table SYS$COMMON:[SYS$LDR]SYSGETSYI.EXE;1
%SDA-I-READSYM,  reading symbol table SYS$COMMON:[SYS$LDR]SYSDEVICE.EXE;1
%SDA-I-READSYM,  reading symbol table SYS$COMMON:[SYS$LDR]MESSAGE_ROUTINES.EXE;1
%SDA-I-READSYM,  reading symbol table SYS$COMMON:[SYS$LDR]EXCEPTION.EXE;1
%SDA-I-READSYM,  reading symbol table SYS$COMMON:[SYS$LDR]LOGICAL_NAMES.EXE;1
%SDA-I-READSYM,  reading symbol table SYS$COMMON:[SYS$LDR]SECURITY.EXE;1
%SDA-I-READSYM,  reading symbol table SYS$COMMON:[SYS$LDR]LOCKING.EXE;1
%SDA-I-READSYM,  reading symbol table SYS$COMMON:[SYS$LDR]PAGE_MANAGEMENT.EXE;1
%SDA-I-READSYM,  reading symbol table SYS$COMMON:[SYS$LDR]WORKING_SET_MANAGEMENT.EXE;1
%SDA-I-READSYM,  reading symbol table SYS$COMMON:[SYS$LDR]IMAGE_MANAGEMENT.EXE;1
%SDA-I-READSYM,  reading symbol table SYS$COMMON:[SYS$LDR]EVENT_FLAGS_AND_ASTS.EXE;1
%SDA-I-READSYM,  reading symbol table SYS$COMMON:[SYS$LDR]IO_ROUTINES.EXE;1
%SDA-I-READSYM,  reading symbol table SYS$COMMON:[SYS$LDR]PROCESS_MANAGEMENT.EXE;1
%SDA-I-READSYM,  reading symbol table SYS$COMMON:[SYS$LDR]ERRORLOG.EXE;1
%SDA-I-READSYM,  reading symbol table SYS$COMMON:[SYS$LDR]PRIMITIVE_IO.EXE;1
%SDA-I-READSYM,  reading symbol table SYS$COMMON:[SYS$LDR]SYSTEM_SYNCHRONIZATION_UNI.EXE;1
%SDA-I-READSYM,  reading symbol table SYS$COMMON:[SYS$LDR]SYSTEM_PRIMITIVES.EXE;1
SDA> e/i @pc
EXE$NAMPID+0000C:  MOVL     04(AP),R0
SDA> e/i .-10;20
%SDA-W-INSKIPPED, unreasonable instruction stream - 3 bytes skipped
EXE$WAKE+0007B:         RSB
EXE$NAMPID:             MFPR          #12,-(SP)
EXE$NAMPID+00003:       CMPL          #00,(SP)+
EXE$NAMPID+00006:       BGEQU         EXE$NAMPID+0000C
EXE$NAMPID+00008:       BUG_CHECK     #06A4
EXE$NAMPID+0000C:       MOVL          04(AP),R0
EXE$NAMPID+00010:       BEQL          EXE$NAMPID+0002D
EXE$NAMPID+00012:       PROBEW        #00,#04,(R0)
EXE$NAMPID+00016:       BEQL          EXE$WAKE+00072
EXE$NAMPID+00018:       MOVL          (R0),R1
EXE$NAMPID+0001B:       BEQL          EXE$NAMPID+0002D
EXE$NAMPID+0001D:       BSBW          EXE$EPID_TO_IPID+0000D
SDA> sh sym bug$/all

Symbols sorted by name
----------------------
BUG$BUILD_HEADE   80002038 => 24A89F16      BUG$_CONSOLRX50 00000640
.
.
.
BUG$_ACPMBFAIL    00000008                  BUG$_CTERM      00000678
BUG$_ACPRECURS    000004B8  => 42494C06     BUG$_CWSERR     000006A0
BUG$_ACPUNSTAK    000004C0  => 00000000     BUG$_DBLERR     000000C8
SDA> e/i .-20;20
%SDA-W-INSKIPPED, unreasonable instruction stream - 2 bytes skipped
EXE$WAKE+0007B:         RSB
EXE$NAMPID:             MFPR          #12,-(SP)
EXE$NAMPID+00003:       CMPL          #00,(SP)+
EXE$NAMPID+00006:       BGEQU         EXE$NAMPID+0000C
EXE$NAMPID+00008:       BUG_CHECK     #06A4
EXE$NAMPID+0000C:       MOVL          04(AP),R0
EXE$NAMPID+00010:       BEQL          EXE$NAMPID+0002D
EXE$NAMPID+00012:       PROBEW        #00,#04,(R0)
EXE$NAMPID+00016:       BEQL          EXE$WAKE+00072
EXE$NAMPID+00018:       MOVL          (R0),R1
EXE$NAMPID+0001B:       BEQL          EXE$NAMPID+0002D
EXE$NAMPID+0001D:       BSBW          EXE$EPID_TO_IPID+0000D
SDA> sh stack
```

Figure 7 contd.

```
Process stacks (on CPU 00)
--------------
Current operating stack (KERNEL):

                7FFE7798  7FFECC58
                7FFE779C  7FFED7D4
                7FFE77A0  7FFE2BDC    CTL$AG_CLIDATA+00180
                7FFE77A4  00000221    BUG$_MODRELNBAK+00001
                7FFE77A8  7FFE77C0    CTL$GL_KSTKBAS+005C0
                7FFE77AC  7FFE77B0    CTL$GL_KSTKBAS+005B0
                7FFE77B0  8118DE1B    EXE$NAMPID+0000C
                7FFE77B4  00C20009

        SP =>   7FFE77B8  000002D8    BUG$_NOTPCB
                7FFE77BC  813A1880
                7FFE77C0  00000000
                7FFE77C4  003C0000
                7FFE77C8  7FF37D78
                7FFE77CC  7FFE77E4    CTL$GL_KSTKBAS+005E4
                7FFE77D0  8118D639    EXE$CMKRNL+0000D
                7FFE77D4  00000004

SDA> e/i 2d8
BUG$_NOTPCB:               MOVL     (SP)+,R2
SDA> e/i 2d8-40;40
BUG$_NONEXSTACP:           HALT
BUG$_NONEXSTACP+00001:     MTPR       #02,#12
BUG$_NONEXSTACP+00004:     MOVL       #00000056,R1
BUG$_NORCVBUF+00003:       JSB        @#V_EXE$ALONONPAGED
BUG$_NOTDDBDDB+00001:      BLBC       R0,BUG$_NOTVVPVCB+00006
BUG$_NOTDDBDDB+00004:      PUSHR      #3F
BUG$_NOTDDBDDB+00006:      MOVC3      #0056,BUG$_OUTSWPERR+00003,(R2)
BUG$_NOTFCBWCB:            POPR       #3F
BUG$_NOTFCBWCB+00002:      MOVW       R1,08(R2)
BUG$_NOTFCBWCB+00006:      MOVB       #02,0A(R2)
BUG$_NOTFCPWCB+00002:      MOVAL      0020(R2),18(R2)
BUG$_NOTIRPAQB:            CLRB       0B(R2)
BUG$_NOTIRPAQB+00003:      BISB2      #80,0B(R2)
BUG$_NOTMTLMTL:            PUSHL      R2
BUG$_NOTMTLMTL+00002:      JSB        @#V_EXE$NAMPID
BUG$_NOTPCB:               MOVL       (SP)+,R2
SDA> e/i @pc-10;80
%SDA-W-INSKIPPED, unreasonable instruction stream - 3 bytes skipped
EXE$WAKE+0007B:  RSB
EXE$NAMPID:                MFPR       #12,-(SP)
EXE$NAMPID+00003:          CMPL       #00,(SP)+
EXE$NAMPID+00006:          BGEQU      EXE$NAMPID+0000C
EXE$NAMPID+00008:          BUG_CHECK  #06A4
EXE$NAMPID+0000C:          MOVL       4(AP),R0
EXE$NAMPID+00010:          BEQL       EXE$NAMPID+0002D
EXE$NAMPID+00012:          PROBEW     #00,#04,(R0)
EXE$NAMPID+00016:          BEQL       EXE$WAKE+00072
EXE$NAMPID+00018:          MOVL       (R0),R1
EXE$NAMPID+0001B:          BEQL       EXE$NAMPID+0002D
EXE$NAMPID+0001D:          BSBW       EXE$EPID_TO_IPID+0000D
EXE$NAMPID+00020:          BEQL       EXE$NAMPID+0008C
EXE$NAMPID+00022:          TSTL       @#CLU$GL_CLUB
EXE$NAMPID+00028:          BEQL       EXE$NAMPID+0008C
EXE$NAMPID+0002A:          BRW        EXE$CHECK_PCB_PRIV+00041
EXE$NAMPID+0002D:          MOVL       08(AP),R3
EXE$NAMPID+00031:          BEQL       EXE$WAKE+0004D
EXE$NAMPID+00033:          PROBER     #00,#08,(R3)
EXE$NAMPID+00037:          BEQL       EXE$WAKE+00072
EXE$NAMPID+00039:          MOVQ       (R3),R2
EXE$NAMPID+0003C:          TSTW       R2
EXE$NAMPID+0003E:          BEQL       EXE$WAKE+00076
EXE$NAMPID+00040:          CMPW       #00FF,R2
EXE$NAMPID+00045:          BLSSU      EXE$WAKE+00076
EXE$NAMPID+00047:          PROBER     #00,R2,(R3)
EXE$NAMPID+0004B:          BEQL       EXE$WAKE+00072
EXE$NAMPID+0004D:          PUSHL      R0
EXE$NAMPID+0004F:          MOVL       @#SCH$GL_MAXPIX,R0
```

Figure 7 contd.

```
EXE$NAMPID+00056:   MOVL    @MMG$AL_SYSPCB+001BC[R0],R1
EXE$NAMPID+0005C:   CMPW    00C6(R1),00C6(R4)
EXE$NAMPID+00063:   BNEQ    EXE$NAMPID+00078
EXE$NAMPID+00065:   CMPB    R2,0138(R1)
EXE$NAMPID+0006A:   BNEQ    EXE$NAMPID+00078
EXE$NAMPID+0006C:   PUSHR   #0F
EXE$NAMPID+0006E:   CMPC3   R2,(R3),0139(R1)
EXE$NAMPID+00074:   POPR    #0F
EXE$NAMPID+00076:   BEQL    EXE$NAMPID+00085
EXE$NAMPID+00078:   SOBGEQ  R0,EXE$NAMPID+00056
EXE$NAMPID+0007B:   BSBW    CWPS$PARSE_PRCNAM
EXE$NAMPID+0007E:   BLBS    R0,EXE$NAMPID+0004F
SDA> ^Z
  Exit

ellis>
```

Figure 8.

```
;^^^^^^^^^^^^^^^^^^^^^^^^^^^^^^^^^^^^^^^^^^^^^^^^^^^^^^^^^^^^^^^^^^
;    Program:        wsblaster
;    Author:         Billy Bitsenbites (Bruce Ellis)
;    Date written:   9/28/87
;    Synopsis:       This program takes a Process Id as input
;                    and adjusts the associated process working
;                    set down to 250 pages.
;    Modifications:  11/11/89  BAE  rearrange the kernel mode
;                    so that the jsb to exe$nampid happens before
;                    the allocation of pool.  This is required
;                    since exe$nampid requires that the code is
;                    called at ipl 0 in Version 5.2.  Also add
;                    checks to guarantee that the process we are
;                    blasting is on our local node.  Future may
;                    include the ability to do this cluster-wide.
;                    Note: that this code was NOT tested in a VAXcluster
;                    configuration, but I am confident that it
;                    will not crash any systems and will work
;                    under the limitations advertised (i.e. node
;                    specific working set blasting.
;                    Also note that the code commented with an ;%%
;                    is probably not necessary and may be removed
;                    if no cluster related problems occur during
;                    execution without them.
;
;      The Hitchhiker's Guide apologizes for any crashes incurred
;      during Version 5.2 execution of this code.  Unfortunately
;      VMS Engineering does not consult the guide on update changes
;      nor were the changes documented in the V5.2 Release Notes.
;      Please note that the code was checked thoroughly before
;      its initial release.
;
;^^^^^^^^^^^^^^^^^^^^^^^^^^^^^^^^^^^^^^^^^^^^^^^^^^^^^^^^^^^^^^^^^^

;Include the system macro library
       .library        /sys$library:lib.mlb/
;Link against the system symbol table
       .link           /sys$system:sys.stb/
;^^^^^^^^^^^^^^^^^^^^^^^^
;Include definitions
;^^^^^^^^^^^^^^^^^^^^^^^^
       $pcbdef         ;Process control block
       $dyndef         ;Dynamic memory types
       $ipldef         ;Interrupt Priority Level
       $acbdef         ;AST Control block
       $pridef         ;Priority boost classes
       $spldef         ;Spinlock

       .macro   check  ?1
       blbs     r0,1
       $exit_s  r0
1:
       .endm    check
```

Figure 8 contd.

```
pid_a: .long   8      ;Ascii descriptor for PID storage
       .address       10$
10$:   .blkb   8
pid:   .blkl   1      ;Storage for binary representation of PID
pmt:   .ascid  /pid> /
pid_arg:              ;argument list for exe$nampid
       .long   1
       .address       pid
       .long   0
lock_adr:
       .address       lock_start
       .address       lock_end
;^^^^^^^^^^^^^^^^^^^^^^^^^^^^^^^^^^^^^^^^^^^^^^^^^^^^^^^^^^^^^^^^^^^
;    User mode code
;^^^^^^^^^^^^^^^^^^^^^^^^^^^^^^^^^^^^^^^^^^^^^^^^^^^^^^^^^^^^^^^^^^^
       .entry  blaster,^m<>
       pushal  pid_a   ;Read in pid
       pushal  pmt     ;  with prompt
       pushal  pid_a
       calls   #3,g^lib$get_input
       check
       pushal  pid     ;Convert pid from Hex Ascii to
       pushal  pid_a   ;  a longword binary value
       calls   #2,g^ots$cvt_tz_l
       check
;^^^^^^^^^^^^^
; Lock down code and data accessed at elevated IPL
;^^^^^^^^^^^^^
       $lkwset_s      inadr=lock_adr
       check
;^^^^^^^^^^^^^^^^^^^^^^^^^^^^^^^^^^^^^^^^^^^^^^^^^^^^^^^^^^^^^^^^^^^
;      Get into kernel mode and blast him
;^^^^^^^^^^^^^^^^^^^^^^^^^^^^^^^^^^^^^^^^^^^^^^^^^^^^^^^^^^^^^^^^^^^
       $cmkrnl_s      routin=negate_him,arglst=pid_arg
       ret
;^^^^^^^^^^^^^^^^^^^^^^^^^^^^^^^^^^^^^^^^^^^^^^^^^^^^^^^^^^^^^^^^^^^
;      Kernel mode code
;      description:
;            1)       Checks the pid and converts to PCB address
;                     and obtains IPID
;            2)       Allocates pool for an ACB, including the
;                     code for the special kernel ast
;            3)       Queues a Special Kernel AST to the process
;
;^^^^^^^^^^^^^^^^^^^^^^^^^^^^^^^^^^^^^^^^^^^^^^^^^^^^^^^^^^^^^^^^^^^
       .entry         negate_him,^m<r2,r3,r4,r5,r6>
lock_start:
;^^^^^^^^^
;Include checks for assumptions made about the csid
;^^^^^^^^^
csid_wid=pcb$s_epid_node_idx+pcb$s_epid_node_seq                   ;%%
;Guarantee that wild card bit follows the csid bit field
        ASSUME PCB$V_EPID_WILD EQ <PCB$V_EPID_NODE_IDX+CSID_WID>    ;%%
;Guarantee that the csid sequence number is adjacent to the index
        ASSUME PCB$V_EPID_NODE_SEQ EQ -                             ;%%
               <PCB$V_EPID_NODE_IDX+PCB$S_EPID_NODE_IDX>            ;%%
        movl   @4(ap),r6               ;%%get epid
        extzv  #pcb$v_epid_node_idx,-  ;%%extract the csid
               #<csid_wid+1>,r6,r6     ;%%pick off csid plus the wild card
                                       ;%% bit if there is any
        cmpw   g^sch$gw_localnode,r6   ;%%is the target process on same node?
        beql   same_node               ;%%if so continue
        movl   #ss$_remote_proc,r0     ;%%else return error status
        brw    scram                   ;%%
same_node:
        jsb    g^exe$nampid            ;find him
        blbc   r0,outta_here           ;on error deallocate the pool
        pushl  r1                      ;Save the ipid for the acb
        movl   #blaster_ast_size,r1    ;Allocate the pool for the
        jsb    g^exe$alononpaged       ; ACB+code
        blbc   r0,scram                ;no pool then leave
;^^^^^^^^^^^^^
```

Figure 8 contd.

```
;Copy the code into pool
;^^^^^^^^^^^^^
        pushr   #^m<r0,r1,r2,r3,r4,r5>
        movc3   #blaster_ast_size,blaster_ast,(r2)
        popr    #^m<r0,r1,r2,r3,r4,r5>
        movw    R1,acb$w_size(r2)           ;Fill in size for later deallocation
        movb    #dyn$c_acb,acb$b_type(r2)   ;set type as ACB
;^^^^^^^^^^^^^
;Fill in the address of the KAST routine
;^^^^^^^^^^^^^
        moval   <blaster_ast_code-blaster_ast>(r2),acb$l_kast(r2)
        clrb    acb$b_rmod(r2)              ;Clear request mode bits
        bisb    #acb$m_kast,acb$b_rmod(r2)  ;Mark as Special kernel AST
        popl    acb$l_pid(r2)               ;copy in his IPID
        movl    r2,r5                       ;R5 must point to ACB for SCH$QAST
        movl    #pri$_ticom,r2              ;give him a big boost
        jsb     g^sch$qast                  ;Queue the AST
        unlock lockname=SCHED,newipl=#0     ;Give up SCHED spinlock
                                            ;that nampid took out
lock_end:
        movl    #ss$_normal,r0              ;success
outta_here:
        ret                                 ;sayonara
scram:  setipl #0                           ;reset IPL
        brb     outta_here                  ;return error status

;^^^^^^^^^^^^^^^^^^^^^^^^^^^^^^^^^^^^^^^^^^^^^^^^^^^^^^^^^^^^^^
;       ACB with code following
;^^^^^^^^^^^^^^^^^^^^^^^^^^^^^^^^^^^^^^^^^^^^^^^^^^^^^^^^^^^^^^
blaster_ast:
acb:    .blkb  acb$k_length                 ;Allocate storage for ACB
old_ws: .blkl  1                            ;saved working set size
blaster_ast_code:
        $adjwsl_s       wsetlm=old_ws       ;get current working set size
        blbc   r0,escape                    ;on error scram
        pushl  r3                           ;save r3
        subl3  #250,old_ws,r3               ;compute the difference between
                                            ;the current working set size
                                            ;and the new size of 250 pages
        blss   escape                       ;if he is already under get out
        mnegl  r3,r3                        ;negate the difference
        $adjwsl_s       pagcnt=r3           ;Adjust down to 250 pages
escape: movl   r5,r0                        ;set up for deallocation
        popl   r3                           ;restore r3
        jmp    g^exe$deanonpaged            ;give up the pool and disappear
        blaster_ast_size=.-blaster_ast
        .end   blaster
$
$
$ mac wsblaster_too
$
$ link wsblaster_too
$
```

Figure 9. SHOW SYSTEM displays before and after running WSBLASTER_TOO.

```
VAX/VMS V5.2  on node LABDOG  16-NOV-1989 05:53:55.59   Uptime  1 18:03:57
  Pid    Process Name    State  Pri    I/O        CPU        Page flts  Ph.Mem
00000021 SWAPPER         HIB     16      0    0 01:00:25.95         0       0
00000062 EVL             HIB      6     92    0 00:00:16.60     38474      46    N
00000025 ERRFMT          HIB      8   1336    0 00:00:17.36        81     114
00000026 OPCOM           HIB      8    103    0 00:00:01.30       261     130
00000027 AUDIT_SERVER    HIB     10     53    0 00:00:09.50      1340     178
00000028 JOB_CONTROL     HIB      9    416    0 00:00:03.68       321     250
00000029 NETACP          HIB     10    291    0 00:00:35.77       338     250
0000004D MULTINET_SERVER HIB      4    120    0 00:00:02.63       299      74
0000002F REMACP          HIB      9     63    0 00:00:00.36        77      44
00000050 SMTP_SYMBIONT   HIB      4     20    0 00:00:01.19       336      38
000000B1 ELLISB          CUR      4   8790    0 00:00:47.50      4590     302
```

Figure 9 contd.

```
000000B2 pig              LEF      6      9    0 00:00:02.07       2161     278     S
00000033 SYMBIONT_0001    HIB      4     24    0 00:00:00.93        227     111
$ r wsblaster_too
pid> B2
$ sh sys
VAX/VMS V5.2  on node LABDOG  16-NOV-1989 05:54:24.74   Uptime  1 18:04:26
  Pid    Process Name     State  Pri    I/O        CPU       Page flts  Ph.Mem
00000021 SWAPPER          HIB     16      0    0 01:00:25.95          0       0
00000062 EVL              HIB      6     92    0 00:00:16.61      38505      46     N
00000025 ERRFMT           HIB      8   1336    0 00:00:17.36         81     114
00000026 OPCOM            HIB      8    103    0 00:00:01.30        261     130
00000027 AUDIT_SERVER     HIB     10     53    0 00:00:09.50       1340     178
00000028 JOB_CONTROL      HIB      9    416    0 00:00:03.68        321     250
00000029 NETACP           HIB     10    291    0 00:00:35.77        338     250
0000004D MULTINET_SERVER  HIB      4    120    0 00:00:02.63        299      74
0000002F REMACP           HIB      9     63    0 00:00:00.36         77      44
00000050 SMTP_SYMBIONT    HIB      4     20    0 00:00:01.19        336      38
000000B1 ELLISB           CUR      4    910    0 00:00:48.13       4643     305
000000B2 pig              LEF      9      9    0 00:00:02.08       2162     250     S
00000033 SYMBIONT_0001    HIB      4     24    0 00:00:00.93        227     111
$
$ r wsblaster_too
pid> 202000B1
%SYSTEM-F-REMOTE_PROC, operation not allowed, process is on remote node
$
$ r wsblaster_too
pid> B7
%SYSTEM-W-NONEXPR, nonexistent process
$
```

Episode 4

Love and Global Sections

The initial Pfffffffftt was followed by the scraping sound of metal against glass. Glug, glug, glug.

Billy slowly examined the glass bottle. With a grin creeping across his face, he took delight in the name Jolt cola.

He appreciated the cola's caffeine and sugar content at 2:45 a.m. For the first time, he was starting to feel like a system programmer.

Other thoughts raced through Billy's mind; he had difficulty concentrating. His mind was thrashing, trying to hold more than it could and getting little real work done.

His projects had been put on hold ever since Dennis Cutlery had been promoted. Middle management in America constantly amazed Billy. As the incompetent were detected, they were moved into positions that were lateral moves or promotions. This behavior leaves businesses with a midmanagement bulge and a dearth of competent support people. In other words, too many chiefs and not enough Indians.

All that Billy knew of his new boss was that he was referred to as Dr. Albino. He also knew he had inherited a system with severe performance and management problems. Billy made efforts to bail out the system in spite of Cutlery's incompetence. At the moment, he didn't care about the speed of the system; his mind focused on other more pressing thoughts.

He needed help. So he went to the gray book and opened the cover of *The Hitchhiker's Guide to VMS*. After the usual whirring and clicking, the book queried Billy.

"Are you ready to attack the problem of process file activity?"

"No," Billy entered.

"Why not?" the *Guide* demanded. "I have spent a great deal of time gathering the information you would require to perform the task."

"Because I, I, I," Billy stuttered into the keyboard. Billy might have been the first person ever to stutter into a keyboard. This startled even Billy. Knowing he had to collect his thoughts, he stopped typing and pondered the answer to the posed question.

Beep, beep, beep.

"Hey, wake up and answer me," the book demanded. Software for the *Guide* had a built-in timer to detect delays in response. This was designed into the *Guide* to improve overall system performance. It has been known for a long time that the slowest component to a computer system is the human on the other end of the terminal, although some debate that the TU58 is actually slower. Any efforts by software to speed up this slug should improve overall system throughput.

Billy snapped to and responded, "I met a girl."

"So what are you doing here?" the *Guide* asked.

"Well, I'm taking night classes at Northeastern, trying to finally get my degree. Between classes, I started talking to this girl in my operating system design class. She works for the university computer department, and she mentioned that she wanted to prove that some of the global sections they were using were being used effectively. Evidently, the new system manager wanted to deinstall some of the images to save some memory. He figured that smaller GBLSECTIONS and GBLPAGES settings would free up memory for processes to use. She thinks that they should remain installed but can't prove it. I told her I would help her out."

Billy chose Northeastern, based on the following entry in the *Guide*:

"Half of Northeastern's night school students are Digital employees trying to get computer science degrees or MBAs."

Billy knew that if you needed to get a problem solved with DEC, it was more important that you knew the right person than the right information. He figured that night classes at Northeastern would kill two birds with one stone. However, he didn't expect to meet the "contact" who occupied his thoughts.

"So you want to know how to determine the effectiveness of global section use?" the *Guide* asked.

"Yes. But how about starting with something a little more fundamental. Like, what exactly is a global section anyway?" responded Billy.

"Before starting, let me tell you that you might want to check the pin connectors on your logic chip. You are in big trouble when you start writing software to impress girls. What ever happened to poetry?

"A global section describes virtual memory that might be shared by processes on a VMS system. Global sections most commonly are created by using the /SHARE qualifier in the INSTALL utility. The qualifier is applied to the ADD command to create global sections for a shared or shareable image.

"A shared image is a program that is going to be run frequently by multiple processes on the system. The global section information allows the processes to share the read-only pages, such as code pages, while maintaining private copies of writable data pages.

"A shareable image is a set of routines or data that will be used by different programs. The run-time library is an example of a shareable image. These images have advantages similar to the shared image. However, they allow the sharing of data that is maintained in program sections with the share (SHR) attribute, such as data stored in a COMMON area. Although this has advantages of its own, if you are not expecting to share the data, this behavior can cause problems when you change someone else's variable on the fly. This can be avoided by the use of the PSECT_ATTR option in a linker options file.

"Shareable images have other benefits, including upgradability and conservation of disk space. We can discuss these topics later if you are interested.

"The other technique for creating global sections is the create and map section system service (SYS$CRMPSC). This system service usually is used by applications developers to create sections that will be used for the sharing of data between processes. This system service also can be used to create process private sections and provides the foundations for image activation," the *Guide* concluded.

"How does VMS support this sharing? Are the pages guaranteed to be memory resident?" Billy wondered.

"No, the page is not guaranteed to be memory resident," the *Guide* answered. "Let us examine process private paging first. Then we will address global paging.

"When you run a program," the *Guide* began, "you first call the image activator system service (SYS$IMGACT). This service will read in the image header of the image file, which is located in the first block or blocks of the image file.

"The image header contains data structures called image section descriptors. These structures describe the virtual layout of sections of the image file that have the same attributes, such as readability versus writability and code versus data. The descriptors contain the starting virtual block number of the section of code or data in the image file, a count of the number of pages in the section, the starting virtual page number of the beginning of the section of virtual memory, and flags describing the attributes of the section.

"At image activation time, these descriptors are used to construct different tables in the process header (PHD). These tables are the process section table (PST) and the P0 and P1 page tables.

"The process section table is a memory resident copy of the image section descriptor with a couple other pieces of information. The additional pieces of information are the address of the channel control block (CCB) and the window control block (WCB). These two structures allow us to perform the I/O operation required to read the block from the image file into a page in memory.

"The page tables contain page table entries that are a longword in size and allow the memory management hardware and the pager to determine the current location of the page."

Billy was beginning to wonder whether love was truly worth this ordeal.

The *Guide* continued, "For sections of code or data that reside in the image file, we build page table entries that have the most significant bit clear. That bit is called the valid bit. Since the bit is clear, the first access of the page will cause a page fault to occur. The pager will be activated by an exception. He will determine that this page is contained in the image file and grab the low word of the page table entry. The word contains a process section table index.

"The process section table index is a negative index into the process section table that allows us to locate the process section table entry (PSTE) for the section of code. We will scan forward through the page table entries and determine whether other pages reside in this section. After we have found out how many pages reside in this section, we will grab the corresponding number of pages from the free page list, make them valid and use the PSTE to initiate a read. Note that several pages might be made valid because of the single hard fault.

"It is also possible that the page is a data page containing uninitialized data. These pages typically would become demand zero pages. A demand zero fault would be resolved by simply taking a page from the free page list, making it valid, and initializing the page to 0. This would be a soft fault, because it does not require an I/O operation to make it valid."

"How does the pager differentiate between process section pages and demand zero pages?" Billy asked.

"The page table entry contains two bits, PTE$V_TYP0 and PTE$V_TYP1. These bits are used to determine the page type.

"Do you have any other questions at this point?" the *Guide* asked.

"None that I can verbalize," Billy responded. "Please continue."

"After the page has been made valid, it is added to the process' working set list. The process may access the valid page with no software intervention. The memory management hardware knows the location of the page because the pager has placed the physical location of the page, i.e., the page frame number (PFN), into the low 21 bits of the page table entry.

"The working set list limits the number of pages a process might own. When the list gets full, the process must invalidate a page before making another one valid. When the page is invalidated, it is placed on the free or modified page list, depending on whether it has been modified or whether it is modifiable."

"Is the page actually moved to these lists?" Billy queried.

"No. The free and modified page lists are described by two arrays that contain the PFN of the previous and next pages in the list. The arrays are located through the addresses PFN$AX_FLINK and PFN$AX_BLINK. The index into the arrays is the PFN of the page. These two arrays and six others form a database called the PFN database. Note that the PFN still is contained in the page table entry," the *Guide* answered.

"I have a couple of questions here," Billy interjected. "First, how does VMS know which list the page is on?"

"The PFN database contains a state array located through PFN$AB_STATE, describing the list that the page resides on," the *Guide* responded.

"My second question is, what is the AX after the dollar sign ($) telling me? AW would be an array of words. AL would be an array of longwords. But what is AX telling me?" Billy wondered.

"In the case of the FLINK and BLINK arrays, we don't know the size until bootstrap time. Prior to version 4.0 of VMS, these arrays were one word in size. This allowed us to describe 32 megabytes of physical memory. When large memory VAX processors were introduced, we needed a larger array. In current releases, when VMS boots, it determines the size of physical memory. If there are 32 megabytes or less, these are word arrays. If there are more than 32 megabytes of memory on the system, these arrays are referenced as longword arrays. You can determine the referencing size to use as an index based on the location

MMG$GW_BIGPFN. If this location is non-zero, then you should use a longword indexing instruction. Otherwise, you should use word indexing instructions," the book answered.

"So, because the page table entry contains the PFN for pages on the free and modified page lists, if we were to reference one of these pages, we could resolve the fault by setting the valid bit and shuffling some pointers in the PFN database. Do I have that right?" Billy wondered.

"You have it right," the *Guide* concurred.

"If the page is written from the modified page list to the page file, it will go to the free list. But the page will not physically move, and the page table entry will still contain the PFN of the page. So, if I touched the page now, I still would get a soft fault. Correct?" said Billy, as he attempted to put the pieces together.

"Correct," the *Guide* responded.

"What happens when the page is pulled off the free list?" asked Billy.

"VMS puts information into the page table entry of the process describing the disk location of the page. That information is either the process section table index or the page file virtual block number," the *Guide* answered.

"So at this point, the process would incur a hard fault, if it accessed the page. Right?" Billy asked.

"Right," the *Guide* acknowledged.

"How does VMS know what to put into the page table entry? And for that matter, because another process may have pulled the page off the free list, how does VMS know where the page table entry is located?" Billy wondered.

"The PFN database maintains a backing store array, describing the disk location of the page. This array is located by indexing off the location pointed to by PFN$AL_BAK. We can locate the page table entry by using the array pointed to by PFN$AL_PTE," the *Guide* replied.

"Okay, I think I have a feel for process private paging, but I still don't have a clue how to attack the global section problem. Let's start with the create and map section system service. The name seems to imply that there are two parts to the service, i.e., creating and mapping. Tell me what's going on with the service, please," Billy requested.

"Creating a section, in the case of a global section, means that you are building three data structures: the global section descriptor (GSD), the global section table entry, and the global page table entries.

"The global section descriptor describes the section by name and contains other information that defines the global section. In particular, the GSD contains the global section table index that allows us to locate the global section table entry. GSDs are allocated out of paged pool. GSDs are maintained in one of two listheads, either EXE$GL_GSDSYSFL for system global sections or EXE$GL_GSDGRPFL for group global sections.

"The GSD contains a usage count that describes how frequently the image has been run since it was last installed. This might be useful to your lady friend. It is accessible from the following command:

```
$INSTALL LIST image/GLOBAL/FULL
```

"The global section table entry basically is identical to the process section table entry, with the following distinctions. The global section table entry contains the address of the global section descriptor instead of the channel control block address. The channel control block address would not make sense here because CCBs are allocated out of process P1 space and there's no guarantee of a P1 space being available with a global section.

"The global section table entry contains a reference count of the number of page table entries currently mapped to the section."

Billy interrupted the *Guide*, "Wouldn't that solve the problem? We could go in and grab the reference count. Wouldn't that tell us whether we were using the sections effectively?"

"No," the *Guide* replied. "The reference count tells us nothing about the memory residence of pages from the section. It only tells that processes are interested in the section. It is possible that none of the pages from the section are in memory, even though the reference count is large. It is also possible that pages for the section are in memory, although the reference count is 0. The reference count simply is used to determine whether it is safe to delete the global section."

Billy was wondering why VMS wasn't written as a haiku. He was seriously considering taking up poetry at this point.

The *Guide* continued, "Remember that the section table entries provide the ability to perform paging I/O. This is their primary function. They also allow us to locate the global pages in the section by providing a count and starting virtual page number.

"The global section table entries are located in the system header. The system header is located through the pointer MMG$GL_SYSPHD.

"The global page table entries work the same as process page table entries, with the exception that the memory management hardware never sees them. They are purely a software construct.

"The global page table entry entries initially contain the global section table index to locate the global section table entry. This index will allow us to perform the I/O operation for the initial hard fault."

"Hold on," Billy demanded. "If the global page table isn't examined by the memory management hardware, how do we generate the initial fault?"

"The structures we have just described are used to create the section. Before you can use the section, you must map to it," the book answered. "Mapping to the section means that the process constructs page table entries that initially contain a global page table index and are invalid. This index allows the pager to locate the page table entry, on a fault, by indexing off the global page table that's pointed to by the location MMG$GL_GPTBASE.

"After we locate the global page table entry, we can resolve the fault in one of three ways, assuming it is a read only page.

"The global page table entry may contain the global section table index. This would mean that we would have to perform a hard fault to make the page valid.

"It could be that the page currently is valid for another process. In this case, the global page table entry would contain the PFN of the page, and the valid bit would be set. Then, all we would need to do is copy up the PFN into the process page table entry. This would show up in $MONITOR PAGE as a global valid fault. There are two big wins here. The fault would be a soft fault, and we'd be guaranteed of sharing pages.

"It also could be that the page currently resides on the free page list. Then, we would have to remove the page from the free list, copy up the PFN, and set the valid bit in both the process and global page table entries. This also would be a soft fault and would show up in $MONITOR PAGE as a free list fault."

Billy wondered whether T.S. Eliot started out this way. He was sure Arthur Rimbaud did.

The *Guide* continued, "Note that after the fault is resolved, the PFN will be stored in both the global and process page table entries."

"Whose working set gets charged for the page? Does the system's?" Billy wondered.

"No, the system's working set doesn't get charged for the actual page; the process' working set gets charged. The only cost to the system's working set is based on the fact that the global page table is pageable. If we also fault on the page containing the global page table entry, the system's working set will be charged for the page of global page table entries," the *Guide* answered.

"So, the global page table is pageable. That seems to imply that there's a small cost for oversizing it," Billy interjected.

"Yes," the book agreed. "In fact, the actual costs for the structures supporting global sections are extremely small. The cost for the global page table in bytes is calculated by dividing the number of global page table entries by 32. The cost for the global section tables is 32 bytes of physical memory for each global section table entry. The global section descriptor cost is insignificant because it's allocated out of paged pool."

"Why don't people just install most of their images?" Billy asked.

"Because they are still operating on a 2-MB mindset," the *Guide* offered.

"Does the page get charged against each process' working set list?" Billy asked.

"Yes," the *Guide* answered.

"That doesn't seem fair," Billy entered.

"That may be true, but the paging mechanics would break down if it were not so. When a global page is removed from the working set, the global page table index is placed back into the process' page table entry immediately."

Billy interrupted, "You mean the PFN is not left in the page table entry when it is displaced, as it would be if it were a process private page?"

"Yes," the *Guide* answered. "The page still might be valid for another process. We could get a global valid fault on the page again."

"How do we determine whether it is time to place the page on the free page list?"

"In the PFN database, the forward link array (i.e., PFN$AX_FLINK) doubles as a share count if the page is a global valid page. The share count array is pointed to by PFN$AX_SHRCNT, which is an overlayed representation of the forward link pointer. When the share count drops to 0, the page is placed on the free list," the *Guide* responded.

"So, we still could get a free list fault," Billy added. "Where on the free page list do the global pages go when an image runs down?"

"Global pages go to the tail of the list unlike process private pages," the *Guide* replied. "This means that the next process running the same image will stand a good chance of locating the pages required to support image activation on the free list. Therefore, it should see much better quality faulting at image activation time.

"Note that when a global page is pulled off the free page list by another process that is not interested in the page, we must replace the global page table entry with the backing store pointer. This mechanism works just like it would for a process private page."

"So," Billy postulated, "the advantages to global sections are that we may reduce memory requirements through the sharing of pages, we may get better quality paging because another process already may have the page valid, and we should get faster image activation time because the pages already might be in memory on the free list or they might potentially be valid."

"That is correct," the *Guide* concurred.

"To write the program to solve my friend's problem, I should determine how many of the pages from the section are memory resident, how many are valid, and how many sharers there are of the global valid pages," Billy proposed.

"Correct," the *Guide* agreed.

"To write the program, I must locate the section by name by scanning through the GSDs and checking for the correct name," Billy entered.

"Yes. The global section name is stored in GSD$T_GSDNAM," the *Guide* added.

Billy examined the data structure layouts in SYS$LIBRARY:LIB.REQ and continued, "The field GSD$W_GSTX contains the global section table index. I can grab that, sign extend it, and back up from the end of the global section table to locate the global section table entry. To locate the end of the global section table, I can jump into the system header by grabbing the address pointed to by MMG$GL_SYSPHD. Then I would offset into the system header by the number of bytes stored in the field PHD$L_PSTBASOFF.

"After I have the global section table entry, I can get the index to the first global page table entry by using the contents of the three low bytes of the field SEC$L_VPXPFC. To determine how many page table entries to examine, I can get the contents of SEC$L_PAGCNT. Then I can index off the location pointed to by MMG$GL_GPTBASE to locate the global page table entry.

"The most significant bit in the page table entry will tell me whether or not the page is valid. If it's valid, I can go to PFN$AX_SHRCNT and grab the share count.

"If the page is not valid, it could be in memory on the free page list. To determine memory residence, I could check the type bits in the page table entry.

"Now I am all done, with the exception of formatting and displaying the information," Billy said proudly.

Then he pondered, "One point where I still need help is synchronization. Do I use spinlocks and interrupt priority level for synchronization?"

The *Guide* answered, "You would use the MMG spinlock for synchronization of the PFN database. You may not use spinlocks to synchronize with global section descriptor access. These structures are allocated out of paged pool. Remember from our earlier discussions that no page faults are allowed at interrupt priority levels greater than 2?

"To synchronize with GSD access, you must take out a mutex."

"What's a mutex?" Billy asked.

"A mutex is a mutual exclusion semaphore," the *Guide* responded. "Given databases that are protected by mutexes are assigned a longword that describes the mutex. The longword is initialized to contain 0 in the high word and -1 in the low word.

"Mutexes allow single writers and multiple readers, though multiple readers typically are rare. When you want to grab the mutex for read access, you would jump to subroutine (JSB) to the routine SCH$LOCKR. For write access, JSB to SCH$LOCKW.

"If you want read access, SCH$LOCKR will check the high word to determine whether the write in progress/write active flag is set. If it is, your process will be placed in an MWAIT state of the type MUTEX. You will compete for the mutex after it has been released.

"If there are no writers or interested writers, you will be granted the mutex. The ownership count in the low word will be incremented. To make it easy to get in and out of the subsystem quickly and to minimize contention, your priority temporarily will be raised to 16.

"When you are finished with the mutex, you would JSB to SCH$UNLOCK. This routine will decrement the ownership count. If the count drops to -1, the mutex will be released, and any processes interested in the mutex will compete for it.

"If you want to write the mutex protected structure, you must check that the write flag is clear and the ownership count is -1. If these conditions are true, you will be granted the mutex. Otherwise, you will wait in a fashion identical to the reader's.

"It is important that you release the mutex before exiting kernel mode. If you did not, in theory, we could have a phantom mutex. VMS will not let this state occur. If you leave kernel mode with an owned mutex, VMS will crash.

"Likewise, it is important that you are not deleted with an owned mutex. To prevent deletion, you should run at interrupt priority level 2 (IPL$_ASTDEL).

"The inputs for the mutex routines are that R0 should contain the address of the mutex and R4 should contain your software process control block (PCB) address. The mutex for global sections is located at EXE$GL_GSDMTX."

"Wow," thought Billy. "Lawrence Ferlinghetti never had it so tough."

"I have one other thing I'd like to work out. The global page table is pageable. So I can't access it at high interrupt priority level. This means that the spinlock for the PFN database must be acquired after I've checked the page table entry. How do I guarantee that the page still is valid?" Billy asked.

"To make sure the page still is described in the PFN database, you could check the page table entry array (i.e., PFN$AL_PTE) entry for the page and make sure it matches the address you started with. To make sure the page still is valid, you could check the bit PFN$C_ACTIVE in the state array of the PFN database, i.e., PFN$AB_STATE," the *Guide* replied.

"Okay," Billy entered. "Let me code this up." (See Figure 10.)

Billy tested the code. It worked. He picked a section that wasn't memory resident. Then he ran the installed program. After running SHOW_SHARE, he saw that most of the pages were memory resident (see Figure 11).

"Thanks, Book," Billy entered.

"You are most welcome," the *Guide* replied.

Suddenly, the door to the computer room burst open. Billy saw a large white-haired man enter. Billy looked at his watch and saw that it was 5:42 a.m.

"What are you doing here?" the white-haired man asked.

WHO IS the white-haired man and what does he want? Will Billy get the girl? Is there a place for poetry in the life of a system programmer? Will Billy ever get to the open file program?

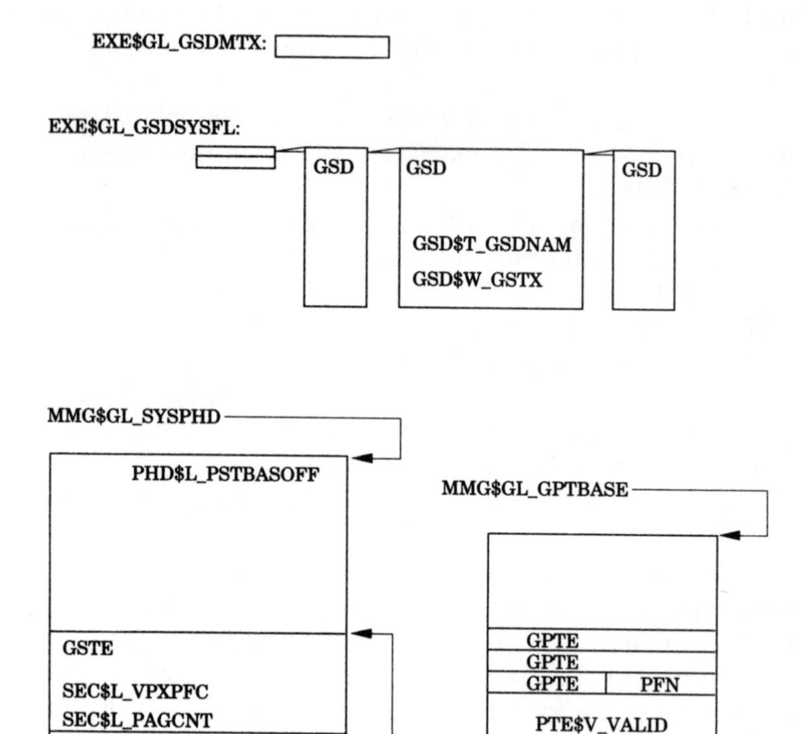

Data structures accessed by SHOW_SHARE.MAR

Figure 10.

```
;*****************************************************************
;       Program:        SHOW_SHARE
;       Author:         Billy Bitsenbites (Bruce Ellis)
;       Date written:   9/22/87
;       Synopsis:       This program receives a section name and
;                       locates all sections named "name_" and
;                       displays the share counts for all pages
;                       mapped by the section.
;*****************************************************************
;include files
        .library        /sys$library:lib.mlb/
        .link           /sys$system:sys.stb/
        $ipldef         ;IPL symbolic definitions
        $secdef         ;Define section table entry offsets
        $gsddef         ;Define global section descriptor offsets
        $ptedef         ;Page table entry offsets
        $pfndef         ;PFN database bit definitions
        $phddef         ;Process header definitions
        .macro  check   ?1
        blbs    r0,1
        $exit_s r0
1:
        .endm   check

;*****************************************************************
;       Format for fao output
;*****************************************************************
fmt:    .ascid  $ Section name: !AC!/!/$-
                $ Total pages: !10UL  Total valid pages: !10UL!/
                $ Total memory resident invalid pages: !10UL !/$-
                $ Pages with share count of 1:     !10UL!/$-
                $ Pages with share count of 2:     !10UL!/$-
                $ Pages with share count of 3:     !10UL!/$-
                $ Pages with share count of 4:     !10UL!/$-
                $ Pages with share count of 5:     !10UL!/$-
                $ Pages with share count of 6:     !10UL!/$-
                $ Pages with share count of 7:     !10UL!/$-
                $ Pages with share count of 8:     !10UL!/$-
                $ Pages with share count of 9:     !10UL!/$-
                $ Pages with share count of 10+:   !10UL!/$
buffer: .long   1024            ;Buffer location for display characters
        .address        10$
10$:    .blkb   1024
pmt:    .ascid  /Image name> /  ;Prompt for section name
lock_start:
max_sections=9                  ;Currently limited to the first 9 sections
images: .blkb   max_sections*40 ;storage for section names
mem_not_valid:
        .blkl   max_sections    ;storage for count of invalid pages which
                                ; are memory resident
mem_valid:
        .blkl   max_sections    ;Count of valid pages
pagecnt:
        .blkl   max_sections    ;Count of total pages in section
share_list:                     ;Count of number of sharers
        .blkl   max_sections*10
img_count:
        .blkl                   ;Count of number of sections
image:  .long   39              ;storage for section name
        .address        image_a
image_a:
        .blkb   39
lock_addr:
        .address        lock_start
        .address        lock_end
;*****************************************************************
;       Code start
;*****************************************************************
        .entry  share,^m<r2,r3,r4,r5,r6,r7>
        pushal  image                   ;Read in section name
        pushal  pmt
        pushal  image
        calls   #3,g^lib$get_input
```

Figure 10 contd.

```
        check
        movzwl    image,r2                  ;append an "_" to the end to
        movb      #^a/_/,image_a(r2)        ; get a name of the form sect_0001
        incl image                          ;make size correspond to included
                                            ; "_"
        $lkwset_s        inadr=lock_addr    ;Lock down the pages accessed at
                                            ; high ipl
        check
;*******************************************************************
;       Get the section info in kernel mode
;*******************************************************************
        $cmkrnl_s        routin=count_share_info
        check
        movl      img_count,r2              ;count of number of sections
        moval     images,r3                 ;section name buffer
        moval     mem_valid,r4              ;count of valid pages
        moval     pagecnt,r5                ;count of pages in the section
        moval     mem_not_valid,r6          ;count of the memory resident
                                            ; but not valid pages
        moval     share_list,r7             ;count of pages shared
;*******************************************************************
;       Format and dump the info one image at a time
;*******************************************************************
fmt_and_dump:
        $fao_s    ctrstr=fmt,outbuf=buffer,outlen=buffer,-
                  p1=r3,p2=(r5)+,p3=(r4)+,p4=(r6)+,p5=(r7),p6=4(r7),-
                  p7=8(r7),p8=12(r7),p9=16(r7),p10=20(r7),p11=24(r7),-
                  p12=28(r7),p13=32(r7),p14=36(r7)
        check
        pushal    buffer
        calls     #1,g^lib$put_output
        movl      #1024,buffer
        addl      #40,r3
        addl      #40,r7
        sobgtr    r2,fmt_and_dump
        ret
;*******************************************************************
;       Kernel mode code to get section counts
;*******************************************************************
        .entry    count_share_info,^m<r2,r3,r4,r5,r6,r7,r8,r9,r10,r11>
        pushl     #ss$_nosuchsec            ;assume ssection is nonexistent
        moval     g^exe$gl_gsdmtx,r0        ;make sure the section does not
        jsb       g^sch$lockr               ;go away while we are looking at it.
        moval     images,r3                 ;section name buffer
        moval     mem_valid,r4              ;count of valid pages
        moval     pagecnt,r5                ;count of pages in the section
        moval     mem_not_valid,r2          ;count of the memory resident
                                            ; but not valid pages
        moval     share_list,r7             ;count of pages shared
        clrl      img_count                 ;count of images <- 0
        assume    gsd$l_gsdfl eq 0
        moval     g^exe$gl_gsdsysfl,r6      ;Get listhead of GSDs
lookup_gsd:
        movl      (r6),r6                   ;get next gsd
        cmpl      r6,#exe$gl_gsdsysfl       ;Are we back at the start
        bneq      check_name                ;if not check the name
        brw       outta_gsds                ;else done
check_name:
        pushr     #^m<r0,r1,r2,r3,r4,r5>    ;save registers for cmpc3
        cmpc3     image,image_a,<gsd$t_gsdnam+1>(r6)       ;check name
        popr      #^m<r0,r1,r2,r3,r4,r5>    ;restore the register
        bneq      lookup_gsd                ;if we do not have the one
                                            ; we are looking for, get next
        movl      #ss$_normal,(sp)          ;Mark that we have found the gsd
        movb      gsd$t_gsdnam(r6),(r3)     ;copy the size into our descriptor
        movzbl    gsd$t_gsdnam(r6),r0       ;save the count
        pushr     #^m<r0,r1,r2,r3,r4,r5>    ;copy the full name back
        movc3     r0,<gsd$t_gsdnam+1>(r6),1(r3)
        popr      #^m<r0,r1,r2,r3,r4,r5>
        addl2     #40,r3                    ;point to next name buffer
        cvtwl     gsd$w_gstx(r6),r8         ;get the section table index
        movl      g^mmg$gl_sysphd,r1        ;get the system header address
        addl2     phd$l_pstbasoff(r1),r1    ;locate the end of the GST
        movl      sec$l_vpxpfc(r1)[r8],r10  ;get the Global page table index
```

Figure 10 contd.

```
        extzv   #sec$v_vpx,#sec$s_vpx,r10,r9
        movl    sec$l_pagcnt(r1)[r8],(r5)+                  ;get the page count
        movl    -4(r5),r11                  ;save the page count as a counter
next_gpte:
        moval   @mmg$gl_gptbase[r9],r10     ;get the pte address
        movl    (r10),r1                    ;get the contents of the pte
        blss    valid                       ;if valid then go process
        bitl    #pte$m_typ0,r1              ;check to see if the page is in
                                            ;memory
        beql    10$
        brw     not_in_mem                  ;if not go process
10$:
        bitl    #pte$m_typ1,r1              ;check to see if the page is in
                                            ; memory
        beql    20$
        brw     not_in_mem                  ;if not go process
20$:    incl    (r2)                        ;increment the count of invalid
                                            ; memory resident pages
        brw     not_in_mem                  ;done with this page
valid:  lock    lockname=MMG,lockipl=#ipl$_mmg              ;synch w/ PFN database
        extzv   #pte$v_pfn,#pte$s_pfn,r1,r1                 ;get the pfn
        cmpl    r10,@pfn$al_pte[r1]         ;is this the same pte
        beqlu   got_right_pte               ;if so continue processing
                                            ; else page is not in memory.
                                            ; This check should
                                            ; almost never occur.
        brw     not_in_mem_ul               ; done with this page
got_right_pte:
        bitb    #<1@pfn$c_active>,-         ;is the page still valid
                @pfn$ab_state[r1]
        beql    still_valid
        incl    (r2)                        ;bump count of not valid but
                                            ; memory resident
        brw     not_in_mem_ul               ;done plus unlock
still_valid:
        tstw    g^mmg$gw_bigpfn             ;determine size of index
        bneq    long_idx                    ;if long index use movl
        movzwl  @pfn$ax_shrcnt[r1],r1       ;get the share count
        brb     inc_cnt                     ;bump the count
long_idx:
        movl    @pfn$ax_shrcnt[r1],r1       ;get the share count
inc_cnt:
        cmpl    #10,r1                      ;if the count is greater than 10 use 10+
        bgtr    use_idx
        movl    #10,r1
use_idx:
        decl    r1                          ;back up for index
        incl    (r7)[r1]                    ;bump the count of sharers
        incl    (r4)                        ;bump the valid count
not_in_mem_ul:
     unlock     lockname=MMG,newipl=#ipl$_astdel            ;unlock pfn data base
not_in_mem:
     incl       r9                          ;use next index
     sobgtr     r11,next_gpte_brw           ;get next gpte
     brw        done_w_gptes                ;this branching scheme
next_gpte_brw:                              ; is to get around byte branching
     brw        next_gpte                   ; problems caused by spinlock macros
done_w_gptes:
     tstl       (r4)+                       ;bump pointers
     tstl       (r2)+
     addl       #40,r7
     incl       img_count                   ;bump the count of images
     cmpl       #max_sections,img_count     ;over quota?
     bleq       maxed_out                   ;if so scram
     brw        lookup_gsd                  ;else get next gsd
outta_gsds:
maxed_out:
     moval      g^exe$gl_gsdmtx,r0          ;give up the mutex
     movl       g^ctl$gl_pcb,r4             ; on the system gsds
     jsb        g^sch$unlock
     popl       r0                          ;set the status
     ret                                    ;scram
;*****************************************************************
lock_end:
     .end    share
```

Figure 11. ***After running SHOW_SHARE, most pages are memory resident.***

```
$ set proc/priv=all
$ install list sys$system:dcl/global/full

DISK$LABSYSRL5:<SYS0.SYSCOMMON.SYSEXE>.EXE
   DCL;1            Open Hdr Shar          Lnkbl
        Entry access count          = 41
        Current / Maximum shared    = 1 / 3
        Global section count        = 1

        System Global Sections
DCL_001         (03000000)            PRM SYS        Pagcnt/Refcnt=169/338
                Owner:        [1,4]
                Protection:  S:RWED,O:RWED,G:RWED,W:RE

$ r show_share
Image name> DCL
Section name: DCL_001
Total pages:         169  Total valid pages:        45
Total memory resident invalid pages:        120
Pages with share count of 1:           45
Pages with share count of 2:            0
Pages with share count of 3:            0
Pages with share count of 4:            0
Pages with share count of 5:            0
Pages with share count of 6:            0
Pages with share count of 7:            0
Pages with share count of 8:            0
Pages with share count of 9:            0
Pages with share count of 10+:          0

$
$ install add sys$system:sda/share
$
$ r show_share
Image name> SDA

Section name: SDA_003

Total pages:          28  Total valid pages:         0
Total memory resident invalid pages:          0
Pages with share count of 1:            0
Pages with share count of 2:            0
Pages with share count of 3:            0
Pages with share count of 4:            0
Pages with share count of 5:            0
Pages with share count of 6:            0
Pages with share count of 7:            0
Pages with share count of 8:            0
Pages with share count of 9:            0
Pages with share count of 10+:          0

Section name: SDA_002

Total pages:         369  Total valid pages:         0
Total memory resident invalid pages:          0
Pages with share count of 1:            0
Pages with share count of 2:            0
Pages with share count of 3:            0
Pages with share count of 4:            0
Pages with share count of 5:            0
Pages with share count of 6:            0
Pages with share count of 7:            0
Pages with share count of 8:            0
Pages with share count of 9:            0
Pages with share count of 10+:          0

Section name: SDA_001

Total pages:           1  Total valid pages:         0
Total memory resident invalid pages:          0
Pages with share count of 1:            0
```

Figure 11 contd.

```
Pages with share count of 2:            0
Pages with share count of 3:            0
Pages with share count of 4:            0
Pages with share count of 5:            0
Pages with share count of 6:            0
Pages with share count of 7:            0
Pages with share count of 8:            0
Pages with share count of 9:            0
Pages with share count of 10+:          0

$ ana/sys


VAX/VMS System analyzer

SDA> sh summ
Current process summary
-----------------------
.
.
.
SDA> exit
$
$ r show_share
Image name> SDA
Section name: SDA_003

Total pages:        28   Total valid pages:        0
Total memory resident invalid pages:        16
Pages with share count of 1:            0
Pages with share count of 2:            0
Pages with share count of 3:            0
Pages with share count of 4:            0
Pages with share count of 5:            0
Pages with share count of 6:            0
Pages with share count of 7:            0
Pages with share count of 8:            0
Pages with share count of 9:            0
Pages with share count of 10+:          0

Section name: SDA_002

Total pages:        369  Total valid page:         0
Total memory resident invalid pages:        198
Pages with share count of 1:            0
Pages with share count of 2:            0
Pages with share count of 3:            0
Pages with share count of 4:            0
Pages with share count of 5:            0
Pages with share count of 6:            0
Pages with share count of 7:            0
Pages with share count of 8:            0
Pages with share count of 9:            0
Pages with share count of 10+:          0

Section name: SDA_001

Total pages:        1    Total valid pages:        0
Total memory resident invalid pages:        0
Pages with share count of 1:            0
Pages with share count of 2:            0
Pages with share count of 3:            0
Pages with share count of 4:            0
Pages with share count of 5:            0
Pages with share count of 6:            0
Pages with share count of 7:            0
Pages with share count of 8:            0
Pages with share count of 9:            0
Pages with share count of 10+:          0

$
```

Episode 5

New Limits

Billy closed *The Hitchhiker's Guide to VMS* and slowly hit the return key several times, hoping that the display would disappear before his new boss made it to his desk.

Billy gazed at the man called Dr. Albino. Dr. Albino stood about six feet two inches, but seemed taller. His hair was relatively short in front, though it extended well below his collar. The funny thing about his name was that his hair was not really white, but a mix of fading brown and silver. His skin, however, was quite pale, as if radiating moonlight. Deep bags shadowed his eyes.

"Hello," said Dr. Albino. He gazed at the nine bottles of Jolt cola lined up across the desk, the Walkman leaking the sounds of Lou Reed, and the listings sprawled in front of the terminal.

"Hi, how are you?" Billy acknowledged.

"Fine," Dr. Albino responded with a pause. "You seem to be quite dedicated. As your current manager, I appreciate that."

"Thanks," mumbled Billy.

"I have spent a little time looking around the systems," the Doctor started.

"Oh no! I'm dead meat," thought Billy.

Dr. Albino continued, "I'm sure that you must realize how screwed up the system performance seems. Well, we are going to do something about improving the current situation. You seem to have the personality of a system programmer, and I am going to need some help. Are you willing to work with me on correcting this mess?"

Billy was shocked. A manager who realized that something was wrong with the system stood before him. And, he really wanted to do something about it. Billy shook for a minute. Between the aftereffects of the Jolt and the shock of the current situation, he couldn't respond.

"I realize that you'll need some support from me. Tell me what you need," Dr. Albino added.

"Sure. I'd love to help you fix this problem," Billy finally answered. "I have a pretty good understanding of VAX MACRO and a feel for VMS internals, but I could use some formal training to help formulate the big picture."

"That'll be no problem. Determine the training that you require. I'll line you up for an internals course from this guy who really seems to know it. I can't remember his name, but he's a big guy with a beard.

"Now, internals is an intense topic, so I'll send you through the course as soon as we can. Then in about six months, we'll send you through again, so you can build on the knowledge you gained in the first pass," Dr. Albino offered.

Billy couldn't believe what he was hearing. Cutlery had hogged the training weeks, leaving no training for Billy. This guy walks in and says he is willing to send him to an internals course, not once but twice. Billy was waiting for Rod Serling to walk through the door any minute.

"What else are you going to need?" Dr. Albino asked.

"Well, to do this right, I'll need to use a privileged account," Billy responded.

"Privileges aren't a problem. Of course, you'll be responsible and held accountable for operating with full privileges.

"One guy who worked with me issued a wildcard delete using an ellipsis. Unfortunately for us, he was positioned at the master file directory and was running with BYPASS privilege. Unfortunately for him, he was working for me.

"Do I make myself clear?"

"I get the message," Billy answered. "Of course, while testing privileged code, there's a chance of crashing the system."

"Crashing is no problem, as long as it doesn't occur during prime time. Crashing doesn't cause permanent damage. Considering the current time, it appears that working on this code during off hours won't be a problem for you," the Doctor replied.

Billy was in a state of total disbelief. He was legitimate for the first time. He could operate with full privileges without sneaking around. He could get real work done, and it would be appreciated. He wanted to slap himself to make sure that he hadn't died and gone to system programmer heaven.

"I have a specific need at this time," Dr. Albino went on. "It will be sort of a test. Take as long as you want, within reason, to complete this task. If you succeed, you will keep the privileges and get the training. If you fail, we'll have to re-evaluate our relationship.

"We have a VAXcluster that's running in a homogeneous mode of operation. However, the hardware is configured heterogeneously. We are memory short on some of the systems in the configuration. I'm working to correct the hardware situation, but this will take time. In the interim, I would like to have you set it up so that the users will log into a given account in which their working sets conform with the largest memory configuration. When users log into a smaller memory configuration VAX, I would like you to have a program that, when run, reduces their working set quota and extent to values that are more reasonable for the system they're logging into.

"Can you do this?" requested Dr. Albino.

"I think so," Billy answered.

"How long do you think it will take you?"

"Give me two days," Billy requested.

Dr. Albino's forehead furled and his eyes widened.

"Are you sure that will be enough time?"

"It should be."

"Well, give yourself three, just in case you need it. And go home for now; you look terrible," the Doctor ordered.

THE NEXT DAY, Billy prepared to attack the problem. He opened the gray tome to the familiar clicking and whirring.

"Book, I need your help," Billy entered.

"Try roses," the *Guide* responded, referring to Billy's previous adventure.

"No, she's not the problem," Billy continued. "I have a project in which I must lower the working set limits of user processes that are logging into smaller memory VAX configurations. Will the WSBLASTER program solve the problem?" (See Figure 8.)

"No," answered the *Guide*. "The WSBLASTER program simply lowered the process' working set list size to temporarily decrease its working set size."

Billy was beginning to wish that he had asked for two weeks, instead of two days, to complete the project.

"You seem to be referring to a working set size and a working set list size. What's the difference?" queried Billy.

"The working set size of a process refers to the number of pages actually owned by a process, whereas the working set list size defines the maximum number of owned pages a process may have in his working set before he must release a page to add a new page. An owned page is a page in process virtual address space or a process header page which a process may access without a page fault," the *Guide* responded.

"So, the working set list size will always be greater than or equal to the working set size?" Billy wondered.

"That's correct. The working set list size bounds the working set size," the *Guide* concurred.

"That does not make sense. If I do:

```
$WRITE SYS$OUTPUT F$GETJPI(pid,"WSSIZE")
```

it shows a value that's larger than the physical memory display in the $SHOW SYSTEM command. The documentation says the WSSIZE item returns the working set size."

"The documentation is wrong," returned the *Guide*. "The WSSIZE item, by our definition, is the working set list size. This value corresponds to the working set size that is displayed in the $SHOW STATUS DCL command. Note that $SHOW STATUS consistently misnames the field.

"The working set size corresponds to the physical memory displays returned by the $SHOW SYSTEM and $SHOW STATUS commands. This value can be calculated by summing the values returned by F$GETJPI(pid,"PPGCNT"), which is the count of the process' private pages in the working set, and F$GETJPI(pid,"GPGCNT"), which is the count of the global pages in the process' working set."

"So, where VMS says working set size, it means working set list size, and where it says physical memory, it means working set size. Boy, are the VMS developers going to be surprised," Billy retorted.

"The relative surprise of the VMS developers is not at issue here. In fact, the formal definition of the working set does not necessarily correspond to physical memory. The working set is the set of pages that a process can access without a page fault," the *Guide* shot back.

"Isn't that technically the same thing as physical memory?" Billy demanded.

"No. The difference in definitions is illustrated when a process is in an outswapped state. The $SHOW SYSTEM display still shows physical memory, even though the process' working set is, in fact, on disk in the swap file. Before the process can be made active again, it must be inswapped. So, a more strict definition might be that the working set size corresponds to the number of pages that a process owns in physical memory while it's in an inswapped state, i.e., a member of the balance set," the *Guide* answered.

"Okay. You made your point. I am beginning to see the difference," Billy admitted. "So, what do I have to do to limit the bounds of the working set size? Couldn't I just call the adjust working set list system service (SYS$ADJWSL)?"

"No. That system service only changes the current list size. The list size is constantly changing," the *Guide* replied.

"So, the change would only be temporary," Billy added. "This is getting confusing. Why do we have the working set anyway?"

"As a process faults and in turn makes more pages valid, the free page list decreases in size. The working set acts as a limit or quota to guarantee that a process doesn't tie up memory needed by other processes on the system," the *Guide* answered.

"Which page replacement algorithm does VMS use?" asked Billy.

"It uses a fundamentally first-in-first-out or FIFO algorithm, as opposed to a whenever-in-never-out or WINO algorithm," replied the Book, showing that even it had the right to a corny sense of humor.

"Why doesn't VMS use a least-frequently-used (LFU) or a least-recently-used (LRU) method?" asked Billy.

"These techniques would require too much excess baggage to carry around and would make the algorithm too complicated. Besides, with soft faults from the free and modified page lists, FIFO doesn't seem so bad. Note, also, that I said VMS uses a fundamentally FIFO mechanism. In fact, most, but not all, VAXs support not-recently-used (NRU) tendencies in the FIFO mechanism.

"Address translation can require several memory fetches to complete. To minimize the overhead of the memory fetch, the VAX maintains an address translation cache called the translation buffer. This cache is limited in size; for instance, a VAX 11/780 supports only 64 process virtual addresses in the cache. When the working set list pointer identifies a page to displace, prior to its displacement, we check to see whether the page is described in the translation buffer.

"If the page is described in the translation buffer, we skip it and look at the next entry in the list. This checking continues until we have located a page that isn't described in the translation buffer or until we have checked the number of entries defined by the special SYSGEN parameter TBSKIPWSL. This mechanism gives the replacement strategy NRU tendencies, because a page described in the translation buffer has been accessed fairly recently," the *Guide* explained.

"Now that I understand why we have the working set list, what do I have to change to restrict the process' working set list size?" Billy persisted.

"You would need to change the WSDEFAULT (or the working set limit), the WSQUOTA, and WSEXTENT quota settings," the *Guide* answered.

"Let me see if I understand how the quotas work. The WSDEFAULT is the amount of memory that VMS gives you at image activation time. Right?" Billy proposed.

"Wrong," the *Guide* corrected. "VMS doesn't give you anything. You have to earn it.

"The WSDEFAULT defines the working set list size at image activation time. Note that the image activator simply builds memory management data structures that allow the pager to load the image on demand."

"Okay," Billy acknowledged. "How does the working set list grow?"

"At QUANTUM end, VMS determines whether the process has also reached the end of its automatic working set adjustment time interval, as defined by the SYSGEN parameter AWSTIME, which is equal to QUANTUM by default. If this is true, we perform what is referred to as automatic working set adjustment (AWSA).

"The first part of the adjustment is performed by checking to see whether the page fault rate is greater than the SYSGEN parameter PFRATH. If the page fault rate is greater than PFRATH, then the working set list is increased by WSINC entries."

Billy interrupted, "Hold on. The units for PFRATH show up as page faults per 10 seconds. QUANTUM is 20 on this system, and the units are in 10 millisecond intervals."

"That's correct. On this system, to calculate the page fault rate, we would take the calculated page fault rate over AWSTIME, multiply it by 1000 and divide by 20, or effectively multiply by 50," the *Guide* responded.

"Well, that means on this system, with PFRATH set to 120, it would only take three page faults over a QUANTUM to be paging a lot. Based on what I read in an article titled 'On VMS Kernel Mode Time' " (see Appendix) Billy recalled, "a soft page fault only takes about 550 microseconds to resolve on a one VUP VAX. So, particularly at image activation time, it should be rare that a process isn't paging a lot.

"On this system, WSINC is set to 150, so VMS gives the process 150 pages when it is paging a lot."

The *Guide* stopped Billy with, "The first point is correct. It does not take much activity to be paging a lot. However, VMS gives you 150 more working set list entries, not 150 more pages. To use those entries, you must fault on pages and make them valid."

"Which means that you are probably going to get an increase at the next QUANTUM end," Billy interjected. "You seem to grow fast."

"Yes, we do," the *Guide* concurred.

"Is there a limit to the growth?" Billy asked.

"Yes. The general limit is defined by WSQUOTA, the working set quota. The process is authorized to grow to its quota under any circumstances. It is considered a commitment. If the quotas are oversized, the system could run out of memory," the *Guide* informed Billy.

"To calculate proper quotas, you could divide the maximum number of processes ever running into the available memory. Is that a fair assumption?" queried Billy.

"Yes, it's fair," the *Guide* responded. "It doesn't, however, compensate for potential sharing of global pages. You could determine the amount of sharing by using the SHOW_SHARE program you wrote for the girl." (See Figure 10.)

"But there's a process on this system whose working set size is larger than its WSQUOTA. Why is that?" asked Billy.

"In version 3 of VMS, the system developed the concept of loans to resolve the problem of a process with a smaller WSQUOTA faulting heavily, even though at the current time, we have a large free list. In this scenario, a version 2 system would have forced the process to generate a large number of soft page faults, if it were memory intensive.

"Under version 3 and greater systems, a process can grow above its WSQUOTA, provided that there are at least SYSGEN parameter BORROWLIM pages on the free page list and the process' working set list hasn't yet reached its WSEXTENT. The area between quota and extent is considered the loan region. If memory becomes tight again, VMS will take back loans, just like the farm credit bureau," the *Guide* replied.

"So doesn't VMS take memory away from the processes?" Billy asked.

"If the process is generating less than PFRATL faults, normalized over AWSTIME," the *Guide* replied, "VMS decreases the working set list size by WSDEC pages. The *Guide* has an entry that notes the significance of the name WS*DEC* and of taking things away from the user community.

"But PFRATL is set to 0 on a default system. So VMS usually never decreases the working set list. Why is that? Is DEC trying to sell more memory?" questioned Billy.

"That might be one man's opinion, but it's not the real reason. If a process were to reach its ideal working set list size, it would generate no faults. This means that if PFRATL were non-zero, the working set list would be decreased eventually. This would force paging, and the process would never sustain its ideal working set list size. This behavior is commonly referred to as oscillation. Setting PFRATL to 0 prevents oscillation and minimizes unnecessary soft paging," the *Guide* replied.

"Why would you set PFRATL to a value larger than 0?" Billy asked.

"Setting PFRATL to 0 makes sense if your system is memory rich, because this would minimize unnecessary CPU time required to resolve soft faults. However, for memory poor systems, you might want it to be non-zero to trade the CPU cycles for balancing the memory load," the *Guide* answered.

"I noticed that on this version 5 system, WSDEC is set to 250. This seems awfully large. Why is it so big?" Billy wondered.

"An assumption is made that PFRATL will always be 0. If you choose to increase it, you should also drop WSDEC to a smaller value. A setting around 35 should be fine.

"The reason WSDEC is so large is based on the following check. If a process reaches QUANTUM end and is not paging a lot, and WSDEC is set to zero, and there are less than the SYSGEN parameter GROWLIM pages on the free page list, and the process is a background process (that is, it has received a PIXSCAN boost in the last 32 QUANTUM intervals), then the process is forced back to its WSQUOTA. This is done by setting the working set list to the maximum of its WSQUOTA or its working set list size minus WSDEC," replied the *Guide*.

The *Guide* continued, "The SYSGEN parameter GROWLIM is also used to freeze the process' loan when memory starts to become tight. If a process' working set is above its quota and less than its working set list size, we make sure that at least GROWLIM pages reside on the free page list prior to allowing the process to add a page to its working set without displacing another."

"I think I have this automatic working set adjustment down," Billy started.

"Note that it would be better to call it automatic working set list adjustment," corrected the *Guide*.

"I stand corrected," an annoyed Billy entered. "One thing that is not totally clear to me is, why is the WSDEFAULT usually set less than the WSQUOTA?"

"That is a good question. There is no good answer, except that they have been set that way since their inception. Over the years, trying to make sense out of the settings, users developed a VMS myth-conception that setting the WSDEFAULT lower than the WSQUOTA conserves memory when small programs were run. Lost was the fact that when an image runs down, its P0 virtual address space is deleted, leaving only the remaining P1 space to occupy the working set. The myth that VMS gives you WSDEFAULT pages at image activation time helped propagate the myth that it was better to have a WSDEFAULT smaller than WSQUOTA."

"So having WSDEFAULT set equal to WSQUOTA should be the way to go?" asked Billy.

"Yes, although in reality, it probably doesn't make much difference, because process working set lists grow relatively quickly. By setting the default less than the quota, you're simply slightly slowing down the image activation time.

"On the off chance that you're running version 2 of VMS, be careful, because setting the default to the quota disables AWSA. In post version 2 VMS systems, there's a bit in the PCB which disables AWSA," the *Guide* replied.

"Actually, the more I think about how all this adjustment stuff operates, the more I think it operates backward," Billy mused. "A process has its image loaded through the pager, so it seems that the majority of the paging will occur at image activation time. Then after the image activity normalizes, it will really need less memory as it accesses localized portions of data and code. So if you analyze the behavior of an image, you'd think that the process should really start out with a large working set list and eventually drop to a smaller, more reasonable working set list size. The AWSA scheme operates under the opposite behavior. Does this seem wrong to you, or am I missing something?" inquired Billy.

"I agree with you wholeheartedly. However, it will probably not be corrected until you go to work at Spit Brook Road. So, you're forced to make the best of what you have now," answered the *Guide*.

"Now we can address my problem. I'm going to need to reset the WSDEFAULT, WSQUOTA, and WSEXTENT. I remember from our earlier discussions that the working set list is maintained in the process header (PHD). Are the limits also stored in the PHD?" started Billy.

"Very good. Yes, they are," concurred the *Guide*.

"I'm looking at the offsets PHD$L_DFWSCNT, PHD$L_WSQUOTA, and PHD$L_WSEXTENT through the system dump analyzer (SDA), and the fields seem to contain values that are larger than the actual settings by 60 odd hexadecimals. What's going on here?"

"The fields that you are examining aren't the values for WSDEFAULT, WSQUOTA, and WSEXTENT; rather, they're longword indexes into the

PHD to locate the areas," explained the *Guide*.

"So, if I take the contents of the PHD$L_WSLIST field and back up by one, I'll get a bias to add to my new settings for the limits. I also see the fields PHD$L_WSAUTH and PHD$L_WSAUTHEXT. What are these fields used for?" Billy asked.

"PHD$L_WSAUTH contains the authorized WSQUOTA, and PHD$L_WSAUTHEXT contains the authorized working set extent. You are authorized to set the actual quota and extent below the authorized values but not above them," responded the *Guide*.

"Why would anyone want to lower the values below the authorized settings?" wondered Billy.

"Who knows? Maybe he saw Ghandi the night before and is just feeling benevolent," offered the *Guide*.

"Fair enough," Billy concurred. "Now if working set list entries, which once were in use, are beyond the new limits of the working set list, the memory management code would have an inconsistency between valid page table entries and the working set list entries which would be ignored. So that I don't mess up the process, I should probably decrease the working set list below the new settings I'm going to establish for the limits. I can use the SYS$ADJWSL system service to implement that decrease.

"To not affect the adjustment, I probably ought to lock down all of my code and data pages into my working set.

"I probably ought to disable AWSA while I'm doing this stuff. How would I go about doing the disable on AWSA?" Billy inquired.

"When you're in kernel mode, just set the bit PCB$V_DISAWS in the field PCB$L_STS," replied the *Guide*.

"Now I should be in the clear. Let me test this out."

Billy wrote and tested the code (see Figure 12). It all worked fine (see Figure 13).

"Thanks again, Book," Billy entered.

"No problem," responded the *Guide*. "By the way, let me know what happens with the girl. The *Guide* might be interested in making an entry on the effects of software on the love life of a young programmer."

Billy went off to show the results of his efforts to Dr. Albino.

IS DR. ALBINO for real? How will Dennis Cutlery's promotion affect Billy? Will Billy get the girl? Whatever happened to the program Billy was going to write to track files that are currently open by a process? Will Billy remain happy to operate under a legitimate set of privileges?

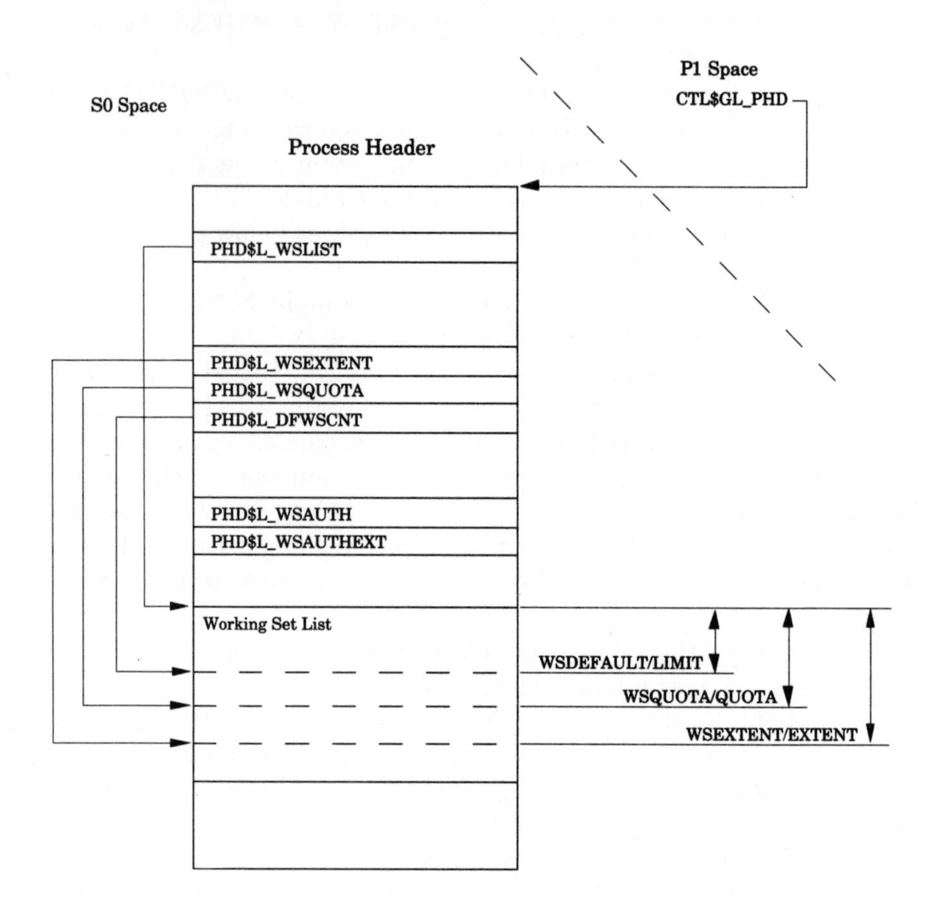

Fields in process header affected by RESET_WS.MAR

Figure 12.

```
;^^^^^^^^^^^^^^^^^^^^^^^^^^^^^^^^^^^^^^^^^^^^^^^^^^^^^^^^^
;       Program:            reset_ws
;       Author:             Billy Bitsenbites (Bruce Ellis)
;       Function:           Resets the WSDEFAULT/WSQUOTA
;                           and authorized WSQTOTA to 512.
;                           Resets the WSEXTENT and authorized
;                           WSEXTENT to 1024.
;^^^^^^^^^^^^^^^^^^^^^^^^^^^^^^^^^^^^^^^^^^^^^^^^^^^^^^^^^
        .library            /sys$library:lib.mlb/
        .link               /sys$system:sys.stb/
        $ipldef
        $phddef             ;define Process header offsets
        $pcbdef             ;define Process Control Block offsets
;^^^^^^^^^^^
;Macro to check status
;^^^^^^^^^^^
        .macro  check       ?1
        blbs    r0,1
        $exit_s r0
1:
        .endm   check
lock_start:
pages: .blkl    1           ;Storage for $ADJWSL calculations
lock_it_all:
        .address            lock_start
        .address            lock_end
;*****************************************
;User mode code
;*****************************************
        .entry  reset_ws,^m<>
        $lkwset_s           inadr=lock_it_all   ;Lock all of the program
        check                                   ; into the working set
        $adjwsl_s           wsetlm=pages        ;Determine the current working
        check                                   ; set list size
        subl    #400,pages                      ;Determine the number of
        blss    skip_adjust                     ; pages required to reduce wsl
                                                ; 400
        mnegl   pages,pages                     ;Negate the value to shrink by
        $adjwsl_s           pagcnt=pages        ;Shrink the working set list
        check
skip_adjust:
        $cmkrnl_s           routin=drop_ws      ;Get into kernel mode and adjust
        ret                                     ;end program

;*****************************************
;Kernel mode code to do the adjustment
;*****************************************
        .entry  drop_ws,^m<r5,r6>
        setipl  #ipl$_astdel            ;Block ^y ast
        clrl    r1                      ;Clear flag to determine whether to
                                        ; re-enable AWSA
        bbcs    #pcb$v_disaws,-         ;set the bit to disable aswa
                pcb$l_sts(r4),10$
        incl    r1                      ;bit was set
10$:    movl    g^ctl$gl_phd,r5         ;get the P1 wndow to the PHD
        cmpl    #400,phd$l_wssize(r5)   ;if ws list > 400 then exit
        bgeq    wsl_ok                  ; else continue
        movl    #ss$_badparam,r0        ;return error status
        brw     sayonara
wsl_ok: movl    phd$l_wslist(r5),r6     ;get the index to the ws list
        decl    r6                      ;back up by one
        addl    #512,r6                 ;determine the index which corresponds
                                        ; to 512 page list sizes
        movl    r6,phd$l_dfwscnt(r5)    ;reset wsdefault to 512
        movl    r6,phd$l_wsquota(r5)    ;reset wsquota to 512
        movl    r6,phd$l_wsauth(r5)     ;reset the authorized quota to 512
        addl    #512,r6                 ;reset bias to 1024
        movl    r6,phd$l_wsauthext(r5)  ;reset authorized wsextent to 1024
        movl    r6,phd$l_wsextent(r5)   ;reset wsextent to 1024
        movl    #ss$_normal,r0          ;set success status
sayonara:
        tstl    r1                      ;was disable awsa bit set?
        bneq    done                    ;if so scram
```

Figure 12 contd.

```
        bicl    #pcb$m_disaws,pcb$l_sts(r4)     ;re-enable AWSA
done:   setipl  #0
        ret                             ;scram
lock_end:
        .end    reset_ws
```

Figure 13. Results of running RESET_WS.

```
$  mac reset_ws
$ link reset_ws
$
$ sh stat
  Status on    4-APR-1990 05:41:56.03     Elapsed CPU :     0 00:00:25.23
  Buff. I/O :       103      Cur. ws. :     512      Open files :          0
  Dir. I/O :        170      Phys. Mem. :  202      Page Faults :      2463
$ sh work
  Working Set       /Limit= 512   /Quota= 1024   /Extent= 4096
  Adjustment enabled    Authorized Quota= 1024  Authorized Extent= 4096
$
$ set proc/priv=cmkrnl
$
$ r reset_ws
$
$ sh stat
  Status on    4-APR-1990 05:42:25.79`    Elapsed CPU :     0 00:00:25.90
  Buff. I/O :       127      Cur. ws. :     512      Open files :          0
  Dir. I/O :        172      Phys. Mem. :  239      Page Faults :      2569
$ sh work
  Working Set       /Limit= 512  /Quota= 512      /Extent= 1024
  Adjustment enabled    Authorized Quota= 512   Authorized Extent= 1024
$
```

Episode 6

Lotsa Lock

The next morning, Billy awoke as the alarm clock blared next to the bed. He looked out the window into the dark of a pre-sunrise morning. He had to scramble to get to the office, because this hour, when most were dreaming, was the ideal time to write and test system programs.

He scrambled around his studio apartment, gathering the documentation he required to complete his work. The last, but most important, item he stuffed into his backpack was *The Hitchhiker's Guide to VMS*.

After a quick shower, he dashed toward the door, tripping over some of the clutter that he never seemed to find the time to clean up. He thought to himself, "If that girl ever does go out with me, I'd better straighten this place up."

With his backpack over his shoulder, he pulled the door shut. As he heard the click, he fumbled through his pockets feeling for his keys. A pained expression spread over Billy's face as he realized that the keys were still on the kitchen table.

Even though he took mass transportation to work, it was a good five miles to the nearest T stop, that is, the Boston subway. As much as he dreaded it, he had to wake the landlord, in the wee hours of the morning and for the third time that week.

He knocked on the landlord's door. The door opened. The landlord stood scratching his back, looking at Billy and said, "Gee, kid, not again?"

Billy shook his head in agreement.

"Maybe if you got a little more sleep, you'd remember your keys," the landlord continued. "Here take this key. After you get your keys, slide this one back under the door."

Billy gratefully accepted the key and raced back to get his own keys. After returning the landlord's key, he dashed off to his car. He thought that a cup of coffee might get him ready to face the rest of the day and headed to the nearest 24-hour convenience store.

Billy got out of the car, carefully remembering to take his keys. He pulled the door to the store; it was locked. He walked back to his car and placed the key into the ignition. Before turning the key, he saw a clerk come to the door and unlock it. Billy dashed out to get the coffee he so badly craved.

With coffee in hand, he walked back to the car. He felt for the keys in his pocket. They weren't there. He finally noticed them in the ignition of the locked car.

Billy went back into the store and got a wire hanger from the clerk. After about 15 minutes of struggling, he opened the car door and headed for the T stop.

As he reached the platform, he noticed that a train had arrived and passengers were piling in. He raced through the turnstyle toward the train. Just as he got there, the doors shut in his face, forcing him to wait another 10 minutes for the next train.

At last, he reached the office. He remembered that he had to check on an outstanding order that was causing problems for one of the users. He entered the order processing application that Dennis Cutlery had purchased, and he requested that the specified order be displayed. He sat and waited, becoming annoyed at the incredibly slow response the application offered him.

Eventually he entered Ctrl-Y and aborted the application. He looked around the system for activity that might be blocking him and saw none. Finally he pulled the gray tome from his backpack and opened it to the all-too-familiar clicking and whirring.

Billy entered, "Hey Book, I'm having a problem. Whenever I try to access a record with this application I'm running, I stall. But nothing seems to be blocking me. Do you have any idea what might be causing the delay?

"Have you checked for a locking problem?" the *Guide* responded.

"Oh man, not another problem with locks. I can't take much more of this," thought Billy.

"What do you mean?" asked Billy.

"One reason you might stall while attempting to access a record is that another process could have accessed the record before you and not released the lock," the *Guide* answered.

Billy went over to the terminal belonging to the user who had asked Billy to check out this record. He saw the record he was trying to access displayed on the terminal. He entered Ctrl-Y and then logged the user off the system.

"Great," Billy thought. "Cutlery was afraid of giving me privileges, and we have terminals all over the building still logged in from the previous day. Wonderful security! I'll have to mention this situation to Dr. Albino."

He got back to his terminal and noticed that the requested record now appeared on his screen.

"It looks like you were correct," Billy told the *Guide*. "However, I'm confused on this locking business. Why do we have locks anyway?"

"Lock management provides synchronization to shared resources, just like the IPL, spinlock, and mutex mechanisms you used earlier," the *Guide* offered. "When you are attempting to read a record, you want to make sure that no other process is simultaneously attempting to change it.

"Locks are requested by calling the enqueue lock request system service ($ENQ) and are released by calling the dequeue lock request system service ($DEQ). These services are called on your behalf when you use the record management services (RMS) to access a shared file.

"Locks are requested on a named resource. The resource can be any operating system entity on which you can agree on a common unique resource name to identify the entity. Processes must cooperate when accessing the entity, or they will break the synchronization," the *Guide* informed Billy.

"So, this is not a lock and key arrangement? Do you mean that I can just go in and access the resource without using the lock manager?" queried Billy.

"Yes," the *Guide* answered. "Knocks might be a better name than locks."

"Huh?" wondered Billy.

"Prior to entering a room, which has a closed door, you, by convention, knock on the door. This saves potential embarrassment for you or for anyone who might be in the room. You could just burst into the room, but this breaks the knocking convention and leads to potential embarrassment. In the case of VMS, ignoring the conventions leads to inaccurate information and potential data corruption."

"Well, what are the benefits of locks over other synchronization techniques, like mutexes and spinlocks?" asked Billy.

"Locks can be requested from any mode; spinlocks and mutexes must be requested from kernel mode," the *Guide* answered.

"One of the benefits of the lock management services is that they allow for locks to be requested in many modes," the *Guide* continued. "The most traditional modes include exclusive (EX) mode requests, which block all other requests, and protected read (PR) mode requests, which allow other readers but block all write requests.

"Concurrent read (CR) mode requests are granted as long as there is not an exclusive mode lock granted on the resource. Protected write (PW) locks are identical to exclusive mode lock requests with the exception that they allow concurrent readers. Concurrent write (CW) requests are granted as long as no protected or exclusive mode requests are currently granted. Null (NL) mode locks are always granted."

"Well, that seems awfully stupid. Why would you have a locking scheme with a mode that could always be granted?" Billy interrupted.

"Null locks are interest locks. You are interested in the resource but do not currently need to access it," the *Guide* replied. "When you are interested in accessing the resource, you can convert the request to a more protected mode and then convert back to null mode when you are finished with the resource."

"What's the advantage of doing the conversion over simply calling $DEQ and later calling $ENQ, if you're interested in the resource?" asked Billy.

"Besides a slight performance gain by doing the conversion, an entity called the value block is preserved between conversions. It might not be preserved if you issued a $DEQ," the *Guide* answered. "The value block allows you to describe changes made to a given resource that another process might be interested in knowing."

"Okay," Billy entered. "I have a basic understanding of the lock manager, but I don't understand why I was being blocked. The other process had read the record and was done with it. Why was there any lock at all?"

"When you open a file, RMS assigns a stream to the file," the *Guide* explained. "RMS supports two types of locking on a stream to a file, automatic and manual locking.

"When a process opens a file for shared read/write access, automatic locking is enabled by default. When automatic locking is enabled, RMS will lock on the record being read or written, until the next operation is performed on the record stream (i.e., another read or write), the record is explicitly unlocked (most languages support an UNLOCK construct in file processing that will translate to a call to the RMS service SYS$RELEASE), or the file is closed.

"Manual locking is enabled by setting the bit RAB$V_ULK in the record options (RAB$L_ROP) field of the record access block (RAB). This action may be supported by high-level language constructs. For instance, COBOL supports an APPLY LOCK-HOLDING clause in its I-O-CON-

TROL section to enable manual locking. You would choose manual locking when more than one record must be processed to complete a transaction.

"When manual locking is enabled, locks on a record stream are held until they are explicitly unlocked individually, by calling SYS$RELEASE (or using the high-level language UNLOCK construct) or by unlocking all records by calling SYS$FREE (or using an UNLOCK ALL construct in the high-level language). They are also released when the file is closed.

"So, in your case, what very likely happened is that the other process read the record and went into an extended wait state by posting a terminal read, without issuing an unlock prior to the wait. This is actually a common problem in application design. As a general rule, an application should always unlock a given record prior to entering an extended wait state," the *Guide* responded.

"What happens to the process requesting the locked record?" Billy wondered.

"In most high-level languages, error status is returned. RMS, however, allows for the process to automatically wait until the record is unlocked. The waiting procedure would be enabled by setting the bit RAB$V_WAT in the record options field of the RAB, that is, in RAB$L_ROP," the *Guide* responded.

"What if the other guy never unlocks the record? Will you wait forever?" Billy queried.

"By default, yes, you will wait forever. You can, however, specify that a timeout be enabled on the wait by setting the bit RAB$V_TMO in RAB$L_ROP and specifying a timeout value, in units of seconds, in the field RAB$B_TMO," the *Guide* replied.

"Why do you hold onto the lock after the record operation has been performed? Aren't you done at that point?" asked Billy.

"You might not be finished with the record," replied the *Guide*. "For example, you might be reading a record with the intent to modify it. Prior to your modification, someone could attempt to read the same record and obtain stale information if we unlocked the record immediately. This is why I said to unlock the record prior to entering an extended wait state.

"If it is a read, modify, and write sequence, the unlock should occur after the write operation. If it is simply a read operation, the unlock should occur immediately following the display of information to the user."

"I can accept that. However, I don't understand why I was forced to stall. The process issued a read and so did I. Because we were both reading, we both should have been granted the lock. Right?" Billy asked.

"Yes, that is correct. However, RMS allows for the setting of bits in the record options field of the RAB. If the read lock bit RAB$V_REA and the record lock bit RAB$V_RLK are clear, RMS takes out an exclusive mode lock on the record. If the record lock bit RAB$V_RLK is set, RMS requests a protected write lock. If the read lock bit RAB$V_REA is set, and the record lock bit RAB$V_RLK is clear, RMS makes a protected read lock request. It also supports a no lock request RAB$V_NLK which causes RMS to temporarily request a concurrent read lock. The no lock request would be blocked by an exclusive lock but would be released before it could block any lock mode once the record has been processed.

"Unfortunately, RMS does not set the corresponding bits based on the attempted access (i.e., read or write) by the application. Most of the compiler writers do not realize that the bits are not dynamically modified. A typical compiler will produce an open statement that has the bit RAB$V_RLK set in the RAB when the file is open for shared read/write access and will make no modifications based on the issuance of a read operation. This implies that when a read is issued by an application, RMS will, typically, take out a protected write lock, blocking other readers. This is probably why your process stalled with two read operations requested," the *Guide* answered.

"How do I go about changing the bits in the RAB?" asked Billy.

"Most languages support a user open option that allows your application to locate the RAB. Some languages, like FORTRAN, support direct access to the RAB of an open file. In FORTRAN, you could use the FOR$RAB construct to locate the RAB. A language like COBOL does not support direct access to the RAB without using something like the routine FDL$PARSE and issuing all I/O requests to the file with calls to SYS$GET and SYS$PUT," replied the *Guide*.

"Let me see if I can write routines that will lock properly. I could write a routine that would set the bits RABV_REA, RABV_WAT, and RAB$V_TMO in the field RAB$L_ROP and clear the bit RAB$V_RLK in the same field for the read routine. I would also have to set the timeout interval in the field RAB$B_TMO

"The write routine would be similar except the bit RAB$V_RLK would have to be set. Does this sound correct?" Billy requested.

"Yes," the *Guide* concurred.

"I can get the address of the RAB from FOR$RAB, but how does VMS identify the correct file?" Billy wondered.

"The argument for FOR$RAB is the logical unit number from the open statement," the *Guide* replied.

"Okay," Billy continued, "how do I get at the RAB symbols from FORTRAN?"

"You would have to include '($RABDEF)' and use a structure defined by the statement RECORD /RABDEF/," responded the *Guide*.

Billy wrote and tested the prototype routines to handle read and write locking properly from FORTRAN (see Figure 14).

"This is great, Book, but suppose some other application is accessing the same file and I'm being blocked. How do I figure out which process is blocking me?" Billy asked. "And for that matter, I might want to know which file I'm trying to access when I'm being blocked."

"To perform those tasks, you will have to learn a little more about the internals of the lock management data structures," replied the *Guide*.

"When a process requests a lock, a structure called a lock block (LKB) is allocated to describe the lock being requested. The LKB describes the requesting process through its process ID, the mode that the lock was requested in, whether the lock has been granted, and so on.

"The lock block is located by using a value called the lock ID. The lock ID is returned to the user process on an $ENQ system service call in the second longword of the lock status block (LKSB) argument. In pre-version 5.3 systems, the lock ID contains a longword index into the lock ID table in the low word, and it has a sequence number to guarantee uniqueness in the high word. The lock ID table is located by using the pointer LCK$GL_IDTBL.

"In version 5.3 and greater systems, the low 18 bits of the lock ID are used as the longword index. The number of bits to use for the index is specified by the constant LKB$C_LKIDSIZ.

"LKBs are also queued to an owner listhead that is maintained in the process control block (PCB) at the offsets PCB$L_LOCKQFL/ PCB$L_LOCKQBL. The queue pointers for the owner queue are not located at the beginning of the LKB, like most of the other queue pointers we have previously seen. The location of these pointers is forced, because the LKB is also used as an AST control block (ACB), and the first two longwords are used as an ACB forward and backward link in the AST queue to the process. To locate the owner queue pointers, you would use the offsets LKB$L_OWNQFL and LKB$L_OWNQBL. To access the LKB, you must back up by LKB$L_OWNQFL bytes to locate its beginning.

"Resource blocks (RSB) describe the resource on which you are requesting locks. The resource block contains the name of the given resource, the value block, and other information pertaining to the resource. The resource block also maintains three queues that describe the current state of outstanding locks on this resource.

"The granted queue maintains a list of locks that have been granted on this resource. Its listhead is located at an offset of RSB$L_GRQFL bytes into the resource block. There is also a wait queue, listing locks that must wait because of incompatibilities with currently granted locks. Its listhead is at RSB$L_WTQFL.

"It is possible that lock conversions may block themselves from being granted. To guarantee that the conversions are granted properly, a separate conversion queue is maintained at RSB$L_CVTQFL.

"The resource block can be located on any given lock by using the offset LKB$L_RSB in the lock block. To locate the resource block by name, VMS hashes on the resource name and other items including the resource name length, UIC group number, access mode, and parent RSB hash value. Hashing takes an input, in this case the resource name and associated baggage, munches it in a function and produces a hash index. The hash index is used as an index into the resource hash table, which can be located through the pointer LCK$GL_HASHTBL.

"The hash index is not guaranteed to be unique, so after we have offset to the longword pointer, we must check the name of the first entry in the list; if we have found the correct resource block, our search is done. Otherwise, we must check the first longword in the resource block (RSB$L_HSHCHN). If this longword is non-zero, we have a collision and must check the next entry in the list which is pointed to by this first longword. More collisions will incur additional CPU time on a look-up, as the scan becomes more sequential."

Billy interrupted, "Two questions, please. First, how can we minimize the number of collisions in the resource hash table?

The *Guide* replied, "A larger table will typically minimize the likelihood of collisions, if the hash function is reasonable. You can increase the size of the resource hash table by increasing the SYSGEN parameter RESHASHTBL. A table which is approximately 60 to 80 percent full is probably an optimally sized table. You can determine the number of resource blocks on the system, at any given point in time, by checking the total resources field in the $MONITOR LOCK display."

"Thanks," Billy said. "Now, is the list maintained as a singly linked list?

"Yes," the *Guide* responded. "However, there is also a backlink pointer located at RSB$L_HSHCHNBK in the resource block. It appears that the developer could not make up his mind on which mechanism to use in maintaining the list."

"I want to write a program to determine which process is blocking me on a given lock request and which resource we are attempting to access," Billy explained. "Knowing the resource would allow me to determine where the application would need to be corrected to resolve the locking problems. Although this would be a general purpose program, handling any given resource, I'm really more interested in RMS locks at this point in time. How does RMS define resource names?"

The *Guide* answered, "When a file is open for shared write access, RMS takes out three types of locks, although there can be additional locks if global buffers are associated with the file. The three locks are for the file, the bucket in which the record ID is contained, and the record being accessed.

"The record lock is the primary lock being held while accessing the record and is the lock held until the next operation on the record stream. Therefore, this lock is probably the one holding you up when you try to access a record. Record locks are always sublocks; the parent lock is the file lock. The general advantages of sublocks are that they cannot be granted until the parent lock has been granted, they must be released before the parent is released, and they only require unique resource names within the sublock hierarchy.

"Record locks are generally easy to identify because they will be sublocks of the file lock and will have eight-byte resource names. The resource name will be the binary representation of the six-byte record file address (RFA) of the record.

"The RFA for a sequential file contains the starting virtual block number (VBN) of the record in the low longword, and, in the next word, we have the starting byte within the block. These fields are actually reversed in the resource name field of the RSB. For a relative file organization, the RFA contains the record number of the record and for indexed files, it contains the bucket VBN of the record, along with the record ID of the record within the bucket.

"The bucket lock has a four-byte resource name that contains the starting virtual block number of the bucket.

"The file lock is identified by a four-byte prefix containing the characters RMS$. Following the prefix, we have the three-word file ID of the file. The file ID uniquely identifies a file on a volume. The file ID is followed by the volume label. Volume labels uniquely identify mounted volumes on a system or within a VAXcluster."

"It appears that we can attack the program now," Billy interjected. "Because we won't be able to perform this from the process that's being hung up, we'll have to obtain the process ID, get into kernel mode, and use EXE$NAMPID to grab the other guy's PCB address. Which spinlock would I use to access the lock database?"

"You would use the system communication services (SCS) spinlock. Take care to release the scheduling (SCHED) spinlock prior to acquiring the SCS spinlock, because the SCHED spinlock is of higher rank than the SCS spinlock," the *Guide* advised.

"This is a pain," Billy complained. "To guarantee synchronization, I will have to unlock the SCHED spinlock, acquire the SCS spinlock, and reacquire the SCHED spinlock long enough to guarantee that the process did not go away in a two-instruction window. After the sanity check, I should be safe, because the process can't be deleted until all locks are released. I will be blocking its deletion by holding the SCS spinlock and blocking access to the lock database. I assume that I could recheck the PCB$L_PID field to make sure that the process is still there?"

"Yes," the *Guide* concurred.

"After all this spinlocking mess, I could get the address of the first lock in the owner queue by using the field PCB$L_LOCKQFL. You said that the owner queue is stored in the middle of the lock block, so to use the LKB symbolic offsets, I will have to compute the beginning address of the lock block. This calculation could be performed by using the following instruction:

```
MOVAL   -LKB$L_OWNQFL(R7),R8
```

To determine whether the lock is being blocked by another process' lock, I have to find out whether the lock has been granted. How would I find out this information?" Billy queried.

"You could check for the constant value LKB$K_GRANTED in the field LKB$B_STATE of the lock block," the *Guide* replied.

"I would want to save the mode in which the lock was requested. What would be the name of this field?" Billy inquired.

"It would be stored in the field LKB$B_RQMODE," the *Guide* responded.

"I assume that the fields LKB$L_RSB and LKB$L_PARENT could be used to locate the RSB and parent RSB for this lock," Billy proposed.

"Correct," the *Guide* concurred.

"Where's the resource name stored?" Billy requested.

"The resource name is stored at the end of the RSB at the offset RSB$T_RESNAM. The size of the resource name is stored in a separate field at RSB$B_RSNLEN, which immediately precedes the resource name," the *Guide* offered.

"Now, to determine who's blocking us, I will have to check through the granted queue in the RSB, using the offset RSB$L_GRQFL. Where in the LKB are the link pointers for the granted queue located?" Billy asked.

"They are located at the field LKB$L_SQFL, which is also in the middle of the LKB, so you will once again have to bias back to the beginning of the lock block," answered the *Guide*.

"Then I can copy back the extended PID (EPID) of the owner of the lock and the grant mode, and I'm done, right?" Billy questioned.

"Wrong," said the *Guide*. "You will want to chain through the list, because it is possible that more than one process can have the lock granted. By the way, the field LKB$B_GRMODE will give you the mode in which the lock is granted."

"You will also have to locate the extended PID from the process' PCB, as the EPID field of the LKB will be reused after the lock has been granted. To locate the EPID, use these instructions:

```
MOVL    LKB$L_PID(R3),R0
MOVL    @SCH$GL_PCBVEC[r0],r0
MOVL    PCB$L_EPID(R0),loc
```

"These instructions will allow you to use the low word of the internal PID to index through the PCB vector table to locate the PCB and grab the extended PID," the *Guide* replied.

"I'll add logic to determine whether up to 10 processes have the resource granted. Then I'll be done, right?" Billy pleaded.

"Wrong," the *Guide* responded again. "What you have now will work fine on a VAX that is not operating in a VAXcluster environment. But the VAXcluster adds new complications. The process that is blocking you might not be executing on your node, and you might not have the master copy of the resource block."

"Huh? Master copy? How does locking work in a VAXcluster environment?" groaned Billy.

"When a process requests a lock in a VAXcluster, we must first determine whether the resource is mastered on a node other than our own. To do this, we must look up the directory node. This look-up is performed by hashing the resource name and indexing into a hash table that describes the cluster system ID (CSID) of the node that maintains the directory information for the resource. It is possible that the node is ours.

"The directory table is located through the pointer LCK$GL_DIRVEC. The table is sized based on each node's LOCKDIRWT SYSGEN parameter setting. The original meaning of LOCKDIRWT was simply the number of entries in the table for directory look-ups. It has evolved to have many additional meanings since version 4.6. We can get into those meanings later after we have discussed resource mastership, if you are interested.

"After we have determined the node that maintains the directory information on this resource, we send a message to the node asking it to perform a directory look-up on the resource to determine whether the resource is currently mastered on a node. If the resource is not currently mastered, the directory node marks the requesting node as the master and notifies that node of the mastership assignment.

"After a node has been designated the master of a resource, all its lock requests on that resource can be handled locally, with no wire transfers, and all other nodes interested in the resource must talk to the master node which arbitrates lock requests. After the master node has lost interest in the resource and no other node is interested in it, a message is sent to the directory node, telling it to drop the mastership description in its lock directory.

"Prior to version 5.2 of VMS, mastership did not move from the current master node unless all interest in the resource was gone. With version 5.2, mastership moves to the node with the highest LOCKDIRWT setting, when the master node is no longer interested in the resource."

"How do we know whether our node is mastering the resource?" Billy asked.

The *Guide* answered, "The lock and resource blocks support two fields, i.e., LKB$W_STATUS, which contains a bit LKB$V_MSTCPY, and RSB$L_CSID. LKB$V_MSTCPY, when set in the LKB$W_STATUS, identifies that this lock block is a master copy of a lock that was requested on a remote node. This representation would not be set in the first pass of your code through the lock blocks. But it would be useful, if you were to go to the node mastering the resource. If this were a master copy, the field RSB$L_CSID would be 0.

"The lock block could also be a local copy. In this case, the LKB$V_MSTCPY bit would be clear and the RSB$L_CSID field would be 0. This case would be true if you were to be mastering the resource on your local node. This is also the case if you are locking in a non-cluster environment.

"If you had a resource mastered on a remote node, the LKB$V_MSTCPY bit would be clear and the RSB$L_CSID field would contain the cluster system ID of the node mastering the resource. In this case, the EPID field would describe the extended process ID of the remote process.

"Note that the LKB$V_MSTCPY bit is represented in the LKB$W_STATUS field. This information conflicts with a statement in the *VMS Internals and Data Structures Version 5 Update Express Volume 1* book by Goldenberg and Kenah which states that the bit is represented in the field LKB$W_FLAGS.

"Although the *VMS Internals* book is a very powerful resource and highly accurate, it is incorrect regarding this bit. Doubters can attempt to write the code using the misinformation or check the file SYS$LIBRARY:LIB.REQ to see that the *Guide* is correct on this point.

"VAXclusters have been a point of confusion since their inception. This results from the secrecy in which Digital has dealt with VAXcluster information. As newer versions of VMS have come out, more code relating to VAXclusters has been removed from the source listings, leading to this confusion as well as an interesting set of myths on how VAXclusters operate. This misinformation will not help clear up these myths."

"So, in the program," Billy observed, "I'm going to need to determine the setting of the LKB$V_MSTCPY bit and the contents of the RSB$L_CSID field to identify which node is mastering the resource. Then, I'll have to manually go over to that node and determine which processes are blocking this process. How do I determine which node to look at in this case, because the PCB of the blocking node might not reside on the master node?"

"The lock block supports a field LKB$L_REMLKID that will give you the lock ID of the LKB being maintained on the master node," the *Guide* answered.

"Then I'm going to need to add logic to the code in order to access the lock block by process ID or lock ID. With the lock ID, I can grab the low 18 bits (in version 5.3+) and index into the lock ID table, located through LCK$GL_IDTBL to locate the lock block. I'll have to check the LKB$L_LKID field to make sure that the sequence number hasn't changed," Billy proposed. "Is there a limit to the size of the lock ID table?

"Yes," answered the *Guide*. "It is limited by the SYSGEN parameter LOCKIDTBL, initially. If the size of the table is exhausted, we add additional LOCKIDTBL entries to a copy of the original table, and we allow it to grow until it hits an absolute upper bound of LOCKIDTBL_MAX entries. The current limit is defined by the contents of the location LCK$GL_MAXID. By the way, because the maximum setting for these parameters grew from 65535 to 262143, the lock ID index grew from 16 bits to 18 bits.

Billy interjected, "It's possible that as soon as I get to the master node, I'll discover that the process blocking me is on another node, right?"

"Yes," answered the *Guide*.

"How do I determine which node the blocking process is on?"

"The field LKB$L_CSID will direct you to the proper node. By the way, you can map CSIDs to node names by using the $SHOW CLUSTER utility," the *Guide* responded

"You know, *Guide*, I'm developing an intense distaste for VAXclusters. Let me collect these thoughts and try to write this program," Billy entered. (See Figure 15.)

Later Billy came back and exclaimed, "It works. But now that I have all this junk, it might be nice to translate the file ID and volume label into a real file specification. How can I do that?"

"Check the help file on the LIB$FID_TO_NAME run-time library procedure. You can write a short program to perform the translation for your purposes," the *Guide* responded.

"I'll check it out. Thanks again," Billy entered.

He then shut the *Guide* and wrote the program to perform file ID to file specification translation. (See Figure 16.) It worked. (See Figure 17.)

WILL BILLY remember his keys? What ever happened to the girl? Has Billy forgotten about the program to examine files open by a process? Will Billy's good fortune with Dr. Albino continue?

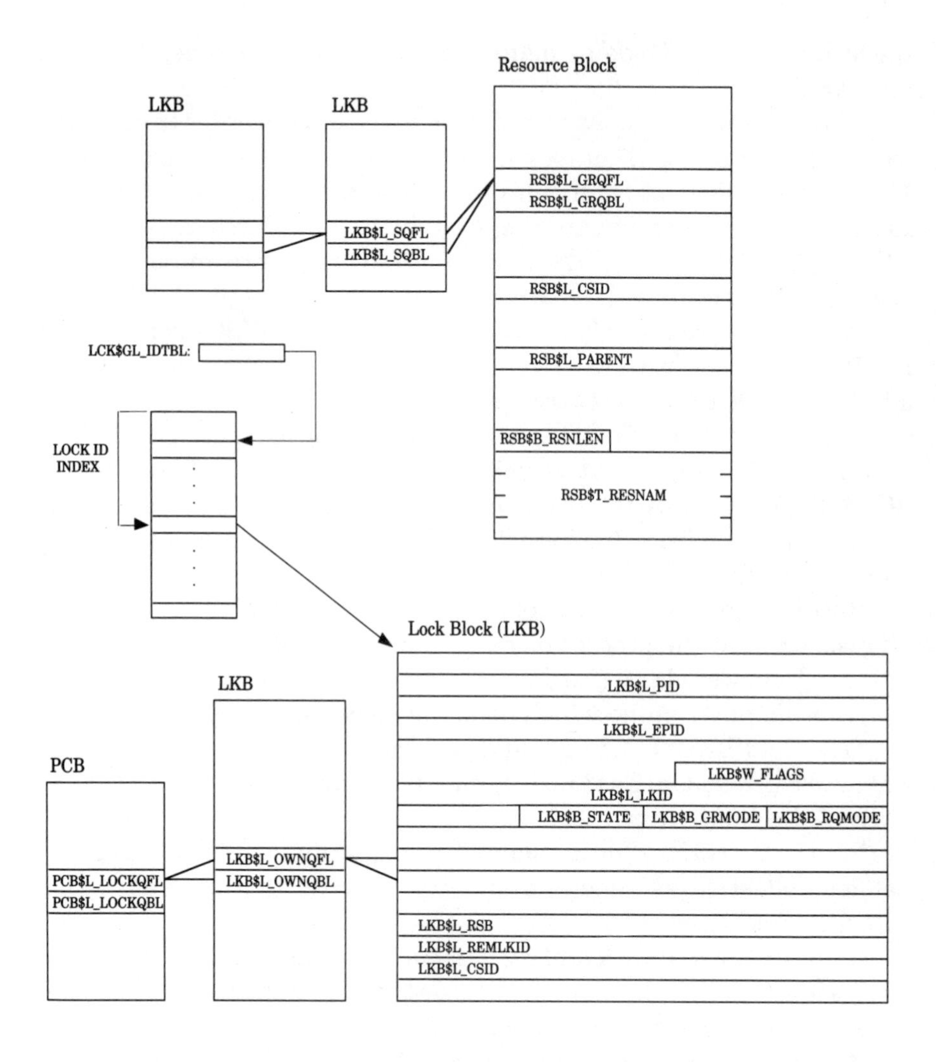

Structures examined by BLOCKING_LOCK.MAR

Figure 14.

```
$ typ idxnostall.for
        program get_idx_stall
        integer s
        character         last*15,first*10,pos*2,hand*1,keyin*15
        character         junk*100
10      format(A15,A10,A2,A1,A100)
        open(unit=1,file='RECS',status='UNKNOWN',form='FORMATTED',
        1       access='KEYED',recordtype='VARIABLE',SHARED)
        keyin='X300           '
        call    read_wait(%val(for$rab(1)))
        read(unit=1,fmt=10,key=keyin,keyid=0) last,first,pos,hand,junk
        call    write_wait(%val(for$rab(1)))
        read(unit=1,fmt=10,key=keyin,keyid=0) last,first,pos,hand,junk
        first='Bruce     '
        rewrite(unit=1,fmt=10) last,first,pos,hand,junk
        end
$
$ typ idxrtn.for
C**********************
C       Subroutine read_wait
C       input:  address of record access block
C       function:         set bits in rab for proper
C                         locking on read with 10
C                         second wait before error status is
C                         returned
C**********************
        subroutine        read_wait(rab)
        include '($rabdef)'
        include '($syssrvnam)'
        record  /rabdef/          rab
        ! clear the record lock bit
        rab.rab$l_rop=ibclr(rab.rab$l_rop,rab$v_rlk)
        ! set the read lock bit
        rab.rab$l_rop=ibset(rab.rab$l_rop,rab$v_rea)
        ! set the bit to wait for a lock
        rab.rab$l_rop=ibset(rab.rab$l_rop,rab$v_wat)
        !enable 10 second time out
        rab.rab$b_tmo=10
        end

C**********************
C       Subroutine write_wait
C       input:  address of record access block
C       function:         set bits in rab for proper
C                         locking on write with 10
C                         second wait before error status is
C                         returned
C**********************
        subroutine        write_wait(rab)
        include '($rabdef)'
        include '($syssrvnam)'
        record  /rabdef/            rab
        ! set the record lock bit
        rab.rab$l_rop=ibset(rab.rab$l_rop,rab$v_rlk)
        ! clear the read lock bit
        rab.rab$l_rop=ibclr(rab.rab$l_rop,rab$v_rea)
        ! set the bit to wait for a lock
        rab.rab$l_rop=ibset(rab.rab$l_rop,rab$v_wat)
        !enable 10 second time out
        rab.rab$b_tmo=10
        end
$
$
$ for idxnostall
$ for idxrtn
$
$ link idxnostall,idxrtn
$
$ def recs b4.idx
$ r idxnostall
$
```

Figure 15.

```
;^^^^^^^^^^^^^^^^^^^^^^^^^^^^^^^^^^^^^^^^^^^^^^^^^^^^^^^^^^^^^^^^^^^^^^^^
;       Program:        blocking_lock
;       Author:         Billy Bitsenbites
;       Date Written:   4/90
;       Function:       This program accepts a PID or lock id
;                       (the lock id is accepted only if the
;                       user skips the entry of the PID)
;                       PID case:       If the user enters a
;                       pid, we use it to locate the list of owned
;                       locks and determine the first blocked lock.
;                       We then determine the process(es) holding
;                       locks which are blocking the process from
;                       accessing the given resource.
;                       We display the resource name the process
;                       is attempting to access, the mode of request
;                       the CSID of the resource, and the REMLKID
;                       field (which is meaningless if CSID=0)
;                       LKID case:      Same as PID case except
;                       we go directly to the lock block by lock
;                       id.  This might be used in the case of
;                       a resource which is mastered on a remote
;                       node.
;
;                       Note:  the only error status returned is
;                       SS$_ABORT.  This status is returned if
;                       1)              The process owns no blocked locks.
;                       2)              If the user enters a bogus lock id.
;                       (If you do not like this behaviour, change
;                       it.  The Guide never made the claim that
;                       it was user friendly.)
;^^^^^^^^^^^^^^^^^^^^^^^^^^^^^^^^^^^^^^^^^^^^^^^^^^^^^^^^^^^^^^^^^^^^^^^^
;Macro to check status
        .macro  check     ?1
        blbs    r0,1
        $exit_s r0
1:
        .endm   check
;Include files
        .library        /sys$library:lib.mlb/
        .link           /sys$system:sys.stb/
        .psect  data    wrt,noshr
;Data structure definitions
        $pcbdef         ;Process control block
        $lkbdef         ;Lock block
        $lckdef         ;need for lock modes
        $rsbdef         ;Resource block
        $ipldef         ;Interrupt priority level
display_buffer_size=1024
display_buffer:                                 ;buffer for fao conversions
        .long   display_buffer_size
        .address        10$
10$:    .blkb   display_buffer_size
lock_start:                                     ;start location for $lkwset
pid:    .blkl   1                               ;process id
kargs:  .long   5                               ;arguments to $cmkrnl
pid_arg=4
        .address        pid                     ;process id address
blank_arg=8
        .long   0                               ;blank argument for exe$nampid
buffer_arg=12
        .address        lock_info_buffer        ;buffer of junk to return from kernel
                                                ; mode
flag_arg=16
flag:   .blkl   1                               ;flag 0=> pid passed 1=> lkid passed
lkid_arg=20
        .address        lkid_b                  ;lock id
;*****************
;buffer of data about locks
;NOTE:  position is assumed any changes will require
;       that you research the code area.
;*****************
lock_info_buffer:
remlkid=0
```

Figure 15 contd.

```
        .blkl   1
lkid=4
        .blkl   1
csid=8
        .blkl   1
rqmode=12
        .blkb   1
resnam_cnt=13
        .blkb   1
resnam=14
resnam_loc:
        .blkb   32
presnam_cnt=46
        .blkb   1
presnam=47
presnam_loc:
        .blkb   32
process_count=79
        .blkb   1
;Info on up to 10 blocking processes
per_process_epid=0
per_process_mode=4
per_process_csid=8
per_process_flags=12
epid_and_grmode=80
        .rept   10
        .blkl   1           ;epid
        .blkl   1           ;grmode
        .blkl   1           ;CSID
        .blkl   1           ;flags
        .endr
per_process_data_size=16
;*****************************
;$FAO format statements
;*****************************
fmt:    .ascid  /RQMODE: !3AC   LKID !8XL  CSID: !8XL  REMLKID: !8XL/
fmt1:   .ascid  $Resource name (ascii) !AF!/$-
$Resource name (hex) !8XL !8XL !8XL !8XL!/$-
$                    !8XL !8XL !8XL !8XL$
fmt2:   .ascid  $Parent Resource name (ascii) !AF!/$-
$Parent Resource name (hex) !8XL !8XL !8XL !8XL!/$-
$                           !8XL !8XL !8XL !8XL$
fmt3:   .ascid  /Blocking PID !8XL  GRMODE: !3AC/
fmt4:   .ascid  /Master copy process is on node with  CSID: !8XL/
;**************
;table for looking up lock modes
;**************
ASSUME LCK$K_NLMODE EQ 0
ASSUME LCK$K_CRMODE EQ 1
ASSUME LCK$K_CWMODE EQ 2
ASSUME LCK$K_PRMODE EQ 3
ASSUME LCK$K_PWMODE EQ 4
ASSUME LCK$K_EXMODE EQ 5
mode_tbl:
        .ascic  /NL /
        .ascic  /CR /
        .ascic  /CW /
        .ascic  /PR /
        .ascic  /PW /
        .ascic  /EX /
pid_a:  .long   8
        .address        10$
10$:    .blkb   8
pmt:    .ascid  /pid> /
pmt1:   .ascid  /LKID> /
lkid_a: .long   8
        .address        10$
10$:    .blkb   8
lkid_b: .blkl   1

;address of code/data to lock down
lock_adr:
        .address        lock_start
```

Figure 15 contd.

```
        .address        lock_end
;*********************************************
;Main program:
;       Prompts for pid/lkid
;       gets into kernel mode and gets lock/resource info
;       displays the junk.
;*********************************************
        .psect  code     nowrt,shr
        .entry  whose_blocking,^m<>
        pushal  pid_a                            ;Do a read with prompt
        pushal  pmt                              ; for the process id.
        pushal  pid_a
        calls   #3,g^lib$get_input
        check
        tstw    pid_a                            ;if did not enter a pid get lkid
        beql    get_lkid
        pushal  pid                              ; else convert the pid to binary
        pushal  pid_a
        calls   #2,g^ots$cvt_tz_l
        check
        brb     got_stuff
get_lkid:                                        ;set flag for kernel mode code
        incl    flag                             ; to process lkid
        pushal  lkid_a                           ;Do a read with prompt for
        pushal  pmtl                             ; the lock id.
        pushal  lkid_a
        calls   #3,g^lib$get_input
        check
        pushal  lkid_b                           ;convert the lock id to binary
        pushal  lkid_a
        calls   #2,g^ots$cvt_tz_l
        check
got_stuff:
        $lkwset_s       inadr=lock_adr           ;lock most everything down
        check
;*************************
;Get into kernel mode and grab the resource/lock info
;*************************
        $cmkrnl_s       routin=find_out_who,arglst=kargs
        check
        moval   lock_info_buffer,r6              ;point to data buffer
        movzbl  rqmode(r6),r8                    ;use request mode as index
        moval   mode_tbl[r8],r8                  ; into display table
;*************************
;format and display mode requested/lock id/csid/remote lock id
;*************************
        $fao_s  ctrstr=fmt,outbuf=display_buffer,outlen=display_buffer,-
                p1=r8,p2=lkid(r6),p3=csid(r6),p4=remlkid(r6)
        check
        pushal  display_buffer
        calls   #1,g^lib$put_output
        check
        movl    #display_buffer_size,display_buffer  ;reset buffer size
;************************
;format and display the resource name
;************************
        movzbl  resnam_cnt(r6),r2                ;size of resource name
        $fao_s  ctrstr=fmt1,outbuf=display_buffer,outlen=display_buffer,-
                p1=r2,p2=#resnam_loc,p3=resnam+12(r6),p4=resnam+8(r6),-
                p5=resnam+4(r6),p6=resnam(r6),p7=resnam+28(r6),-
                p8=resnam+24(r6),p9=resnam+20(r6),p10=resnam+16(r6)
        check
        pushal  display_buffer
        calls   #1,g^lib$put_output
        check
        movl    #display_buffer_size,display_buffer   ;reset buffer size
;************************
;format and display the parent resource name
;************************
        movzbl  presnam_cnt(r6),r2
        $fao_s  ctrstr=fmt2,outbuf=display_buffer,outlen=display_buffer,-
                p1=r2,p2=#presnam_loc,p3=presnam+12(r6),p4=presnam+8(r6),-
                p5=presnam+4(r6),p6=presnam(r6),p7=presnam+28(r6),-
```

Figure 15 contd.

```
                p8=presnam+24(r6),p9=presnam+20(r6),p10=presnam+16(r6)
        check
        pushal  display_buffer
        calls   #1,g^lib$put_output
        check
        movl    #display_buffer_size,display_buffer ;reset buffer size
;************************
;format and display epid and mode of blocking processes
;(up to 10)
;if master copy then display csid
;************************
        movzbl  process_count(r6),r11               ;set process count
        moval   epid_and_grmode(r6),r7              ;get address of per process buffer
next_process_user:
        movl    per_process_mode(r7),r8             ;get mode owned
        moval   mode_tbl[r8],r8                     ;get mode string address
        $fao_s  ctrstr=fmt3,outbuf=display_buffer,outlen=display_buffer,-
                p1=(r7),p2=r8
        check
        pushal  display_buffer
        calls   #1,g^lib$put_output
        check
        movl    #display_buffer_size,display_buffer   ;reset buffer size
        bbc     #lkb$v_mstcpy,12(r7),skip_csid      ;if not master skip csid
        $fao_s  ctrstr=fmt4,outbuf=display_buffer,outlen=display_buffer,-
                p1=8(r7)
        check
        pushal  display_buffer
        calls   #1,g^lib$put_output
        check
        movl    #display_buffer_size,display_buffer   ;reset buffer size
skip_csid:
        addl    #per_process_data_size,r7           ;point to next data segment
        decl    r11                                 ;decrement process count
        beql    done                                ;if out scram
        brw     next_process_user                   ; else get next process
done:
         ret
;*************************************************
;Kernel mode code to return lock/resource data
;       inputs: 4(ap)       pid
;               8(ap)       null
;               12(ap)      user buffer
;               16(ap)      flag (0=pid passed,1=lkid passed)
;               20(ap)      lkid
;       outputs:          user buffer filled
;                         r0= ss$_normal/ss$_abort
;*************************************************
        .entry  find_out_who,^m<r2,r3,r4,r5,r6,r7,r8,r9,r10,r11>
        movl    buffer_arg(ap),r11                  ;set return buffer address
        tstl    flag_arg(ap)                        ;if pid passed then process
        beql    use_pid                             ; else
        brw     use_lkid                            ; process lock id
use_pid:
        jsb     g^exe$nampid                        ;get pcb address from pid
        blbs    r0,ok_proc                          ;if we have it continue
        brw     err_out                             ; else scram
ok_proc:
        movl    pcb$l_epid(r4),r6                   ;save his pid
        unlock  lockname=SCHED                      ;give up sched spinlock
                                                    ; so we can grab SCS
                                                    ; spinlock at correct rank
                                                    ; leave ipl at 8

ASSUME IPL$_SCS EQ IPL$_SCHED
        lock    lockname=SCS                        ;get spinlock for locks
        lock    lockname=SCHED                      ;re-acquire sched spinlock
        cmpl    pcb$l_epid(r4),r6                   ;is he still there?
        beql    still_there                         ; if so continue
        unlock  lockname=SCHED                      ;release owned locks
        brw     err_out_release_locks               ;else scram
still_there:
        unlock  lockname=SCHED                      ;release owned locks
        moval   pcb$l_lockqfl(r4),r6                ;get owner queue address
```

Figure 15 contd.

```
        cmpl    (r6),r6                             ;if no locks scram
        bneq    10$
        brw     no_locks
10$:    movl    r6,r7                               ;save listhead address
next_lock:
        movl    (r7),r7                             ;get next lock
        cmpl    r6,r7                               ;if back at listhead scram
        bneq    20$
        brw     no_locks
20$:    moval   -lkb$l_ownqfl(r7),r8      ;locate the beginning of lock block
process_lock:
        cmpb    #lkb$k_granted,lkb$b_state(r8)      ;if granted skip
        bneq    process_wait_on_lock
        brb     next_lock
process_wait_on_lock:

        movzbl  lkb$b_rqmode(r8),rqmode(r11)        ;save request mode
        movl    lkb$l_lkid(r8),lkid(r11)            ;save lock id
        movl    lkb$l_remlkid(r8),remlkid(r11)      ;save remote lock id
        movl    lkb$l_rsb(r8),r8                    ;get resource block address
        movl    rsb$l_csid(r8),csid(r11)            ;get csid of master (if any)
        movl    rsb$l_parent(r8),r10                ;get parent resource block
        beql    skip_parent                         ;if none skip copying name
        movzbl  rsb$b_rsnlen(r10),r0                ;copy parent resource name
        movb    r0,presnam_cnt(r11)                 ; to user buffer
        movc3   r0,rsb$t_resnam(r10),presnam(r11)
skip_parent:
        movzbl  rsb$b_rsnlen(r8),r0                 ;copy resource name to
        movb    r0,resnam_cnt(r11)                  ; user buffer
        movc3   r0,rsb$t_resnam(r8),resnam(r11)
        clrl    r5                                  ;clear process counter
        movl    #10,r1                              ;handle up to 10 processes
        moval   rsb$l_grqfl(r8),r9                  ;get granted queue
        movl    r9,r10                              ;save listhead address
        moval   epid_and_grmode(r11),r2             ;get per process buffer
next_process:
        movl    (r10),r10                           ;get next granted lock
        cmpl    r10,r9                              ;if done scram
        beql    done_with_procs
        moval   -lkb$l_sqfl(r10),r3                 ;locate start of lock block
        bbs     #lkb$v_mstcpy,lkb$w_status(r3),skip_epid
        movl    lkb$l_pid(r3),r0                    ;get pid to determine epid
        movzwl  r0,r0                               ;get index into pcb vector tbl
        movl    @sch$gl_pcbvec[r0],r0               ;get his pcb address
        movl    pcb$l_epid(r0),(r2)+                ;get his epid
        brb     got_epid
skip_epid:
        movl    lkb$l_epid(r3),(r2)+                ;if remote copy epid field
got_epid:
        movzbl  lkb$b_grmode(r3),(r2)+              ;copy mode granted
                                                    ;if not master skip csid/
                                                    ; flags
        bbc     #lkb$v_mstcpy,lkb$w_status(r3),skip_master
        movl    lkb$l_csid(r3),(r2)+                ;copy csid of master
        movzwl  lkb$w_flags(r3),(r2)+               ;copy flags
        brb     skip_add
skip_master:
        addl    #8,r2                               ;point to next buffer
skip_add:
        incl    r5                                  ;increment count of processes
        sobgtr  r1,next_process                     ;get next process
done_with_procs:
        movb    r5,process_count(r11)               ;return process count

        movl    #ss$_normal,r0                      ;beat it
err_out_release_locks:
        unlock  lockname=SCS,preserve=YES,newipl=#0
err_out:
        ret
no_locks:
        unlock  lockname=SCS,preserve=YES,newipl=#0
        movl    #ss$_abort,r0                       ;no locks
        ret
```

Figure 15 contd.

```
;************************
;process using lock id
;************************
use_lkid:
        movl    @lkid_arg(ap),r7          ;get the lkid
        lock    lockname=SCS
        extzv   #0,#lkb$c_lkidsiz,r7,r8   ;extract the index
        cmpl    r8,lck$gl_maxid           ;if bogus index scram
        bgtru   no_locks
        movl    @lck$gl_idtbl[r8],r8      ;get the lock block
        cmpl    r7,lkb$l_lkid(r8)         ;correct lkid?
        bneq    no_locks                  ;if not scram
        cmpb    #lkb$k_granted,lkb$b_state(r8)      ;if granted scram
        beql    no_locks
        brw     process_wait_on_lock
lock_end:
        .end    whose_blocking
```

Figure 16.

```
;**************************************************
;       Program:          trans_fid
;       Author:           Billy Bitsenbites (Bruce Ellis)
;       Date written:     4/90
;       Function:         translates device name and fid
;                         to file specification.
;**************************************************
        .macro  check     ?1
        blbs    r0,1
        $exit_s r0
1:
        .endm   check
trans_loc:                                ;location for converted file id pieces
        .blkl   1
fid:    .blkw   3                         ;file id
devnam: .long   255                       ;device name
        .address          10$
10$:    .blkb   255
file_spec:                                ;file specification
        .long   255
        .address          10$
10$:    .blkb   255
;prompts
pmt1:   .ascid  /Device name> /
pmt2:   .ascid  /First word of fid  (hex)> /
pmt3:   .ascid  /Second word of fid  (hex)> /
pmt4:   .ascid  /Third word of fid  (hex)> /
;Prompt table
pmt_table:
        .address          pmt2
        .address          pmt3
        .address          pmt4
fid_a:  .long   4                         ;ascii representation of fid
        .address          10$
10$:    .blkb   4
        .entry  trans_fid,^m<>
        pushal  devnam                    ;read with prompt device name
        pushal  pmt1
        pushal  devnam
        calls   #3,g^lib$get_input
        check
        movl    #3,r6                     ;get three pieces of fid
        moval   pmt_table,r7              ;point to prompt table
        moval   fid,r8                    ;point to file id storage
trans_loop:
        movl    #4,fid_a                  ;reset file id buffer size
        pushal  fid_a                     ;read with prompt the file id piece
        pushl   (r7)+
        pushal  fid_a
        calls   #3,g^lib$get_input
        check
        pushal  trans_loc                 ;convert it to binary
```

Figure 16 contd.

```
        pushal  fid_a
        calls   #2,g^ots$cvt_tz_l
        check
        movw    trans_loc,(r8)+          ;copy to file id buffer (binary)
        sobgtr  r6,trans_loop            ;get next piece
        pushal  file_spec                ;file specification size
        pushal  file_spec                ;file speification
        pushal  fid                      ;file id
        pushal  devnam                   ;device name
        calls   #4,g^lib$fid_to_name     ;get file spec
        check
        pushal  file_spec                ;spill the file spec
        calls   #1,g^lib$put_output
        ret
        .end    trans_fid
```

Figure 17. Output from running BLOCKING_LOCK.MAR and TRANS_FID.MAR.

```
$sh sys/s
VAX/VMS V5.3  on node LABDOG  28-APR-1990 19:39:28.38   Uptime  8 03:12:17
  Pid    Process Name    State  Pri      I/O       CPU        Page flts Ph.Mem
000000FD ELLISB_1        LEF      5       33   0 00:00:00.80      213    201  S
000000FE ELLISB_2        LEF      5       33   0 00:00:00.73      213    201  S
$set proc/priv=cmkrnl
$r blocking_lock
pid>  fd
%SYSTEM-F-ABORT, abort
$
$r blocking_lock
pid>  fe
RQMODE: PW    LKID 12500063  CSID: 00000000  REMLKID: 48385B4B
Resource name (ascii) ........
Resource name (hex) 00000000 00000000 00000007 00000000
                    00000000 00000000 00000000 00000000
Parent Resource name (ascii) RMS$.......LABUSER     ...
Parent Resource name (hex) 53554241 4C020000 000206E2 24534D52
                           00000000 00000000 00202020 20205245
Blocking PID 000000FD  GRMODE: PW
$
$!The process with pid FD is blocking our access to the
$!record with RFA of 7 in the file with file id (6E2,2,0) (hex)
$!on the device with label LABUSER
$
$r blocking_lock
pid>
LKID> 12500063
RQMODE: PW    LKID 12500063  CSID: 00000000  REMLKID: 48385B4B
Resource name (ascii) ........
Resource name (hex) 00000000 00000000 00000007 00000000
                    00000000 00000000 00000000 00000000
Parent Resource name (ascii) RMS$.......LABUSER     ...
Parent Resource name (hex) 53554241 4C020000 000206E2 24534D52
                           00000000 00000000 00202020 20205245
Blocking PID 000000FD  GRMODE: PW
$
$sh dev d

Device                  Device           Error    Volume         Free  Trans Mnt
 Name                   Status           Count     Label        Blocks Count Cnt
DUA0:                   Online               0
DUA1:                   Online               0
DUB0:                   Mounted              0  LABSYSRL5      1047381   152   1
DUB1:                   Mounted              0  LABUSER         211644     5   1
DUC0:                   Online               1
$r trans_fid
Device name> dub1
First word of fid  (hex)> 6e2
Second word of fid  (hex)> 2
Third word of fid  (hex)> 0
LABUSER:[USERS.ELLISB]JUNK.;1
$
```

Episode 7

Fragmented Thoughts

Billy walked out of work into the sunshine of a warm spring Thursday afternoon. An ominous, almost odious, feeling overcame his emotions. Depression doesn't wear well on most and looked almost ugly on his face.

The feeling of depression was, as it usually is, inexplicable in origin. Perhaps, on this fine spring day, all that surrounded him seemed more alive than he felt.

He had made monumental progress in the development of his understanding of VMS. Yet, there was no one to share his feeling of accomplishment. Sure, Dr. Albino had expressed his gratitude for a job well done, but he did not, nor did he care to, understand the inner workings or the elegance of the code Billy had written.

Billy made his way to the T stop for the Red Line, referred to as the Dead Line by many Boston commuters. He took the train to the Kendall Square exit. A few MIT students passed him, in a world all their own.

Billy had to break some of the tension. He stopped at a package store, picked up a few bottles of beer and headed for a more secluded section of the Charles River bank. After he found a place away from the mainstream, he sat down, opened a beer, and watched the rowing teams shoot along the river.

He noticed the straight path with which they rowed and was impressed at the precision with which the rowing was synchronized. He thought, "Why can't people write code in the same fashion, precise and to the point? Instead, the industry is producing tons of slop. Programmers don't seem to take the time to understand what's going on in the system they're coding in. How can they write efficient code without a fundamental understanding of system architecture?

"The world would be better off if the industry spent as much money and time developing system-friendly users as it does on developing user-friendly systems."

Billy finished his beer and headed back to the Dead Line. He rode the T to Harvard Square. The atmosphere there was substantially more lively. He ate dinner at a German restaurant around the corner from the T stop, ordering Wiener schnitzel and a few foreign beers.

After eating, Billy went to a club located in the lower level of a building just down the street. He paid the cover charge and went in to watch the band. He had been there one night when Jorma Kaukonen and Jaco Pastorious were supposed to play. Jaco didn't show up because he drank too much wine on a boat earlier in the day. Billy got in for half price that night.

He regretted not seeing Jaco; now, he'd never see him, because Jaco died later on. "But Jaco Pastorious will be remembered. Who'll remember Billy Bitsenbites?" Billy mumbled despondently.

He danced a little and bent some girl's ear with the wonders of coding in kernel mode. It didn't bother him that she eventually walked away while Billy was in the middle of a sentence. He had put away a few more beers since entering and was starting to feel good.

He was about to leave when he realized that no more immediate projects lay before him at work. He thought long and hard about what to do next, but nothing inspired him.

He left the bar, moving in the general direction of the T stop. He staggered a couple steps to the right, a step forward, a step to the left. He continued to weave, making little progress toward the T stop. Billy wasn't a regular beer drinker, and the alcohol was hitting him hard. He noticed that the trip, which was typically a quick jog, was taking a painstakingly long time, primarily because he couldn't walk a straight path.

He found a coffee shop. He sat eating a doughnut, drinking a cup of coffee, and attempting not to get arrested, when he thought, "If I'm having these problems making it home because I can't walk straight, what happens when I access a fragmented file that isn't on the system straight? I'll have to discuss this with the *Guide* tomorrow."

The next morning, Billy dragged into work. He opened the gray tome to an unusually loud, but familiar, clicking and whirring.

"Can I help you?" asked the *Guide*.

"Yeah, you can keep the noise down a little," Billy entered.

"Not feeling well today?" the *Guide* asked after automatically reducing the volume.

"Hung over," Billy responded.

"Too bad," consoled the *Guide*. "If it helps you feel better, you are in good company. Rumors logged in the *Guide* mention that, though this information is completely unsubstantiated, a prominent RSX developer went through several cases of beer a week while designing his version of the RSX operating system.

"Maybe you do have what it takes to become a system programmer after all.

"What did you want me for anyway?"

"I was wondering about accessing fragmented files. Isn't it more expensive than accessing a contiguous file? If it is more expensive, how much more expensive is it?" Billy entered slowly, adding, "The key click on this terminal interface is rattling my brain. Can you turn it off, please?"

The key click was turned off.

"Yes," responded the *Guide*. "Accessing a fragmented file is more expensive than accessing a contiguous file. To understand the general effects of accessing a fragmented file, we must first discuss the general components of a disk transfer.

"When the first read (i.e., call to SYS$GET) from disk is performed through the record management services (RMS), RMS reads in a number of blocks. The number of blocks read is defined by the bucket size of the file for indexed or relative files; for sequential files, RMS reads a buffer, whose size is defined by the multiblock count. The multiblock count is not a characteristic of the file. It is instead defined by the program by setting the field FAB$B_MBC in the file access block. If this field is set to 0, RMS uses the process default multiblock count as set either with the command:

```
$SET RMS/BLOCK=n
```

or with the system default as defined initially by the SYSGEN parameter RMS_DFMBC (which defaults to 16 blocks), or RMS overrides the count with the command:

```
$SET RMS/SYSTEM/BLOCK=n.
```

"After reading the blocks into the P1 space buffer, RMS obtains the record and returns it to the user buffer. On subsequent reads, RMS looks into the buffer to determine whether it has already read the record. If the record has been read, RMS returns the record to the user buffer without having to issue another I/O request. Otherwise, on the call to SYS$GET, RMS reads the blocks or buckets that correspond to the record your process requested."

Billy interjected, "So when you perform a read operation, you aren't necessarily issuing an I/O operation."

"Correct," the *Guide* concurred.

"I know that the I/O request would be performed by the SYS$QIO system service. How does that work, generally?" asked Billy.

"When you issue a $QIO, 12 arguments are passed to the service. The first six arguments are the event flag number (EFN), channel address (CHAN), I/O status block address (IOSB), address of the AST routine, if any (ASTADR), AST parameter (ASTPRM), and the function that you want this request to perform (FUNC). These arguments are the device and function independent arguments.

"The other six arguments with those meaningful names (i.e., P1, P2, P3, P4, P5, and P6) are the device and function dependent arguments. The writer of the device driver defines the passing conventions for these arguments, based on the function you specified. For instance, if you want to perform a read from a file, like RMS would have had to perform, you use the function IO$_READVBLK. For this function, the P1 argument contains the address of the user buffer, the P2 argument contains the count of the number of bytes that you wish to transfer, and the P3 argument contains the starting virtual block at which you wish to read. A driver other than the disk driver might define these arguments in a different way.

"Note that $QIO is running in process context, and the driver will later be running in system context. When you are running in system context, you cannot access P0 or P1 space, and you cannot incur page faults. So, to pass information to the driver, $QIO allocates an I/O request packet (IRP) out of non-paged pool. The IRP contains fields that describe the I/O request, such as the PID of the requesting process, the event flag to set upon completion, the size of the transfer, and so on.

"After $QIO has pre-processed the device and function dependent arguments, it locates a table called the function decision table (FDT). The FDT contains two initial quadwords. The first quadword contains a legal function mask, with bits set defining which functions this driver can process. If the program specifies an invalid function, $QIO returns with an error status of SS$_ILLFUNC.

"The quadword following the legal function mask contains a buffered function mask. This mask defines which functions will be processed as buffered I/Os. All other functions will be considered direct I/Os. This mask allows $QIO to perform operations like determining whether to charge the buffered I/O limit (BIOLM) or the direct I/O limit (DIOLM). On a buffered I/O, $QIO also converts virtual requests to logical requests, automatically if the function is a buffered function. This implies that the driver will never see a IO$_READVBLK or IO$_WRITEVBLK function that has been marked as buffered.

"What's the difference between a buffered and direct I/O?" Billy queried. "Is this the same as direct memory access (DMA) versus programmed I/O?"

The *Guide* replied, "No. DMA and programmed I/O are hardware distinctions, determining whether the device will transfer a block of data followed by an interrupt, in the case of a DMA transfer, or whether the CPU will transfer a byte or word at a time with an interrupt on each transfer, in the case of programmed I/O.

"Direct I/O implies that we will transfer directly to the process' P0 or P1 space buffer. This requires that the buffer be locked into memory, which in turn implies that the process is not an outswap candidate. We would only want to choose to perform direct I/O if we had a guaranteed completion time on the I/O request, as in the case of a disk or tape transfer.

"If we were to perform direct I/O to a terminal, and the user left the terminal logged in overnight, sitting at the dollar sign prompt, we could not swap his process, even though he would be the most ideal candidate for swapping, because of his inactivity. So, instead of performing direct I/O, we would perform a buffered I/O operation. In buffered I/O, we allocate an intermediate buffer from non-paged pool and perform the transfer to and from this buffer. This mechanism allows the process to be fully swappable and pageable for the duration of the I/O, although the buffer would be guaranteed to be memory resident.

"Buffered I/O is typically performed on devices such as terminals, mailboxes, printers, and communications devices, which do not have a guaranteed completion time. The extended QIO procedures (XQP) also perform buffered I/Os to disk. The XQP, sometimes fondly referred to as the exempt from quality-control procedures, due to version 4 problems, replaced the pre-V4.0 anxiety creating process (just kidding, actually the ancillary control process or ACP) in servicing file system requests."

After that long-winded response, Billy, for the first time that day, wished for another beer.

"Okay, Book, let's get back to the FDT routines," Billy suggested.

The *Guide* responded, "After checking these first two quadwords, $QIO checks a quadword function selection mask to determine whether the bit, corresponding to the passed function, is set. If it's set, $QIO ships off to a routine whose address is an associated longword. This procedure is repeated until we find a quadword with this bit set.

"The routine that we located through the FDT is referred to as an FDT routine. The FDT routine is responsible for processing the P1 through P6 arguments. It is the last place in the driver that the driver writer is guaranteed to be in process context. This implies that the driver writer must incur all page faults and touch any process virtual address space required prior to leaving these routines. These routines run at IPL 2 to block process deletion while we own pool.

"In the case of a disk transfer, the FDT routines are responsible for translating the virtual block in a file to a logical block on disk, as disk controllers have no real understanding of the file system. The translation is performed by examining a data structure referred to as a window control block (WCB) that contains mapping pointers. The mapping pointers describe the location of extents logically on a disk. An extent is a set of logically contiguous blocks allocated to the same file.

"The mapping pointers are six bytes in size and describe the starting logical block and size of the extent on disk. The WCB is constructed at the file open, using mapping pointers read from the file header of the file.

"Because the WCB is allocated from non-paged pool, we limit its initial size. The size is defined at the file open by filling in the field FAB$B_RTV, from the file access block, with the desired number of mapping pointers. If this field is null, we use the number specified by the /WINDOW qualifier in the MOUNT command for the volume. If the qualifier was not specified, we use the value corresponding to the SYSGEN parameter ACP_WINDOW and add 1 to it. The default setting for this parameter is 7, so we default to 8 mapping pointers in a WCB."

"What if the file is so fragmented that it takes more than eight mapping pointers to be described?" Billy asked.

"If we attempt to access beyond the mapped portion of the file, we discard the existing mapping pointers and remap the file from the block that we are attempting to access. This operation is called a window turn," answered the *Guide*.

"I assume that the file header would have to be reread to complete the window turn. This means that you would be performing an I/O to get the information required to complete the initial I/O request," Billy interrupted.

"That is correct," the *Guide* agreed.

"So, this is one level of additional overhead that I have to deal with when accessing a badly fragmented file. What can I do to minimize the number of window turns, short of making the files more contiguous?" asked Billy.

"You can increase the size of the window control block. If you are not sure how many mapping pointers to specify, you may stick -1 in the FAB$B_RTV field and the XQP will map the entire file, regardless of its discontiguousness."

The WCB will be marked as a cathedral window, by setting the bit WCB$V_CATHEDRAL in the field WCB$B_ACCESS. If we need more space to describe the mapping pointers than can be described in the WCB, we allocate another WCB and chain them together.

"This procedure eats up additional pool and should be considered a Bandaid and not a solution to fragmentation problems, as other performance issues will come up later. Larger WCBs also take up more non-paged pool," the *Guide* answered.

"Is there any way to determine the amount of pool being used by the WCBs?" Billy requested.

"You can use an unsupported-undocumented-can-go-away-at-any-time feature of VMS. The command:

```
$SHOW DEVICE/FILES/WINDOWS
```

gives you a count of the number of WCBs associated with each open file, as well as the size in bytes of each WCB. A C in the Win. Cnt. field implies that this is a cathedral window," the *Guide* offered.

"Back to the flow of I/O, where does the FDT routine go from the translation of virtual block number (VBN) to logical block number?" Billy requested.

"After we have mapped the extent, $QIO places the starting LBN in the field IRP$L_MEDIA of the IRP and dispatches off to the driver routine, called the start I/O routine, to set up the disk controller for the I/O," the *Guide* explained.

"What if the transfer is a large virtual request that's logically discontiguous?" Billy asked.

"If the transfer is logically discontiguous, we describe the initial segment of the transfer in the I/O request packet (IRP)," answered the book. "Additional segments are described in IRP extensions (IRPEs), which are chained off of the IRP.

"The IRP contains an original byte count IRP$L_OBCNT and an accumulated byte count IRP$L_ABCNT. The accumulated byte count is initialized to 0 and increased by the size of the segment after the transfer has completed. If the accumulated byte count is less than the original, the I/O completion code remaps the IRP, using information described in the IRPE, so that it points to the next segment. We then transfer control back to the beginning of the start I/O routine and continue the process until the entire transfer has completed," the *Guide* replied.

"Wow," Billy exclaimed and continued, "So one I/O request could effectively become many requests to the physical disk. In other words, this is another level of overhead because of fragmented files. Can we track all this stuff?"

"Yes," the *Guide* answered. "This breaking up of a transfer is known as a split I/O or a split transfer. Split transfers can be tracked by using $MONITOR IO. By the way, window turns can also be tracked, using $MONITOR FCP."

"Is this information provided on a per-disk basis?" asked Billy.

"No," the *Guide* answered. "It is only available systemwide, unless you purchase products like the VAX Performance Advisor (VPA) or the System Performance Monitor (SPM), which are sold by Digital."

"That stinks," Billy responded. "You have to pay extra to determine how messed up your disks are after you already had to pay for the stupid product that screwed up the disks in the first place."

"Sorry, that is beyond the control of the *Guide*," the book stated.

"What does the start I/O routine do?" asked Billy.

"Generally, it sets up the controller for the transfer, fields the I/O completion interrupt, performs any necessary error processing, and requests I/O completion," answered the *Guide*.

"So, are split transfers and window turns the only real cost for fragmentation?" Billy asked.

"No," the *Guide* replied. "The most important cost is based on the physical processing of the disk drive.

"The disk drive is made of surfaces that are divided into concentric circles referred to as tracks. The tracks are, in turn, divided into 512-byte sectors, which correspond to the logical blocks of a volume. The surfaces or platters are aligned one above the next. If you were to cut a perpendicular line through a track on the surface, all the tracks that it intersected would form a cylinder.

"To transfer data from the disk, a set of read/write heads that move in parallel must be positioned over the correct cylinder boundary. This operation is referred to as a seek operation. The seek is a mechanical operation and therefore slow. In fact, the seek is typically the slowest component of a disk transfer. The seek takes about 55 to 60 percent of the overall transfer time on a typical disk transfer.

"The more fragmented your file is, the more you will seek."

Billy wanted to seek an aspirin about now, but the *Guide* continued.

"After the seek has completed, you perform a track selection and wait for the starting block of the transfer to rotate under the heads. This component of the transfer is known as rotational latency. Latency is limited by the speed at which the disk rotates, usually 3,600 revolutions per minute.

"Rotational latency is the next slowest component of a disk transfer, taking roughly 15 percent of the transfer time on a typical disk transfer. Once again, fragmentation tends to accentuate the overhead of latency.

"The transfer across the wire is the next slowest component. It is limited by the electronic transfer from the controller across a given I/O bus and any associated bus arbitration. The cost is roughly 10 percent of the transfer; it can be more for larger transfers. A typical transfer is assumed to be about three blocks in size."

"So, the big three costs for fragmentation are window turns, split transfers, and the physical overhead of seeks and rotational latency," Billy summarized. "How do I go about making my files more contiguous?"

"The best way to maintain contiguity is to create the files contiguously from the start. This can be done by creating the files with either the contiguous or contiguous-best-try options and preallocating space for them on disk at the time of creation," the *Guide* said.

"What's the difference between contiguous and contiguous-best-try?" asked Billy.

The *Guide* answered, "The file system scans through the volume bitmap, which is stored in the file [000000]BITMAP.SYS, for a set of contiguous blocks large enough to support your allocation request. (Note that this information may be available in the file system caches.) If it locates this required extent, the file system allocates the space and assigns it to your file.

"If the bitmap does not describe a contiguous extent which is large enough to support your request, the file system returns error status.

"On a contiguous-best-try option, the file system scans the bitmap on three passes grabbing the three largest extents, if necessary. After the three passes, it uses a first-fit algorithm to grab any additional blocks required to store the file."

"What else can I do to minimize fragmentation?" Billy asked.

"You can specify a larger extend size for files at file creation time or through $SET RMS/EXTEND. If you ask for more blocks at once, they are more likely to be contiguous, even if VMS performs first-fit allocation.

"If the disk is already fragmented, you can use either $COPY/CONTIGUOUS or the backup utility (i.e., backup and restore) to make existing files contiguous. Another alternative is to purchase a disk defragmentation tool," the *Guide* stated.

"How can I determine the level of fragmentation within an existing file?" Billy queried.

"You can use the DUMP/HEADER command and count the mapping pointers," offered the *Guide*.

"Hey, Book, I have a lot of files out there and that would take forever. Isn't there a directory qualifier that will tell me the number of mapping pointers in the file header?" Billy demanded.

"No," the *Guide* replied.

"Well, I want to write one. Where do I start?" Billy requested.

"To perform the task you are asking about, you will have to learn a little more about Files-11," the *Guide* started.

"What's Files-11?" Billy demanded.

"The VMS file system is named Files-11 ODS-2. It is an extension of the RSX-11 operating system's file system, which was named Files-11 ODS-1. The ODS part stands for On-Disk Structure," the *Guide* responded.

"Let us start with some general concepts and provide some definitions here. A volume is typically a disk and is described by a logical block number (LBN). The logical block numbers are organized starting with LBN 0 located at the beginning of the volume and growing to LBN X-1, where X is the size of the volume in blocks.

"Files are contained on volumes. Files are described by virtual block number (VBN). The files grow from VBN 1 to VBN X, where X is the size of the file in blocks.

"The VBNs of a file are not required to be logically contiguous. So, we must have a mechanism for locating files on a given volume. That mechanism is implemented by the mapping pointers.

"They describe extents. An extent is a set of logically contiguous blocks on a volume, which are allocated to the same file. Space for the extents is allocated in units defined by the cluster size of the volume. The cluster size is defined by the $INITIALIZE DCL command, which is used to define the Files-11 characteristics of the volume.

"The clusters on the volume define an allocation quantity. If you ask for a block on the volume, you receive N contiguous blocks, where N is the cluster size of the volume.

"The clusters on a volume are described by the volume bitmap, which is stored in the file [000000]BITMAP.SYS. The first block of this file contains a structure called the storage control block (SCB), not to be confused with the system control block, another SCB. After the SCB, we have the bitmap, which contains one bit per cluster on the volume, marking whether the given cluster is in use or available.

"The mapping pointers are stored in the file header of the file. The file headers are allocated from a file called the index file, i.e., [000000]INDEXF.SYS. The index file is the single most important file on a Files-11 volume.

"The first block of the index file (i.e., VBN 1) corresponds to the first block on the volume (i.e., LBN 0). This block is the boot block. It is unused, except on a VAX 11/750 without a CI port, where it is used to locate the primary bootstrap program (i.e., VMB.EXE) on the system disk.

"The next block in the index file and on the volume is the home block. The home block describes the Files-11 characteristic required to mount the volume. These characteristics include the volume label, user identification code (UIC) protection, owner UIC, and so on.

"In the first block of the third cluster of the index file, we store the backup home block. It is skewed to a different track, sector, and cylinder to minimize the chances of losing it, should the home block go bad. If the backup home block is being used, the $MOUNT command will warn you. This is a good time to back up the given disk.

"The first block in the fourth cluster of the index file contains a backup copy of the index file's header.

"The next cluster is the start of the index bitmap. The index bitmap contains one bit per file header on the volume, describing whether the header is in use or available. This must be scanned to locate a free header when creating a new file, although caches typically eliminate the need to perform this scan.

"Following the index bitmap, we have the header blocks. All file headers are one block in size, aligned on block boundaries. If more information is required to describe the file than can fit into one block, an extension header is allocated to contain this information. A file can have multiple extension headers."

Billy stopped the *Guide* with, "What information requires an extension header?"

"Two things typically force the need for extension headers. First is when the system manager has gone crazy with access control list entries. Second is when the file is extremely fragmented, and the mapping pointers do not fit into one header block," answered the *Guide*.

"I assume that this would cause additional overhead in accessing the file," Billy postulated.

"Yes," the *Guide* concurred. "To complete the open, all header blocks must be read in, when a file is opened up. Therefore, there would be additional I/Os required to complete the file open."

"How's the header of a given file located?" Billy demanded.

"I was getting to that," the *Guide* snapped back and continued.

"Files have a file ID that uniquely identifies the file on the volume. The file ID is made up of three values, namely the header number, the sequence number, and the relative volume number. Internally, this is a three-word entity, whose format is described by the macro $FIDDEF.

"The header number is a block index, away from the block preceding the first file header, used to locate the header block. The header number is described by 24 bits. The low word of the header number is stored in the first word of the internally represented file ID. The offset to this field is defined by the symbol FID$W_NUM. The third byte of the header number is stored in the last byte of the file ID, offset by FID$B_NMX.

"Because headers are reused, we need to guarantee that a process does not access a file by file ID, which has already been deleted. So, we maintain a sequence number. This is the second word of the internally represented file ID, i.e., FID$W_SEQ. It is incremented when the file is deleted, so that the next file using the header block will have a higher sequence number.

"If you are using bound volume sets, created with the $MOUNT/BIND DCL command, the last number contains the relative volume number, which is an index into a table called the relative volume table (RVT). This index identifies which member of the bound volume set holds the index file that contains the header block for this file. If the file is not on a bound volume set, the relative volume number is 0.

This information is stored in the byte located at the offset FID$B_RVN."

"How do I determine the file ID of a file so that I can locate the file header to complete the open request?" Billy asked.

"When you open a file by name, we must perform a directory look-up," the *Guide* answered. "Directories are files that are created contiguously, with a bit set in the file header marking the file as a directory. They are maintained as sequential file organizations with variable length records.

"The records are sorted alphabetically by file name and file type. The records contain the version limit on the file, flags, the name stored as an ASCII counted string, and a list containing the version number and file ID of each file with the given file name.

"The format of the directory record is defined by the macro $DIRDEF. The list entries, containing the file ID and version number, have independent offsets defined by the same macro.

"There are two gotchas associated with using the directory symbolic definitions to access the record. If you use RMS to get the record, your directory record offsets are off by two bytes. These two bytes define the record size. So, you have to back up by 2 on each of the base offsets.

"The other gotcha is that the file name size is rounded to the next even byte boundary. On odd sized file names, there will be a null byte padding the name string."

The *Guide* has the following entry on the term gotcha: "*Although the term gotcha was not coined by Elinor Woods, a great RMS instructor, she says it in such a unique way as to add new meaning to gotcha. The* Guide *wishes to thank Elinor for this additional contribution to the understanding of VMS and RMS.*"

The *Guide* continued, "For your purposes, you will need to use the offsets DIR$B_NAMECOUNT to locate the size of the file name and DIR$T_NAME to locate the name. You will have to calculate the start of the file ID/version list. After you have located the list, the offsets DIR$W_VERSION will get you to the version number of the file and DIR$W_FID to locate the file ID."

"So, I can open the directory file, read each record and, for each version of a given file, I can use the header number to locate the block in the index file containing the file header. Does this sound correct?" Billy proposed.

"Yes," the *Guide* concurred.

"After I open the index file, how do I determine the VBN that the headers are offset from?" Billy asked.

The *Guide* replied, "You have to read it in the home block. That's at VBN 2 of the index file.

"The home block offsets are defined by the macro $HM2DEF. Two fields are required to calculate the bias for the header number index from the file ID. These fields contain the index bitmap starting virtual block number HM2$W_IBMAPVBN and the size in blocks of the index bitmap, HM2$W_IBMAPSIZE. *(The* Guide *is proud to note that this is the only place within it where you will find the letters I, B, and M strung together contiguously.)*

"To calculate this bias, you have to sum the size and starting VBN of the index bitmap; decrementing this value yields the bias. You add the header number to this bias to locate the VBN of the desired header block."

"After I read the header block, how do I locate the mapping pointers?" Billy asked.

The *Guide* answered, "The file header is broken into four general pieces, namely the header area, the identification area, the map area, and the access control list area. The header area, whose offsets are defined by the macro $FH2DEF, is fixed at the start of the header block.

"To locate the other three pieces of the file header, you use the word offsets for map area FH2$B_MPOFFSET, ident area FH2$B_IDOFFSET, and ACL area FH2$B_ACOFFSET.

"Before assuming that the header block is valid, you should probably check the field FH2$W_FID_SEQ against your sequence number to make certain that this is the correct header block.

"There is no count of mapping pointers stored in the file header, so you have to count them yourself. To conserve space, the mapping pointers can be either one, two, three, or four words in size. You can determine the size by extracting the high two bits of the first word of the mapping pointer. These bits will be equal to one less than the number of words in the mapping pointer.

"The format of mapping pointers is defined by the macro $FM2DEF. To determine the location and size of the mapping pointer bits, you can use the symbols FM2$V_FORMAT and FM2$S_FORMAT.

"You need to check for an extension header next. The field FH2$W_EXT_FID contains the file ID of the extension header. If there is not an extension header, the field contains 0. You need to continue counting until you run out of extension headers."

Billy's head was throbbing, and his stomach was churning. He wanted to leave, but there was still unfinished business. He asked, "How can I open the directory file, using the directory specification, without a bunch of logical name translations and sophisticated parsing?"

The *Guide* offered, "You could construct a file access block (FAB) and a name block (NAM) that would describe the directory specification and feed it to the RMS routine SYS$PARSE. SYS$PARSE will return the directory file ID in the field NAM$W_DID of the name block.

"The directory ID could be copied to the file ID field of the name block NAM$W_FID. You could, then, clear the directory ID field, call SYS$OPEN to open the file, and call SYS$CONNECT to connect the record stream. After the connect, you can read the records by using the routine SYS$GET.

"The details of these routines are described in the *Record Management Services Reference Manual.*"

"We're kind of cheating here, using the directory file directly to get the file IDs," Billy observed. "What does the file system have to do to get to the directory?"

"The file system has to start at the master file directory of the volume or volume set to locate the file ID, and in turn the file header, of the user file directory. The user file directory must be searched in similar fashion for any subdirectories identified in the file specification, until we get to the lowest level of directory. Opening a file at that point requires processing to access the file header that is similar to your code.

"The master file directory is named [000000]000000.DIR. It catalogs itself and has a known file ID of (4,4,0)."

"Why does the master file directory's file ID have a sequence number of 4?" Billy asked.

"It is a sanity check, used to guarantee a valid Files-11 volume, which is carried over from RSX days," answered the *Guide*.

Billy said, "I'm planning to read the index file using the SYS$QIO system service. Can't I open the index file using a call to SYS$QIO, also?"

"Yes," the *Guide* answered. "You assign a channel to the device containing the directory. Then, you issue a $QIO, using the ACP function IO$_ACCESS and the function modifier IO$M_ACCESS. This function value tells the XQP to open the file.

"You have to tell a little white lie and pass the address of the FIB. Just kidding. The FIB is a file information block, whose offsets are defined by the macro $FIBDEF."

Billy wanted to find the guy who coded *Just kidding* into the *Guide* and strangle him. His headache left no tolerance for stupid jokes.

The *Guide* continued, "You will have to place the file ID of the index file in the field FIB$W_FID of the FIB. The index file has a known file ID of (1,1,0).

"After this $QIO, you can issue $QIOs, using the same channel number as passed to the access function to perform your reads."

"Other than formatting the output, it looks like I'm done with the program. Let me try it out. Thanks again, Book," Billy stated.

He wrote the program (see Figure 18) and tested it (see Figure 19). It worked as advertised. Billy was as ecstatic as he could be in his current state. He could not celebrate too long because his stomach erupted. He raced to the men's room and went home to sleep it off over the weekend.

WILL BILLY recover from his beer bout? Will he quit drinking or follow Charlie Matco's bawdy path? Where are Dr. Albino, Dennis Cutlery, and the girl? What's next in Billy's venture further into VMS?

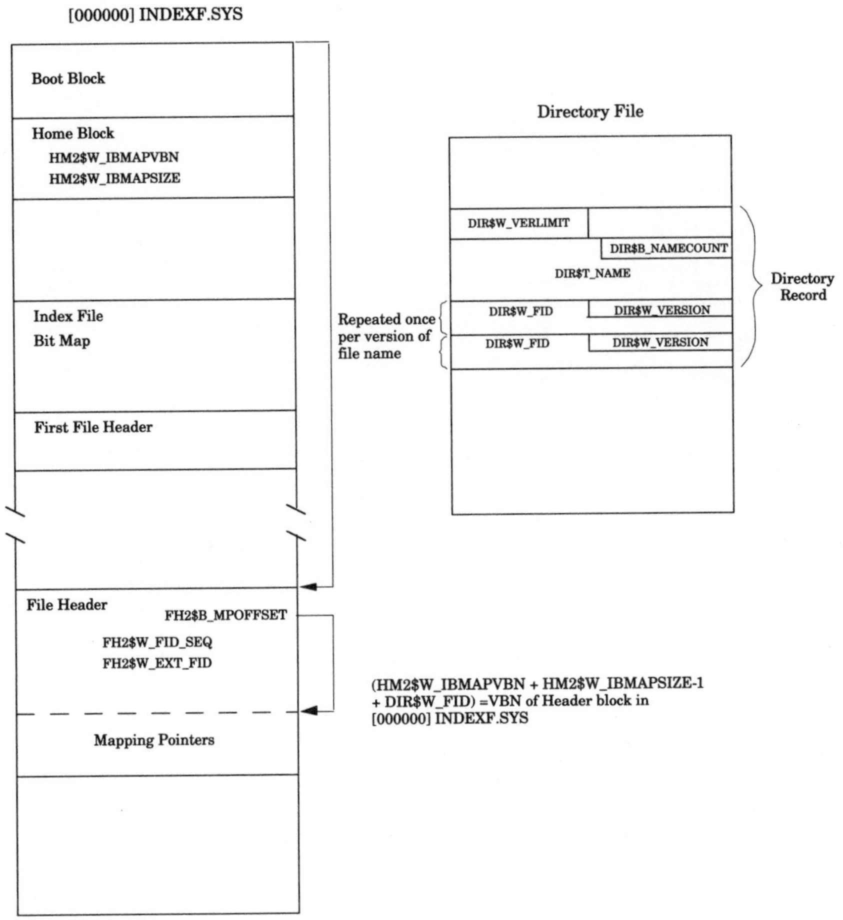

[000000] INDEXF.SYS

Boot Block

Home Block
HM2$W_IBMAPVBN
HM2$W_IBMAPSIZE

Index File
Bit Map

First File Header

File Header
FH2$B_MPOFFSET
FH2$W_FID_SEQ
FH2$W_EXT_FID

Mapping Pointers

Directory File

DIR$W_VERLIMIT
DIR$B_NAMECOUNT
DIR$T_NAME
DIR$W_FID
DIR$W_VERSION
DIR$W_FID
DIR$W_VERSION

Directory Record

Repeated once per version of file name

(HM2$W_IBMAPVBN + HM2$W_IBMAPSIZE-1 + DIR$W_FID) =VBN of Header block in [000000] INDEXF.SYS

INDEXF and directory usage for COUNT_FRAG.MAR

Figure 18.

```
;^^^^^^^^^^^^^^^^^^^^^^^^^^^^^^^^^^^^^^^^^^^^^^^^^^^^^^^^^^^^^
;       Program:          Count_frag
;       Author:           Billy Bitsenbites (Bruce Ellis)
;       Date written:     5/5/90
;       Function:         Prompts for a directory specification,
;                         opens the directory file, and uses the
;                         file id of the files cataloged in the
;                         directory to count the number of file
;                         headers and mapping pointers for each
;                         file.  Note:  no fancy wildcard processing
;                         was included in the interest of brevity.
;                         In typical Guide style, if you want it
;                         then add it.
;^^^^^^^^^^^^^^^^^^^^^^^^^^^^^^^^^^^^^^^^^^^^^^^^^^^^^^^^^^^^^
;Macro to check status
        .macro  check     arg=r0,?1
        blbs    arg,1
        $exit_s arg
1:
        .endm   check
;Include system macro library
        .library          /sys$library:lib.mlb/
        $dirdef           ;Directory record symbolic definitions
        $fabdef           ;File Access Block definitions
        $rabdef           ;Record Access Block definitions
        $namdef           ;Name Block definitions
;Fab for $PARSE to parse directory specification to fid/did
fab_parse:
        $fab    FNA=dir_spec,FOP=NAM,-
                NAM=dir_nam_blk
;Fab for directory file open
fabl:   $fab    FAC=<GET>,FOP=NAM,-
                MRS=512,ORG=<SEQ>,RFM=<VAR>,-
                SHR=<SHRGET>,NAM=dir_nam_blk
;Rab for directory file processing
RAB1:   $rab    FAB=FAB1,-
                RBF=BUF,RSZ=512,UBF=BUF,USZ=512,-
                ROP=<RLK,WAT>
;Name block for processing directory fid/did
dir_nam_blk:
        $nam    ESA=dir_spec_p,ESS=nam$c_maxrss
;Record buffer
buf:    .blkb   512
;record number counter
line_counter:   .long    0,0
;format statement for file name
file_fmt:       .ascid   /!AC;!UW/
;full format for output
fmt:    .ascid  /!50AS !9UL !9UL/
;file name descriptor
file_desc:
        .long   255
        .address          10$
10$:    .blkb   255
indexf_channel:           ;Storage for indexf channel number
        .blkl   1
header_bias:              ;Bias from first header for use with file id
        .blkl   1
pointer_cnt:              ;count of mapping pointers
        .blkl   1
header_cnt:               ;count of file headers
        .blkl   1
pmt:    .ascid  /Directory spec>/        ;prompt for directory spec
dir_spec_d:               ;storage for full directory spec
        .long   nam$c_maxrss
        .address          dir_spec
dir_spec:
        .blkb   nam$c_maxrss
dspd:
        .blkl   1
        .address          dir_spec_p
dir_spec_p:
        .blkb   nam$c_maxrss
```

Figure 18 contd.

```
device_name:
        .blkl   1           ;device name descriptor
devnam_adr:
        .blkl   1
;display buffer
out_buf:.long   512
        .address            10$
10$:    .blkl   512
;^^^^^^^^^^^^^^^^^^^^^^^^^^^^^^^^^^^^^^^^^^^^^^^^^^^^^^^^^^^^
;       Main code
;       Function:       Prompts for directory spec, opens directory
;                       file by file id, reads each record, obtains
;                       the count of headers, and displays counts.
;^^^^^^^^^^^^^^^^^^^^^^^^^^^^^^^^^^^^^^^^^^^^^^^^^^^^^^^^^^^^
        .entry  file,^m<>
        pushal  dir_spec_d                          ;Read with prompt
        pushal  pmt                                 ; directory specification
        pushal  dir_spec_d
        calls   #3,g^lib$get_input
        check
        movb    dir_spec_d,fab_parse+fab$b_fns      ;parse directory spec
        $parse  fab=fab_parse
        check
        bbs     #nam$v_exp_name,-                   ;Don't handle file name
                dir_nam_blk+nam$l_fnb,no_exp
        bbs     #nam$v_exp_ver,-                    ;Don't handle versions
                dir_nam_blk+nam$l_fnb,no_exp
        bbs     #nam$v_exp_type,-                   ;Don't handle types
                dir_nam_blk+nam$l_fnb,no_exp
        bbs     #nam$v_wildcard,-                   ;don't handle wildcard
                dir_nam_blk+nam$l_fnb,no_exp
        brb     dir_ok
no_exp: movl    #ss$_badirectory,r0                 ;beat it
        ret
dir_ok: movzbl  dir_nam_blk+nam$b_esl,dspd          ;get size of complete string
        subl2   #2,dspd                             ;skip trailer
        pushal  dspd                                ;spill the directory spec
        calls   #1,g^lib$put_output
        movl    dir_nam_blk+nam$w_did,-             ;Reset dir id to file id
                dir_nam_blk+nam$w_fid
        movw    dir_nam_blk+4+nam$w_did-            ;Reset rest of file id
                ,dir_nam_blk+nam$w_fid+4
        clrl    dir_nam_blk+nam$w_did               ;clear the directory id
        clrw    dir_nam_blk+nam$w_did+4
        movzbl  dir_nam_blk+nam$b_dev,device_name   ;Build device name
        movl    dir_nam_blk+nam$l_dev,devnam_adr    ; descriptor
        $open   fab=fabl                            ;open the direcory file
        check
        $connect        rab=rabl                    ;connect the record stream
        check
        pushal  device_name                         ;pass device name
        pushal  header_bias                         ;pass file header bias
        pushal  indexf_channel                      ;pass the channel address to store
        calls   #3,open_indexf                      ;open the index file
1:      $get    rab=rabl                            ;read the first record from the dir
        cmpl    #rms$_eof,r0                        ;at end?
        bneq    check_error                         ;if not check for other errors
        brw     done                                ; else scram
check_error:
        check                                       ;
        moval   buf,r7                              ;move record address to register
        movzwl  rab$w_rsz+rabl,r6                   ;get the record size
        ASSUME dir$w_verlimit EQ 2
        subl    #<dir$t_name-2>,r6                  ;drop count by size of fixed overhead
        movzbl  <dir$b_namecount-2>(r7),r8          ;get the size of the file name
        blbc    r8,skip_inc                         ;if even don't round
        incl    r8                                  ;round to even number of bytes
skip_inc:
        subl    r8,r6                               ;drop count by size of file name
        divl    #8,r6                               ;determine the number of versions
        addl3   r8,#<dir$t_name-2+buf>,r9           ;determine the start the fids
process_versions:
        pushal  header_cnt                          ;push location to store header count
```

Figure 18 contd.

```
        pushal  pointer_cnt                            ;push location to store pointer count
        pushal  dir$w_fid(r9)                          ;pass file id
        pushal  header_bias                            ;pass header bias
        pushal  indexf_channel                         ;pass channel of indexf.sys
        calls   #5,count_pointers                      ;count the pointers
        ediv    #22,line_counter,r10,line_counter      ;Printed 22 lines?
        tstl    line_counter                           ;if not skip line header
        bneq    skip_header                            ; else print line header
        jsb     dump_page_header
skip_header:
        movab   <buf+dir$b_namecount-2>,r4             ;get size of file name
;*********
;Format the file name/header count/pointer count
;*********
        $fao_s  ctrstr=file_fmt,outbuf=file_desc,outlen=file_desc,-
                p1=r4,p2=dir$w_version(r9)
        $fao_s  ctrstr=fmt,outbuf=out_buf,outlen=out_buf,-
                p1=#file_desc,p2=pointer_cnt,p3=header_cnt
        pushal  out_buf                                ;spill file info
        calls   #1,g^lib$put_output
        incl    line_counter
        movl    #255,file_desc
        movl    #512,out_buf                           ;reset buffer size
        addl    #8,r9                                  ;get next version of file
        sobgtr  r6,process_versions_br                 ;process next version of file
        brb     next_file
process_versions_br:
        brw     process_versions
next_file:
        brw     1                                      ;get next file
done:
        movl    #ss$_normal,r0                         ;sayonara
        ret

;^^^^^^^^^^^^^^^^^^^^^^^^^^^^^^^^^^^^^^^^^^^^^^^^^
;Dump page header
;^^^^^^^^^^^^^^^^^^^^^^^^^^^^^^^^^^^^^^^^^^^^^^^^^
LF=10
CR=13
page_hdr:       .ascid  $File                                  $-
                        $               Ptr cnt.   Hdr cnt.$<LF><CR>-
                        $____                                  $-
                        $               _______    ________$
dump_page_header:
        pushal  page_hdr
        calls   #1,g^lib$put_output
        rsb

 ;^^^^^^^^^^^^^^^^^^^^^^^^^^^^^^^^^^^^
;       Subroutine:     open_indexf
;       Function:       opens the indexf.sys file
;       Inputs:         4(ap)   channel address
;                       12(ap)  device name
;       Outputs:        8(ap)   header bias
;^^^^^^^^^^^^^^^^^^^^^^^^^^^^^^^^^^^^
        $fibdef                         ;File information block offsets
        $hm2def                         ;Home block offsets
chan_arg=4
bias_arg=8
dev_arg=12
i_fid:  .word   1,1,0                   ;file id of indexf.sys
fibd:   .long   fib$k_length            ;file info block descriptor
        .address        fib
fib:    .blkb   fib$k_length            ;file information block
iostat: .blkq   1                       ;io status block
block:  .blkb   512                     ;home block buffer
        .entry  open_indexf,^m<r6,r8,r9>
;Assign channel to device
        $assign_s       devnam=@dev_arg(ap),chan=@chan_arg(ap)
        check
        moval   fib,r6                  ;get fib descriptor
        movl    i_fid,fib$w_fid(r6)     ;set up fid in fib
;******************
```

Figure 18 contd.

```
;Open indexf.sys
;******************
        $qiow_s chan=@chan_arg(ap),func=#<io$_access!io$m_access>,-
                iosb=iostat,p1=fibd
        check                                   ;Check status
        check   iostat
;****************
;Read the home block
;****************
        $qiow_s chan=@chan_arg(ap),func=#io$_readvblk,iosb=iostat,-
                p1=block,p2=#512,p3=#2
        check                                   ;Check status
        check   iostat
        movzwl  hm2$w_ibmapvbn+block,r8         ;get index bitmap VBN
        movzwl  hm2$w_ibmapsize+block,r9        ; and size
        addl    r8,r9                           ;compute header bias
        decl    r9
        movl    r9,@bias_arg(ap)                ;return header bias
        movl    #ss$_normal,r0                  ;scram
        ret
;^^^^^^^^^^^^^^^^^^^^^^^^^^^^^^^^^^^^^^^^^^^^^^^^^^^^^^^^^^
;       Subroutine:     count_pointers
;       Function:       counts the number of mapping pointers
;                       and file headers in a file.
;       Inputs:         4(ap)   channel number address for index file
;                       8(ap)   header bias
;                       12(ap)  file id of file
;       Outputs:        16(ap)  count of mapping pointers
;                       20(ap)  count of file headers
;^^^^^^^^^^^^^^^^^^^^^^^^^^^^^^^^^^^^^^^^^^^^^^^^^^^^^^^^^^
        $fh2def         ;Base file header offsets
        $fiddef         ;file id offsets
        $fm2def         ;mapping pointer offsets
header_num:
        .blkb   4       ;local storage for header number
ios:    .blkq   1       ;io status block
header_block:           ;storage for header block
        .blkb   512
fid_arg=12
ptr_arg=16
hdr_arg=20
        .entry  count_pointers,^m<r2,r3,r4,r6,r7,r8,r9>
        movl    fid_arg(ap),r6                  ;Get file id address
        movw    fid$w_num(r6),header_num        ;Get file header number
        movzbw  fid$b_nmx(r6),header_num+2
        addl3   @bias_arg(ap),header_num,r7     ;add bias to header number
        movl    #1,@hdr_arg(ap)                 ;assume 1 header
        clrl    @ptr_arg(ap)                    ;clear count of pointers
;****************
;Read header block
;****************
        $qiow_s chan=@chan_arg(ap),func=#io$_readvblk,iosb=ios,-
                p1=header_block,p2=#512,p3=r7
        check                                   ;check call status
        check   ios                             ;check completion status
        cmpw    header_block+fh2$w_fid_seq,fid$w_seq(r6)      ;check seq #
        beql    got_header
        movl    #ss$_nosuchfile,r0              ;if seq # wrong abort
        brw     err_out_counter
got_header:
        moval   header_block,r9                 ;get header block buffer address
next_ext_header:
        movzbl  fh2$b_mpoffset(r9),r2           ;locate mapping pointers
        mull2   #2,r2                           ; using word offset
        addl    r9,r2                           ;
next_mapping_ptr:
        movw    (r2)+,r3                        ;get next pointer
        beql    no_more_pointers                ;if none scram
        extzv   #fm2$v_format,#fm2$s_format,r3,r4  ;determine format
        mull2   #2,r4                           ;skip based on word count of pointer
        addl    r4,r2                           ;
        incl    @ptr_arg(ap)                    ;bump the pointer count
        brw     next_mapping_ptr
```

Figure 18 contd.

```
no_more_pointers:
        movaw   fh2$w_ext_fid(r9),r6                  ;get extension header file id
        movw    fid$w_num(r6),header_num
        movzbw  fid$b_nmx(r6),header_num+2
        tstl    header_num                            ;extension header?
        beql    done_with_pointers                    ;if so calculate the VBN of
        addl3   @bias_arg(ap),header_num,r7           ; the header block
        beql    done_with_pointers                    ;if none scram
        incl    @hdr_arg(ap)                          ; else bump header count
;*****************
;Read extension header
;*****************
        $qiow_s chan=@chan_arg(ap),func=#io$_readvblk,iosb=ios,-
                p1=header_block,p2=#512,p3=r7
        check                                         ;check appropriate status
        check   ios
        moval   header_block,r9                       ;reset header address
        brw     next_ext_header                       ;get next header block
done_with_pointers:

        movl    #ss$_normal,r0
err_out_counter:
        ret                                           ;Sayonara
        .end    file
```

Figure 19. Output of COUNT_FRAG.MAR.

```
$
$mac count_frag
$link count_frag
$
$r count_frag
Directory spec>sys$login
DUB1:[USERS.ELLISB]
%SYSTEM-F-NOPRIV, no privilege for attempted operation
$set proc/priv=sysprv
$
$r count_frag
Directory spec>sys$login:
DUB1:[USERS.ELLISB]

File                                       Ptr cnt.   Hdr cnt.
____                                       ________   ________
B2.IDX;1                                       2          1
B24.IDX;1                                      4          1
B3.FDL;2                                       1          1
B3.IDX;1                                       1          1
B4.IDX;1                                       0          1
BADJUNK.DAT;1                                  0          1
BADJUNK.IDX;2                                  1          1
BIG2.IDX;4                                     1          1
BIG2.IDX;3                                     1          1
BIG2.LOG;1                                     1          1
BIG3.DAT;8                                     6          1
BIG3.DAT;7                                     3          1
BIG3.DAT;6                                     4          4
BIG_CODE.EXE;2                                 1          1
BIG_CODE.MAR;1                                 1          1
BIG_FILE.DAT;4                                 3          1
BIG_FILE.DAT;3                                22         10
BIG_FILE.FDL;3                                 1          1
BIG_FILE.FDL;2                                 1          1
BIG_FILE.IDX;1                                 3          1
BLAST_MTX.EXE;1                                1          1
BLAST_MTX.MAR;1                                1          1

File                                       Ptr cnt.   Hdr cnt.
____                                       ________   ________
BLOCKING_LOCK.EXE;31                           1          1
BLOCKING_LOCK.MAR;43                           1          1
BLOCKING_LOCK.OBJ;36                           1          1
```

Figure 19 contd.

```
CACHE.DAT;2                                     1         1
CACHES.DAT;2                                    1         1
CEB.EXE;1                                       1         1
CEB.MAR;2                                       1         1
COPY.COM;1                                      1         1
COUNT_FRAG.EXE;6                                1         1
COUNT_FRAG.EXE;5                                1         1
COUNT_FRAG.EXE;4                                1         1
COUNT_FRAG.EXE;3                                1         1
COUNT_FRAG.EXE;2                                1         1
COUNT_FRAG.EXE;1                                1         1
COUNT_FRAG.MAR;5                                1         1
COUNT_FRAG.MAR;4                                1         1
COUNT_FRAG.MAR;3                                2         1
COUNT_FRAG.MAR;2                                2         1
COUNT_FRAG.MAR;1                                2         1
COUNT_FRAG.OBJ;6                                1         1
COUNT_FRAG.OBJ;5                                2         1
COUNT_FRAG.OBJ;4                                2         1

File                                         Ptr cnt.  Hdr cnt.
____                                         ________  ________
COUNT_FRAG.OBJ;3                                2         1
COUNT_FRAG.OBJ;2                                2         1
COUNT_FRAG.OBJ;1                                1         1
CREATE_BIG.COM;2                                1         1
CREATE_BIG.LOG;2                                1         1
CREATE_SUB.COM;2                                1         1
CREATE_SUB.LOG;3                                1         1
FILE.DAT;1                                      1         1
FILE.EXE;4                                      1         1
FILE.FDL;2                                      1         1
FILE.IDX;2                                      1         1
FILE.MAR;7                                      1         1
FORCREATE.COM;2                                 1         1
X.EXE;5                                         1         1
X.MAR;10                                        1         1
XYZ.DAT;1                                       0         1
XYZ.IDX;1                                      31         1
$
$r count_frag
Directory spec>x.dat
%SYSTEM-W-BADIRECTORY, bad directory file format
$
$
$r count_frag
Directory spec>[*...]
%SYSTEM-W-BADIRECTORY, bad directory file format
$
```

Episode 8

Heavy Traffic

Monday morning, Billy gazed at the radio on the dashboard of his dust encrusted Datsun B-210. He then looked at the traffic on the Mass Pike. The radio didn't work, and the traffic was motionless.

He wished he could look ahead at the traffic problems which were occurring. If the radio had worked, he could have tuned into a traffic report. He might have taken Route 9 or some other way back from Marlborough.

He really disliked driving in the Boston area. It was a city where you learned to drive offensively, a city where the car with the most dents took the right-of-way, and the only city that Billy knew of where drivers made left turns on red lights.

He normally drove the minimum distance to the T and rarely ventured onto the Mass Pike. But, today he had to run to Marlborough to pick up a tape, containing some form of online transaction processing software, that Dr. Albino had to test for Dennis Cutlery. Billy hoped that the software processed transactions faster than the state police removed wrecks.

He left the Pike in favor of Route 128 north, figuring that if he could just make it to Route 2, he could sneak into Boston on the side streets. Unfortunately for Billy, the traffic on Route 128 was even worse than that on the Pike. Billy wondered whether the Boston Marathon became popular because it was a faster mode of transportation than driving in the Boston area.

Eventually, Billy exited Route 128 to Route 2. Luckily, Route 2 was much less busy than his other choices. He moved along at a pretty good clip, until he came up behind a pair of trucks that were traveling side by side, tying up both lanes of the highway. He slowed up, waiting for the truck on the left to pass the one on the right. He creeped along, waiting and waiting.

He was so frustrated that he eventually pulled off the highway and drove to the nearest T stop. He took the T into work.

When he arrived at the office building, he waited in the lobby for an elevator to take him to the 42nd floor. The elevators at work did not inform the waiting passengers of the current floor and movement of the elevator car. Anxiously, Billy pressed the arrow pointing up, located next to the elevator doors. He pressed it several times, hoping that, in some

way, the elevator would speed its pace at his demand.

Billy looked through the glass doors of the office building and noticed the girl from Northeastern. He thought about chasing after her to find out whether she liked the SHOW_SHARE program (see Figure 10) that he had given her. Instead, he decided that he had better get to work.

As he looked back at the elevator door, he saw it shut before him. He had missed the window of opportunity. He waited several more minutes for the elevator to come down again and took it to his work area.

He handed the tape to Dr. Albino and asked, "What's this software, anyway?"

Dr. Albino responded, "It is online transaction processing (OLTP) software for DECwindows systems. Do you want to test it out?"

"No thanks," Billy answered, "I don't do windows. Besides, the concept of real-time OLTP on a windowing system sounds like an oxymoron to me."

Dr. Albino cracked the first smile that Billy had seen on his face and asked, "So, what are you working on currently?"

"Some of the users have mentioned that the system is running slow. I've been trying to put as many fingers in the dyke as I can, but, as soon as I do, new leaks start to drip somewhere else," Billy replied.

"Well, attack one problem at a time, and eventually we'll get this system straightened out. By the way, I got you signed up for a VMS internals course that's being offered in a couple of months," the Doctor commented.

"Thanks. That'll be great," Billy responded.

Billy logged into the system and waited for the dollar sign prompt. He waited and waited, hitting the return key impatiently, similar to the way he'd been pressing the elevator button. He was annoyed at the amount of time that he had to wait. He knew that he needed to investigate the systemwide login command procedure that Dennis Cutlery had produced. As he waited, he wondered why Digital decided to use the dollar sign as the default prompt character. It looked like the same dollar sign that glowed from the Digital salesman's eyes as he entered Cutlery's office.

Billy finally received the prompt and, looking for a file, issued a $DIRECTORY command. He waited some more. Then he wrote down the file name, so that he wouldn't have to experience this wait again.

"Ah, computers and the paperless society — the great American myth," thought Billy, as he scribbled down the file specification.

Billy decided to investigate the system performance, using the $MONITOR utility. He used the MODES class first and noticed plenty of idle CPU cycles.

Next, he used $MONITOR DISK and noticed some fairly high I/O rates on several of the disks. He wondered about the wait time on the disks and used the qualifier /ITEM=ALL on the same monitor class. Many of the disks were incurring high queue depths, meaning that users were noticeably waiting for their I/Os to complete.

Perhaps, some of the disk I/Os could be split transfers, caused by disk fragmentation. There was no way to tell, as the split transfer rate was only reported as a systemwide rate, using $MONITOR IO. This inability to isolate split transfer rates on a per-disk basis annoyed Billy.

Perhaps the transfers were large in size. He remembered that larger transfers will increase the time to complete an I/O. He granted that the seek and rotational characteristics were the most costly components in a typical disk transfer. However, large transfers can still tie up access to the disk drive and controller for an extended period of time.

He wished that he could determine the size of transfers being performed to the disk, allowing him to determine the type of traffic to the drive. Like the way that the trucks slowed him down on the open highway, large transfers could slow down I/O requests to a disk. However, no VMS utility told him the size of transfers to a disk drive. This was particularly annoying to Billy, as he noted that $MONITOR MSCP would at least tell him a range of transfer sizes to mass storage control protocol (MSCP) served disks.

The performance tools available within VMS were like Billy's car radio. Because it was broken, Billy couldn't get a traffic report. Likewise, the information that he required to make intelligent decisions on altering disk traffic didn't seem to be available.

He was sure that there must be some way to obtain the information he wanted. He opened the gray tome, marked *The Hitchhiker's Guide to VMS*, listening to the almost annoying whirring and clicking.

"May I help you?" the *Guide* asked.

"Yes," Billy replied. "VMS seems to lack sophisticated disk performance analysis tools. With Dennis Cutlery managing Dr. Albino's budget, I know that we won't be purchasing any layered performance analysis tools. So, I was wondering whether you might be able to help me write some kind of tool that will allow me to track certain characteristics of disk I/O requests."

"Sure, no problem," the *Guide* responded. "What kind of information would you like to obtain on the disk I/O requests?"

Billy entered, "I'm interested in tracking the size of each transfer to the disk. I would also like to track the number of split transfers on a per-disk basis. Is there some code that I could write to provide this information?"

"Sure," the *Guide* replied. "One technique that you could use is provided by an unsupported-undocumented-can-go-away-at-any-time module called IOPERFORM. The code for this module appears in the VMS source listings."

"What kind of work would be required, on my behalf, to use this interface?" Billy asked.

"If you check the code, you will find that you will have to construct data structures that will track certain pieces of information from four different points in the flow of the driver. You will also have to create a process to grab the structures and save the information," the *Guide* responded.

"That is great, but I do not see a reason to have a process log this information. Why write a performance tool to track disk activity that causes more disk I/O activity? Is there no way to grab this information and log it in real-time, in memory which is accessible systemwide?" Billy countered.

"Well, you could intercept the I/O request at some point in the driver code," the *Guide* started.

"Yeah," Billy interrupted. "I remember from our last conversation that the driver processes the P1 through P6 arguments from SYS$QIO in the function decision table (FDT) routines. The P2 argument contains the size of the transfer. You also mentioned that the FDT routines could be located through a driver table called the function decision table. So, I could modify the table to point to my code and pick off the P2 argument on each request. Sound good?"

The *Guide* empathized with Billy, but overruled his plan with, "That is a nice try. However, there are two things wrong with using the technique that you proposed. First, when you are in the FDT routine, you cannot guarantee that the I/O will not exit with error status prior to actually performing the I/O operation.

"Second, your technique leaves no easy way to track the number of split transfers that are occurring on the given disk drive. Nice try, though."

Dejected, Billy entered, "So does this mean that there is no way possible to determine this information?"

"No. Before you so rudely interrupted me, you might have noted that I did say that you could, in fact, intercept the I/O at a given point within the driver code. Do you remember where the driver is sent after the FDT routines are finished processing the I/O request?" the *Guide* interrogated.

"Yes, I think so," Billy answered. "Didn't it enter the driver start I/O routine next?"

"Very good," complimented the *Guide*. "The start I/O routine is located through a table called the driver dispatch table (DDT). Now, if you were to allocate some non-paged pool, copy your code into the pool, save the address stored in the field DDT$L_START, and replace it with the address of your code, you could intercept each I/O operation that is sent to the disk drive. This interception would guarantee that the I/O operation was initiated to the disk, although it may not have completed properly."

"I can live with that. It sounds good," Billy acknowledged. "Now, how do I locate the DDT?"

"The DDT, for a given device driver, can be located through the unit control block (UCB) for the given device unit. The field UCB$L_DDT contains a pointer to the DDT for the driver processing this device unit," answered the *Guide*.

Billy was getting frustrated. He felt like he was always getting only a small piece of the picture. But, he continued, "That is just great, but how do I locate the UCB of the device unit, and for that matter, what is it used for besides locating the DDT?"

The *Guide* responded calmly, "The UCB is the heart of the device driver. The driver uses the UCB to locate the majority of its other data structures. It describes which fork and device spinlocks will be used for synchronization. It contains the unit number of the device and maintains the context of any information that should be saved from one thread of code to the next.

"The UCB is located by the SYS$ASSIGN system service and pointed to by a data structure, referred to as a channel control block (CCB), which is 16 bytes in size and stored in your process' P1 space. The assign channel system service constructs the CCB. The channel number, returned to the caller of the assign channel system service, is a negative displacement into the CCB table, used to locate the CCB for the device to which you assigned the channel.

"The channel number is also used by the SYS$QIO system service to locate the UCB. In addition to containing the pointer to the start I/O routine, the DDT also contains a pointer to the FDT, which QIO uses to perform legal and buffered function processing as well as dispatching off to the FDT routines.

"To locate the UCB, the assign channel system service chains through data structures that correspond to the different pieces of the device specification. Consider a device name of the form DDCU:. The DD portion of the device specification defines the device type, or effectively which driver will be processing your request.

"The C portion of the device specification defines the controller to which you are referring. The assign channel system service uses this portion of the device specification to chain through controller data structures, referred to as device data blocks (DDBs). These structures, along with all other driver-related structures, form the I/O database.

"The DDBs are maintained in a singly linked list. The first DDB in the list is located by the pointer stored in the system memory location IOC$GL_DEVLIST. The link pointers to the next DDB are stored in the field DDB$L_LINK. You know that you have reached the end of the list when the link field contains a 0 forward link pointer.

"To determine whether you have located the proper DDB, you compare the device name through the controller designation (i.e., the DDC portion of the device name) to the ASCII counted string stored in the field DDB$T_NAME. If they match, you have located the proper DDB, describing the controller corresponding to your device name.

"Next, you must use the U portion of the device name to chain through the UCBs for the given device name. The UCBs are also maintained in a singly linked list. The first UCB, for the given controller, is located through the field DDB$L_UCB. Subsequent UCBs, in the chain, are located through the link pointer stored in the field UCB$L_LINK. Once again, you have reached the end of the list when the link pointer contains 0."

Billy wished that the rush-hour traffic had moved as quickly as this explanation. The *Guide* continued relentlessly.

"To determine whether you have reached the correct unit, you should compare the U portion of the DDCU: device name against the binary representation of the unit number stored in the field UCB$W_UNIT of the unit control block."

To give himself time to absorb this explanation, Billy slowly typed the following question, "That handles the case of a locally connected device. What happens when a disk is being served through a hierarchical storage controller (HSC) or, for that matter, through the mass storage control protocol (MSCP) on another VAX?"

"In the case of an expensive device whose name contains one dollar sign, we must determine which node in a VAXcluster is serving the device to our node. The naming convention, in this case, is of the form NODE$DDCU:. The NODE portion of the device specification corresponds to the system communication services (SCS) node name of the node serving the device," the *Guide* explained.

"Internally, nodes in a VAXcluster, which are known to us, are described by data structures referred to as system blocks (SBs). The SBs are maintained in a doubly linked list with a listhead at the memory location SCS$GQ_CONFIG.

"When chaining through the SBs, we must compare the node name portion of the device specification against the field SB$T_NODENAME. If the fields match, we have identified the proper node.

"After we have located the proper SB, we can go to the field SB$L_DDB and chain through the DDBs for all controllers served by the given node. The search path, at this point, for the given UCB is identical to the search path taken on the locally connected device," the *Guide* explained.

"What if the device name contains two dollar signs?" Billy asked.

"If it is a really expensive device (just kidding) that is accessible through multiple paths, we must check the allocation class. The naming convention, in this case, is of the form $ALLO$DDCU:, where ALLO corresponds to the allocation class of the device. The allocation class is a number in the range from 1 to 255. It is assigned, as an arbitrary value, to be the same for all nodes through which the device is accessible. For instance, two HSCs with disks dual-ported between them should be assigned the same allocation class.

"To perform the look-up on a device, with an allocation class assigned to the nodes to which it is connected, requires that we chain through all DDBs off of all SBs. We continue the search until one of the DDBs, whose controller designation matches also, contains a matching allocation class in the field DDB$B_ALLOCLS."

"This seems like a lot of work," Billy complained.

"Actually, you make life a lot easier on yourself by using a jump to subroutine (JSB) instruction to transfer control to a routine called

IOC$SEARCHDEV, which will perform the look-up for you," the *Guide* offered.

A perturbed Billy slammed into the keyboard, "Why didn't you simply tell me this in the first place?"

"Chill out, dude," the *Guide* countered. "If I had told you about the routine in the first place, the only thing that you would have learned is the calling mechanism for the routine."

Billy admitted that the book did make a valid point on this issue and said, "Okay, sorry. Now, what do I have to do to get this routine to work properly for me?"

The *Guide* replied, "You should request a mutex on the I/O database, in a similar fashion to the technique that you used in the SHOW_SHARE program (see Figure 10). The mutex for the I/O database is stored at the location IOC$GL_MUTEX.

"The required input for IOC$SEARCHDEV is that R1 should contain the address of an ASCII string descriptor that describes the name of the device that you are trying to look up.You must also own a mutex on the I/O database. Other inputs may include flags in R2 and the address to receive the lock value block in R3. For more information on this routine, take a look at IOC$SEARCHDEV in the module IOSUBPAGED in the source listings.

"The output from IOC$SEARCHDEV has R1 containing the address of the UCB for the device you are looking up. R0 contains success status. Other outputs include R2 that points to the device data block (DDB) and R3 that points to the system block (SB)."

"How do I synchronize access to the UCB and DDT?" Billy asked.

The *Guide* replied, "You can use the FORKLOCK macro to acquire a spinlock on data structures accessed at the fork IPL, which corresponds to the fork level of your device. The field UCB$B_FLCK contains a spinlock index.

"Spinlocks are required here because the start I/O routine runs as a fork process. A fork process, unlike a typical scheduling process, is scheduled by an interrupt service routine, typically associated with the device driver. To schedule the fork process, the interrupt service routine saves minimal context (i.e., R3, R4, and the PC) in a fork block, typically a subset of the UCB. It then places the UCB on a fork queue associated with a given fork IPL (i.e., 6, 8, 9, 10, or 11) and requests an interrupt at that IPL. The queues for fork processing are located in the per-CPU database (CPUL_SWIQFL/CPUL_SWIQBL).

"When the fork interrupt occurs, a piece of code called the fork dispatcher yanks a fork block out of the queue, re-establishes R3 and R4, sets R5 to point to the fork block, and issues a JSB to the saved PC. This procedure continues until the fork queue is empty.

"The start I/O routine is also entered directly from the SYS$QIO/FDT code, if the driver is not busy, as determined by checking the bit UCB$V_BSY in the field UCB$W_STS.

The fork lock blocks all fork process-related activity at that fork IPL and allows you to modify structures that may be accessed at fork level, like the DDT."

"Okay," Billy entered, "after I have looked up the device UCB and copied my code into non-paged pool, I can save the actual start I/O entry point, replacing it with my code. I should probably save off the unit number, to compare the unit being processed, as one driver handles many units and controllers.

"How do I determine the size of the requested transfer?"

The *Guide* answered, "The size of the transfer is stored in the field IRP$L_BCNT of the I/O request packet (IRP) describing the current request. The IRP can be located through register R3.

"You should be careful to check read and write functions before assuming that you have a valid byte count. The function code is stored in the field IRP$W_FUNC. It is contained in a set of contiguous bits starting at the bit position corresponding to the symbol IRP$V_FCODE and has a size, in bits, corresponding to the symbol IRP$S_FCODE."

"Actually," Billy stated, "knowing whether the request is a read or write might be useful information. The documentation on volume shadowing states that if there is a ratio of three read operations, or better, to each write to a shadow set, you may receive a performance boost using shadowing."

The *Guide* explained, "Because members of the shadow set are logically identical, reads allow us to keep the two sets of read-write heads active on the disk drives simultaneously, as the reads can be satisfied by either member of the shadow set. We also may seek on the member of the shadow set which is closest to being on cylinder."

"Up to this point," Billy admitted, "I wasn't able to obtain the information needed to determine whether shadowing would buy anything from a performance standpoint.

"How do I determine whether the request is a split transfer?" Billy asked.

"After a transfer has completed, the accumulated byte count IRP$L_ABCNT is increased by the size of the transfer and compared against the original byte count IRP$L_OBCNT. If these fields are not the same, the start I/O routine is re-entered to transfer the next split and so on, until the transfer is complete. So, you can simply check for a non-zero value in the IRP$L_ABCNT field to determine whether you are processing a split transfer.

"You should also check the bit IRP$V_VIRTUAL in the field IRP$W_STS. If this bit is not set, the request was not a virtual block request and could not be a split transfer."

"So," Billy proposed, "I can log the size in blocks of each transfer, by dividing the size in bytes of each transfer by 512, log this information in memory, and write another program to pick up and display the counts. Therefore, I will not have to perform any disk transfers to track the information. I need help on a couple of details, however.

"How can I keep track of the location of the code and data in pool? Also, it might be interesting to keep track of the number of paging and swapping I/Os to the disk. Is this information available?"

The *Guide* replied, "To keep track of your code and data in non-paged pool, you can use the location EXE$GL_SITESPEC. It is a site-specific longword and is not used by VMS. You can have it point to your pool. Unfortunately, there is only one site-specific longword, so if you need to track a number of locations in system space, you must design the logic to link them all together.

"The paging and swapping I/O requests are differentiated from all others by the bits IRP$V_PAGIO and IRP$V_SWAPIO, respectively, being set in the status word of the IRP, i.e., IRP$W_STS."

"So, all I have to do is dispatch off to the real start I/O routine, and the first program is done," Billy observed. (See Figure 20.) "Then I need a display program (see Figure 21) and an unload program (see Figure 22), and I am done. Let me try it out," Billy stated. (See Figure 23.)

Billy came back a little later and told the *Guide*, "They work. Thanks a lot, Book. Now, I can track file activity and figure out what to move around."

"No problem," the *Guide* responded.

WILL BILLY EVER WRITE the program to track open files, or is he just blowing smoke? Does the girl like the SHOW_SHARE program? Does she like Billy? Can OLTP really be done on windowing systems?

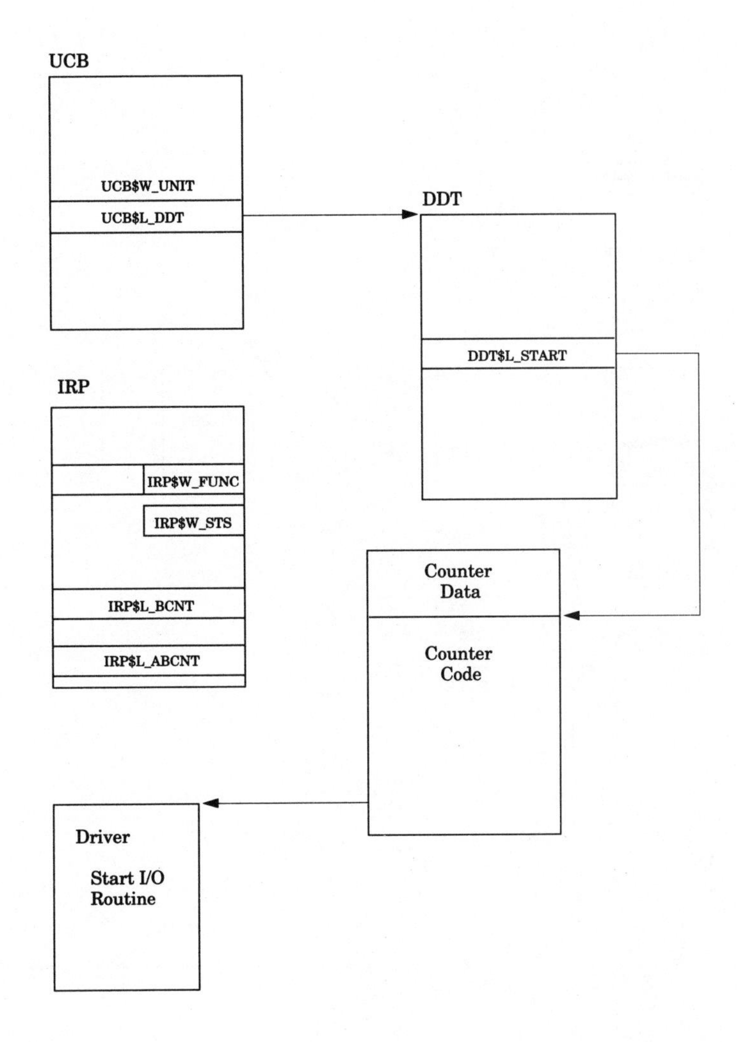

Structures used in LOAD_BLOCK_COUNTER.MAR

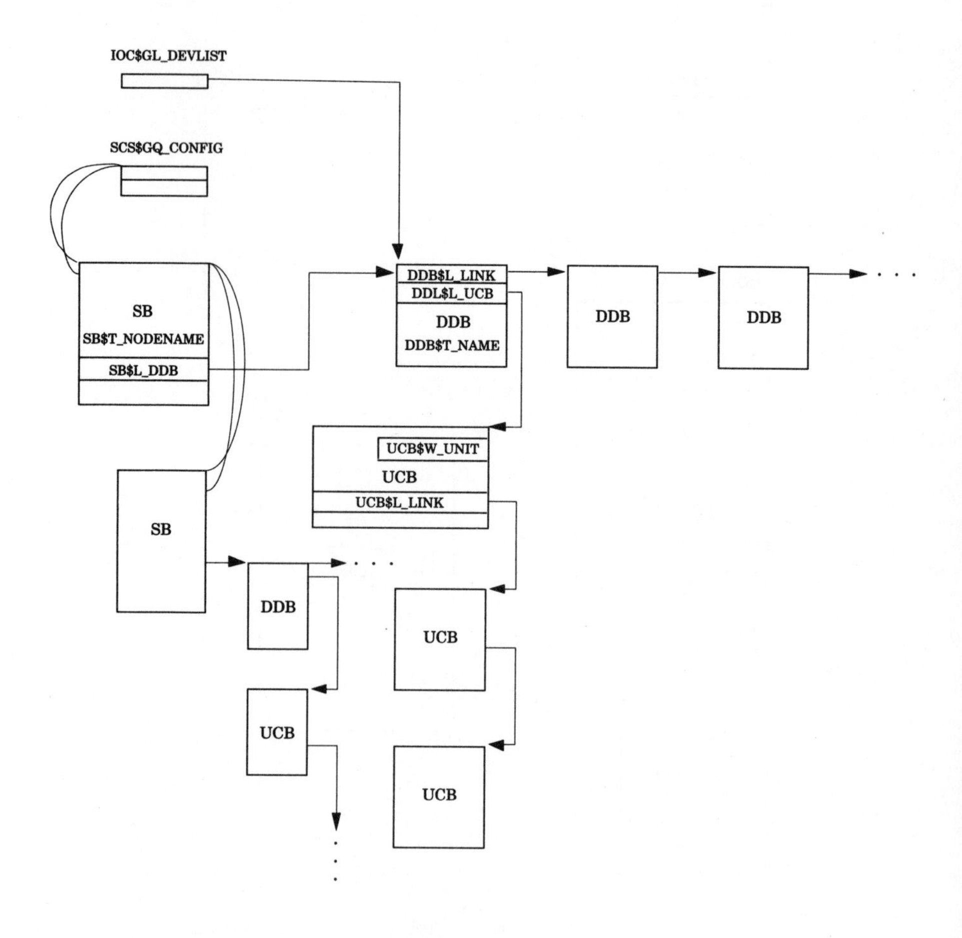

I/O database structures associated with device name

Figure 20.

```
;^^^^^^^^^^^^^^^^^^^^^^^^^^^^^^^^^^^^^^^^^^^^^^^^^^^^^^^^^^^
;       Program:            load_block_counter.mar
;       Author:             Billy Bitsenbites (Bruce Ellis)
;       Date written:       Sometime in January 1986
;       Synopsis:           This guy prompts for a disk device name
;                           and looks up its UCB address.  He
;                           then allocates a chunk of non-paged pool
;                           and copies the monitoring code into the
;                           allocated pool.  To get the code activated
;                           he saves the start i/o address from the
;                           DDT and moves the address of the code
;                           in pool to the start i/o address in the
;                           DDT.  When the start i/o entry point
;                           is entered, the code has the address of the
;                           IRP passed to it in R3.  He checks for
;                           paging, swapping, and split i/os.  He also
;                           counts the number of read, writes and the
;                           size of each.
;
;       Modifications:
;               BAE 9/24/87: Add code to count the split i/os.
;               BAE 5/90:    Update synchronization for V5.
;
;^^^^^^^^^^^^^^^^^^^^^^^^^^^^^^^^^^^^^^^^^^^^^^^^^^^^^^^^^^^



        .library        /sys$library:lib.mlb/
        .link           /sys$system:sys.stb/
        $ddtdef
        $ucbdef
        $irpdef
        $ipldef
header=12                                        ;12 byte header for the pool
devnam: .long   15                               ;storage for the disk device name
        .address        10$
10$:    .blkb   15
dev_prompt:                                      ;Prompt for device name
        .ascid  /enter disk to be monitored:/
l_adr:  .address        l_s
        .address        l_e
        .entry  load_block_ctr,^m<>
;^^^^^^^^^^^^^^^^^^^^^^^^^^^^^^^^^^^^^^^^^^^^^^^^^^^^^^^^^^^
;       Get device name to monitor
;^^^^^^^^^^^^^^^^^^^^^^^^^^^^^^^^^^^^^^^^^^^^^^^^^^^^^^^^^^^
        pushal  devnam                           ;pass the length address
        pushal  dev_prompt                       ;pass the prompt
        pushal  devnam                           ;address of desc. to store device name
        calls   #3,g^lib$get_input               ;Get the device name
        blbs    r0,lab1
        $exit_s r0
lab1:   $lkwset_s       inadr=l_adr              ;lock code running at high ipl
        blbs    r0,lab2
        $exit_s r0
;^^^^^^^^^^^^^^^^^^^^^^^^^^^^^^^^^^^^^^^^^^^^^^^^^^^^^^^^^^^
;       Load the code to monitor disk activity
;^^^^^^^^^^^^^^^^^^^^^^^^^^^^^^^^^^^^^^^^^^^^^^^^^^^^^^^^^^^
lab2:   $cmkrnl_s       routin=kernel_setup
        ret
;*********************************************************************
;       Kernel mode setup code
;*********************************************************************
        .entry  kernel_setup,^m<r2,r3,r4,r5>
;^^^^^^^^^^^^^^^^^^^^^^^^^^^^^^^^^^^^^^^^^^^^^^^^^^^^^^^^^^^
;       Grab a write mutex on the i/o database
;^^^^^^^^^^^^^^^^^^^^^^^^^^^^^^^^^^^^^^^^^^^^^^^^^^^^^^^^^^^
        moval   g^ioc$gl_mutex,r0       ;Grab a write mutex on the
        jsb     g^sch$lockw             ; i/o database (Note this code
                                        ; assumes that the change mode
                                        ; dispatcher has set up R44 to point
                                        ; to the PCB)
```

Figure 20 contd.

```
;^^^^^^^^^^^^^^^^^^^^^^^^^^^^^^^^^^^^^^^^^^^^^^^^^^^^^^^^^^^^
;       Search  for ucb address of this device
;^^^^^^^^^^^^^^^^^^^^^^^^^^^^^^^^^^^^^^^^^^^^^^^^^^^^^^^^^^^^
        moval   devnam,r1                   ;Pass the address of the device name
                                            ; descriptor.
        jsb     g^ioc$searchdev             ;Search the i/o database for the UCB
        blbs    r0,no_dev_error             ;If error scram
                                            ; of the device (r1<-UCB address)
        pushl   r0                          ;save status
        brw     dev_error
no_dev_error:
        pushl   r1                          ;Save the ucb address
        movl    #code_len+header,r1         ;else grab a chunk of pool to
        jsb     g^exe$alononpaged           ; load the code into
        blbs    r0,no_pool_error            ;on error scram
        pushl   r0                          ;save error status
        brb     pool_error
no_pool_error:
        movzwl  r1,8(r2)                    ;init the size field for deallocation
        movl    r2,g^exe$gl_sitespec        ;save the pointer to pool
;^^^^^^^^^^^^^^^^^^^^^^^^^^^^^^^^^^^^^^^^^^^^^^^^^^^^^^^^^^^^
;       Copy the code into pool
;^^^^^^^^^^^^^^^^^^^^^^^^^^^^^^^^^^^^^^^^^^^^^^^^^^^^^^^^^^^^
        pushr   #^m<r0,r1,r2,r3,,r4,r5>
        movc3   #code_len,pool_code_start,12(r2)
        popr    #^m<r0,r1,r2,r3,,r4,r5>
        popl    r1                          ;restore the ucb address
l_s:    forklock        ucb$b_flck(r1)      ;Synch with driver at Fork ipl
        movl    ucb$l_ddt(r1),r5            ;get the driver dispatch table address
        movl    ddt$l_start(r5),header(r2)          ;save actual start i/o
;^^^^^^^^^^^^^^^^^^^^^^^^^^^^^^^^^^^^^^^^^^^^^^^^^^^^^^^^^^^^
;       reset the start i/o to point to our code
;^^^^^^^^^^^^^^^^^^^^^^^^^^^^^^^^^^^^^^^^^^^^^^^^^^^^^^^^^^^^
        moval   get_block_info-pool_code_start+header(r2),ddt$l_start(r5)
;^^^^^^^^^^^^^^^^^^^^^^^^^^^^^^^^^^^^^^^^^^^^^^^^^^^^^^^^^^^^
;       Save the unit number of the disk
;^^^^^^^^^^^^^^^^^^^^^^^^^^^^^^^^^^^^^^^^^^^^^^^^^^^^^^^^^^^^
        movzwl  ucb$w_unit(r1),unit-pool_code_start+header(r2)
        forkunlock      lock=ucb$b_flck(r1),newipl=#ipl$_astdel
l_e:    pushl   #ss$_normal                 ;set success status
dev_error:
pool_error:
        moval   g^ioc$gl_mutex,r0           ;Free up the mutex on the io database
        movl    g^ctl$gl_pcb,r4             ;
        jsb     g^sch$unlock                ;get status
        popl    r0
        ret

;^^^^^^^^^^^^^^^^^^^^^^^^^^^^^^^^^^^^^^^^^^^^^^^^^^^^^^^^^^^^
;^^^^^^^^^^^^^^^^^^^^^^^^^^^^^^^^^^^^^^^^^^^^^^^^^^^^^^^^^^^^
;       Pool code to check each i/o request processed by
;       the start i/o routine
;^^^^^^^^^^^^^^^^^^^^^^^^^^^^^^^^^^^^^^^^^^^^^^^^^^^^^^^^^^^^
;^^^^^^^^^^^^^^^^^^^^^^^^^^^^^^^^^^^^^^^^^^^^^^^^^^^^^^^^^^^^

pool_code_start:
saved_start:    .blkl   1
read_count:     .long   0
read_lengths:   .long   0[129]
write_count:    .long   0
write_lengths:  .long   0[129]
paging_ios:     .long   0
swap_ios:       .long   0
unit:           .long   0
splits:         .long   0
get_block_info:
        pushr   #^m<r2>
        cmpw    unit,ucb$w_unit(r5)         ;this the unit to be monitored?
        beql    ours                        ;
        brw     exit                        ;if not scram
ours:   bbc     #irp$v_pagio,irp$w_sts(r3),no_page          ;Paging i/o?
        incl    paging_ios                                  ;if so increment count
no_page:
```

Figure 20 contd.

```
        bbc     #irp$v_swapio,irp$w_sts(r3),no_swap          ;Swapping i/o?
        incl    swap_ios                                     ;if so increment count
no_swap:
        extzv   #io$v_fcode,#io$s_fcode,irp$w_func(r3),r2    ;get function
;^^^^^^^^^^^^^^^^^^^^^^^^^^^^^^^^^^^^^^^^^^^^^^^^^^^^^^^^^^^^
;       Check for reads
;^^^^^^^^^^^^^^^^^^^^^^^^^^^^^^^^^^^^^^^^^^^^^^^^^^^^^^^^^^^^
        cmpb    #io$_readvblk,r2          ;Read virtual?
        beql    handle_reads
        cmpb    #io$_readlblk,r2          ;Read logical?
        beql    handle_reads
        cmpb    #io$_readpblk,r2          ;Read physical?
        beql    handle_reads
;^^^^^^^^^^^^^^^^^^^^^^^^^^^^^^^^^^^^^^^^^^^^^^^^^^^^^^^^^^^^
;       Check for writes
;^^^^^^^^^^^^^^^^^^^^^^^^^^^^^^^^^^^^^^^^^^^^^^^^^^^^^^^^^^^^
        cmpb    #io$_writevblk,r2          ;Write virtual?
        beql    handle_writes
        cmpb    #io$_writelblk,r2          ;Write logical?
        beql    handle_writes
        cmpb    #io$_writepblk,r2          ;Write physical?
        beql    handle_writes
        brw     exit

handle_reads:
        incl    read_count                ;increment read count
        movl    irp$l_bcnt(r3),r2         ;determine the size
        divl2   #512,r2                   ;Compute the size in blocks
        cmpl    r2,#127                   ;if > 127 blocks note in 127
        blequ   ok1
        movl    #128,r2
ok1:    incl    read_lengths[r2]          ;increment size counter
        brw     check_splits
handle_writes:
        incl    write_count               ;increment write count
        movl    irp$l_bcnt(r3),r2         ;determine the size
        divl2   #512,r2                   ;Compute size in blocks
        cmpl    r2,#127                   ;if > 127 then set to 127
        blequ   ok2
        movl    #128,r2
ok2:    incl    write_lengths[r2]         ;increment write size counter
check_splits:
;^^^^^^^^^^^^^^^^^^^^^^^^^^^^^^^^^^^^^^^^^^^^^^^^^^^^^^^^^^^^
;       If not a virtual i/o then it cannot be a split i/o.
;^^^^^^^^^^^^^^^^^^^^^^^^^^^^^^^^^^^^^^^^^^^^^^^^^^^^^^^^^^^^
        bbc     #irp$v_virtual,irp$w_sts(r3),exit
        tstl    irp$l_abcnt(r3)                   ;If accumulated byte count
                                                  ; is 0 this is either not a split
                                                  ; i/o or it is the first pass
                                                  ; prior to the split so skip it.
        beql    exit
        incl    splits                            ; else increment split count
exit:   popr    #^m<r2>
        jmp     @saved_start                      ;Goto driver start i/o routine
pool_code_end:
code_len = pool_code_end-pool_code_start          ;amount of pool to allocate

        .end    load_block_ctr
```

Figure 21.

```
;^^^^^^^^^^^^^^^^^^^^^^^^^^^^^^^^^^^^^^^^^^^^^^^^^^^^
;       Program:        dump_block_counts
;       Author:         Billy Bitsenbites (Bruce Ellis)
;       Date written:   Sometime in January
;
;       Synopsis:       This guy dumps the block counts
;                       monitored by the load_block_counter
;                       program.
;^^^^^^^^^^^^^^^^^^^^^^^^^^^^^^^^^^^^^^^^^^^^^^^^^^^^
        .macro  check    ?1
        blbs    r0,1
```

Figure 21 contd.

```
        blbs    r0,1
        $exit_s r0
1:
        .endm   check
        .library        /sys$library:lib.mlb/
        .link   /sys$system:sys.stb/
long=4
base=12
c_off=base
saved_start=c_off
c_off=c_off+long
read_count=c_off
c_off=c_off+long
read_lengths=c_off
c_off=c_off+<long*129>
write_count=c_off
c_off=c_off+long
write_lengths=c_off
c_off=c_off+<long*129>
paging_ios=c_off
c_off=c_off+long
swap_ios=c_off
c_off=c_off+long
splits=c_off+<long>
c_off=c_off+<2*long>

data:   .blkb   c_off                    ;Data returned from block counter

general_fmt:
        .ascid  -
        /Read:!10UL Writes:!10UL Paging ios:!10UL Swapping ios:!5UL/
split_fmt:
        .ascid  /Split ios on this disk: !10UL/
line_fmt:
        .ascid  /!AD:!10UL!10UL!10UL!10UL!10UL/
pre_list:
        .ascii  /   0 -   4/
pre_len=.-pre_list
        .ascii  /   5 -   9/
        .ascii  /  10 -  14/
        .ascii  /  15 -  19/
        .ascii  /  20 -  24/
        .ascii  /  25 -  29/
        .ascii  /  30 -  34/
        .ascii  /  35 -  39/
        .ascii  /  40 -  44/
        .ascii  /  45 -  49/
        .ascii  /  50 -  54/
        .ascii  /  55 -  59/
        .ascii  /  60 -  64/
        .ascii  /  65 -  69/
        .ascii  /  70 -  75/
        .ascii  /  75 -  79/
        .ascii  /  80 -  85/
        .ascii  /  85 -  89/
        .ascii  /  90 -  94/
        .ascii  /  95 -  99/
        .ascii  / 100 - 104/
        .ascii  / 105 - 109/
        .ascii  / 110 - 114/
        .ascii  / 115 - 119/
        .ascii  / 120 - 124/
        .ascii  / 125 - 128+/
buffer: .long   80
        .address        10$
10$:    .blkb   80
nlines=25
read_header:
        .ascid  /Breakdown of Reads by block size:/
write_header:
        .ascid  /Breakdown of writes by block size:/
;^^^^^^^^^^^^^^^^^^^^^^^^^^^^^^^^^^^^^^^^^^^^^^^^^^^^^^^^^^^^^^^^^^^^^^^^^^^
;       Program to format and dump block counts
```

Figure 21 contd.

```
;^^^^^^^^^^^^^^^^^^^^^^^^^^^^^^^^^^^^^^^^^^^^^^^^^^^^^^^^^^^^^^^^^^^^^^^^
        .entry  dump_block_counts,^m<>
        $cmkrnl_s        routin=return_counts
        check
;^^^^^^^^^^^^^^^^^^^^^^^^^^^^^^^^^^^^^^^^^^^^^^^^^^^^^^^^^^^^^^^^^^^^^^^^
;       Format and spill general information
;^^^^^^^^^^^^^^^^^^^^^^^^^^^^^^^^^^^^^^^^^^^^^^^^^^^^^^^^^^^^^^^^^^^^^^^^
        $fao_s  ctrstr=general_fmt,outbuf=buffer,outlen=buffer,-
                p1=data+read_count-
                p2=data+write_count,p3=data+paging_ios,p4=swap_ios
        check
        pushal  buffer
        calls   #1,g^lib$put_output
        check
        movl    #80,buffer
;^^^^^^^^^^^^^^^^^^^^^^^^^^^^^^^^^^^^^^^^^^^^^^^^^^^^^^^^^^^^^^^^^^^^^^^^
;       Format and spill split io information
;^^^^^^^^^^^^^^^^^^^^^^^^^^^^^^^^^^^^^^^^^^^^^^^^^^^^^^^^^^^^^^^^^^^^^^^^
        $fao_s  ctrstr=split_fmt,outbuf=buffer,outlen=buffer,-
                p1=data+splits
        check
        pushal  buffer
        calls   #1,g^lib$put_output
        check
;^^^^^^^^^^^^^^^^^^^^^^^^^^^^^^^^^^^^^^^^^^^^^^^^^^^^^^^^^^^^^^^^^^^^^^^^
;       Format and spill read header
;^^^^^^^^^^^^^^^^^^^^^^^^^^^^^^^^^^^^^^^^^^^^^^^^^^^^^^^^^^^^^^^^^^^^^^^^
        movl    #80,buffer
        pushal  read_header
        calls   #1,g^lib$put_output
        check
;^^^^^^^^^^^^^^^^^^^^^^^^^^^^^^^^^^^^^^^^^^^^^^^^^^^^^^^^^^^^^^^^^^^^^^^^
;       Format and spill each line of read information
;^^^^^^^^^^^^^^^^^^^^^^^^^^^^^^^^^^^^^^^^^^^^^^^^^^^^^^^^^^^^^^^^^^^^^^^^
        movl    #nlines,r5
        moval   pre_list,r3
        moval   data+read_lengths,r2
dump_read:
        $fao_s  ctrstr=line_fmt,outbuf=buffer,outlen=buffer,p1=#10-
                p2=r3,p3=(r2),p4=4(r2),p5=8(r2),p6=12(r2),p7=16(r2)
        check
        pushal  buffer
        calls   #1,g^lib$put_output
        check
        addl    #pre_len,r3
        addl    #4*5,r2
        movl    #80,buffer
        sobgtr  r5,dump_read
;^^^^^^^^^^^^^^^^^^^^^^^^^^^^^^^^^^^^^^^^^^^^^^^^^^^^^^^^^^^^^^^^^^^^^^^^
;       Format and spill last line of read information
;^^^^^^^^^^^^^^^^^^^^^^^^^^^^^^^^^^^^^^^^^^^^^^^^^^^^^^^^^^^^^^^^^^^^^^^^
        $fao_s  ctrstr=line_fmt,outbuf=buffer,outlen=buffer,p1=#10-
                p2=r3,p3=(r2),p4=4(r2),p5=8(r2),p6=#0,p7=#0
        check
        pushal  buffer
        calls   #1,g^lib$put_output
        check
;^^^^^^^^^^^^^^^^^^^^^^^^^^^^^^^^^^^^^^^^^^^^^^^^^^^^^^^^^^^^^^^^^^^^^^^^
;       Format and spill write header
;^^^^^^^^^^^^^^^^^^^^^^^^^^^^^^^^^^^^^^^^^^^^^^^^^^^^^^^^^^^^^^^^^^^^^^^^
        pushal  write_header
        calls   #1,g^lib$put_output
        check
        movl    #nlines,r5
        moval   pre_list,r3
        moval   data+write_lengths,r2
;^^^^^^^^^^^^^^^^^^^^^^^^^^^^^^^^^^^^^^^^^^^^^^^^^^^^^^^^^^^^^^^^^^^^^^^^
;       Format and spill each line of write information
;^^^^^^^^^^^^^^^^^^^^^^^^^^^^^^^^^^^^^^^^^^^^^^^^^^^^^^^^^^^^^^^^^^^^^^^^
dump_write:
        $fao_s  ctrstr=line_fmt,outbuf=buffer,outlen=buffer,p1=#10-
                p2=r3,p3=(r2),p4=4(r2),p5=8(r2),p6=12(r2),p7=16(r2)
        check
```

Figure 21 contd.

```
        pushal  buffer
        calls   #1,g^lib$put_output
        check
        addl    #pre_len,r3
        addl    #4*5,r2
        movl    #80,buffer
        sobgtr  r5,dump_write
;^^^^^^^^^^^^^^^^^^^^^^^^^^^^^^^^^^^^^^^^^^^^^^^^^^^^^^^^^^^^^^^^^^^^^^
;       Format and spill last line of write information
;^^^^^^^^^^^^^^^^^^^^^^^^^^^^^^^^^^^^^^^^^^^^^^^^^^^^^^^^^^^^^^^^^^^^^^
        $fao_s  ctrstr=line_fmt,outbuf=buffer,outlen=buffer,p1=#10-
                p2=r3,p3=(r2),p4=4(r2),p5=8(r2),p6=#0,p7=#0
        check
        pushal  buffer
        calls   #1,g^lib$put_output
        check
        ret


;^^^^^^^^^^^^^^^^^^^^^^^^^^^^^^^^^^^^^^^^^^^^^^^^^^^^^^^^^^^^^^^^^^^^^^
;       Return block counter information
;^^^^^^^^^^^^^^^^^^^^^^^^^^^^^^^^^^^^^^^^^^^^^^^^^^^^^^^^^^^^^^^^^^^^^^
        .entry  return_counts,^m<r2,r3,r4,r5>
        movl    g^exe$gl_sitespec,r2      ;Check to see if block counter
        beql    accvio                    ; is loaded.
        movc3   #c_off,(r2),data          ;copy the data up from pool
        movl    #ss$_normal,r0
exit:   ret                               ;fini
accvio: movl    #ss$_accvio,r0
        brb     exit

        .end    dump_block_counts
```

Figure 22.

```
;^^^^^^^^^^^^^^^^^^^^^^^^^^^^^^^^^^^^^^^^^^^^^^^^^^^^^^^^^^^^
;       Program:         Unload_block_counter
;       Author:          Billy Bitsenbites (Bruce Ellis)
;       Synopsis:        Cleans up after disk monitor.
;^^^^^^^^^^^^^^^^^^^^^^^^^^^^^^^^^^^^^^^^^^^^^^^^^^^^^^^^^^^^
        .library         /sys$library:lib.mlb/
        .link            /sys$system:sys.stb/
        $ddtdef
        $ucbdef
        $irpdef
header=12
devnam: .long   15
        .address         10$
10$:    .blkb   15
dev_prompt:
        .ascid  /enter disk to be unmonitored:/
        .entry  unload_block_ctr,^m<>
;^^^^^^^^^^^^^^^^^^^^^^^^^^^^^^^^^^^^^^^^^^^^^^^^^^^^^^^^^^^^^
;       Get device name to unload monitor for
;^^^^^^^^^^^^^^^^^^^^^^^^^^^^^^^^^^^^^^^^^^^^^^^^^^^^^^^^^^^^^
        pushal  devnam
        pushal  dev_prompt
        pushal  devnam
        calls   #3,g^lib$get_input
        blbs    r0,lab
        $exit_s r0
;^^^^^^^^^^^^^^^^^^^^^^^^^^^^^^^^^^^^^^^^^^^^^^^^^^^^^^^^^^^^^
;       Unload the code to monitor disk activity
;^^^^^^^^^^^^^^^^^^^^^^^^^^^^^^^^^^^^^^^^^^^^^^^^^^^^^^^^^^^^^
lab:    $cmkrnl_s        routin=kernel_setup
        ret
;**********************************************************************
;       Kernel mode setup code
;**********************************************************************
        .entry  kernel_setup,^m<r2,r3,r4,r5>
        tstl    g^exe$gl_sitespec         ;if not loaded scram
```

Figure 22 contd.

```
        bneq    cont
        movl    #ss$_accvio,r0
        ret
cont:
;^^^^^^^^^^^^^^^^^^^^^^^^^^^^^^^^^^^^^^^^^^^^^^^^^^^^^^^^^^
;       Grab a write mutex on the i/o database
;^^^^^^^^^^^^^^^^^^^^^^^^^^^^^^^^^^^^^^^^^^^^^^^^^^^^^^^^^^
        moval   g^ioc$gl_mutex,r0
        jsb     g^sch$lockw
;^^^^^^^^^^^^^^^^^^^^^^^^^^^^^^^^^^^^^^^^^^^^^^^^^^^^^^^^^^
;       Search  for ucb address of this device
;^^^^^^^^^^^^^^^^^^^^^^^^^^^^^^^^^^^^^^^^^^^^^^^^^^^^^^^^^^
        moval   devnam,r1
        jsb     g^ioc$searchdev
        blbs    r0,no_dev_error         ;If error scram
        pushl   r0
        brb     dev_error
no_dev_error:
        movl    g^exe$gl_sitespec,r0    ;save the pointer to pool
;^^^^^^^^^^^^^^^^^^^^^^^^^^^^^^^^^^^^^^^^^^^^^^^^^^^^^^^^^^
;       reset the start i/o to point to original and deallocate code
;^^^^^^^^^^^^^^^^^^^^^^^^^^^^^^^^^^^^^^^^^^^^^^^^^^^^^^^^^^
        movl    ucb$l_ddt(r1),r5        ;get the driver dispatch table address
        movl    header(r0),ddt$l_start(r5)      ;save actual start i/o
        jsb     g^exe$deanonpaged       ;give up the pool
        clrl    g^exe$gl_sitespec       ;mark the sitespec as unused
        pushl   #ss$_normal
dev_error:
        moval   g^ioc$gl_mutex,r0       ;Free up the mutex on the io database
        movl    g^ctl$gl_pcb,r4
        jsb     g^sch$unlock
        popl    r0
        ret
        .end    unload_block_ctr
```

Figure 23. Output from running block_counter programs.

```
$mac load_block_counter
$link load_block_counter
$
$mac dump_block_counts
$link dump_block_counts
$
$mac unload_block_counter
$link unload_block_counter
$
$r load_block_counter
enter disk to be monitored:dub0:
%SYSTEM-F-NOPRIV, no privilege for attempted operation
$set proc/priv=cmkrnl
$
$r load_block_counter
enter disk to be monitored:dub0:
$
$dir/out=nl: sys$system:
$
$r dump_block_counts
Read: 6       Writes: 0      Paging ios: 4      Swapping ios: 0
Split ios on this disk: 0
Breakdown of Reads by block size:
   0 -   4:         0          2          1          0          0
   5 -   9:         0          0          1          1          0
  10 -  14:         0          0          0          0          0
  15 -  19:         0          0          0          0          1
  20 -  24:         0          0          0          0          0
  25 -  29:         0          0          0          0          0
  30 -  34:         0          0          0          0          0
  35 -  39:         0          0          0          0          0
  40 -  44:         0          0          0          0          0
  45 -  49:         0          0          0          0          0
  50 -  54:         0          0          0          0          0
```

Figure 23 contd.

```
   55 -  59:        0         0         0         0         0
   60 -  64:        0         0         0         0         0
   65 -  69:        0         0         0         0         0
   70 -  75:        0         0         0         0         0
   75 -  79:        0         0         0         0         0
   80 -  85:        0         0         0         0         0
   85 -  89:        0         0         0         0         0
   90 -  94:        0         0         0         0         0
   95 -  99:        0         0         0         0         0
  100 - 104:        0         0         0         0         0
  105 - 109:        0         0         0         0         0
  110 - 114:        0         0         0         0         0
  115 - 119:        0         0         0         0         0
  120 - 124:        0         0         0         0         0
  125 - 128:        0         0         0         0         0
Breakdown of writes by block size:
    0 -   4:        0         0         0         0         0
    5 -   9:        0         0         0         0         0
   10 -  14:        0         0         0         0         0
   15 -  19:        0         0         0         0         0
   20 -  24:        0         0         0         0         0
   25 -  29:        0         0         0         0         0
   30 -  34:        0         0         0         0         0
   35 -  39:        0         0         0         0         0
   40 -  44:        0         0         0         0         0
   45 -  49:        0         0         0         0         0
   50 -  54:        0         0         0         0         0
   55 -  59:        0         0         0         0         0
   60 -  64:        0         0         0         0         0
   65 -  69:        0         0         0         0         0
   70 -  75:        0         0         0         0         0
   75 -  79:        0         0         0         0         0
   80 -  85:        0         0         0         0         0
   85 -  89:        0         0         0         0         0
   90 -  94:        0         0         0         0         0
   95 -  99:        0         0         0         0         0
  100 - 104:        0         0         0         0         0
  105 - 109:        0         0         0         0         0
  110 - 114:        0         0         0         0         0
  115 - 119:        0         0         0         0         0
  120 - 124:        0         0         0         0         0
  125 - 128:        0         0         0         0         0
$
$
$r unload_block_counter
enter disk to be unmonitored:dub0:
$
```

Episode 9

What's Open?

It finally happened. Billy asked the girl for a date. They decided to go on a picnic on Memorial Day afternoon.

As soon as he made the date, Billy realized he had made a mistake. He was so nervous asking her out that he wasn't thinking clearly. The time of the date conflicted with the start of the fourth game of the NBA Eastern conference finals.

Billy's major interest outside of work was sports. In particular, he was an avid Chicago sports fan, ingrained from his youth, with allegiance to the Cubs, Bulls, Bears, and Black Hawks.

The series pitted Michael Jordan and the Bulls against the Bad Boys of Detroit. The Bulls were the underdog in the series, having fallen to a two game to one disadvantage. Billy relished the role of underdog that his Chicago teams seemed to acquire naturally. Had Bill Wirtz, P.K. Wrigley, and George Halas not been so cheap, he could have grown up with winners. Instead, he faced the hardened understanding that he would have to work hard to succeed in spite of the obstacles presented by their own financially short-sighted nature. In his mind, he saw himself as a software engineering version of Ernie Banks, hitting a lot of unnoticed home runs.

Billy could not cancel the date, not after he had written software for her and agonized over asking her out. So he called her and recommended that they go, instead, to a sports bar near Harvard Square. She agreed to the new plan. It was unfortunate that Billy had not also come across *The Hitchhiker's Guide to Social Graces*.

They spent the afternoon talking and watching the Bulls. In spite, or perhaps because, of his preoccupation with the basketball game, their conversation moved smoothly, with little discussion of computers and work. She did, however, thank him for the program which he had written for her, which would probably have a more lasting effect than the roses Billy gave her, now wilting on the bar from the heat, smoke and lack of water.

Billy enjoyed the game as the Bulls headed to victory. He noticed that the Bulls were more effective in getting Jordan free for a shot. In the earlier games, the Pistons had blocked his path to the basket constantly, by double and triple teaming him. In this game, though, Michael took the ball at the point, spreading the defense and opening a lane for him to take the ball to the basket.

Billy's mind wandered to his performance problems. He could quickly determine which files were fragmented and the type of I/O traffic to the disks. But to improve performance, he had to distribute files across the disk drives, allowing him to spread the I/Os and open a clear lane to the read/write heads of the disk drives. If he could keep more heads active simultaneously, more concurrent I/Os could be processed.

The Bulls had gotten Joe Dumars off Jordan. Likewise, Billy had to know which files were hot. If he knew which files were active, he would also know which files to move to the lightly loaded disk drives. He knew he would have to, at last, write the program he intended to write a while ago, the one that would show the files that were open by a process.

He was so excited about writing this program that he barely remembered to kiss his date good bye.

Billy rushed to the office and opened the grey tome, titled *The Hitchhiker's Guide to VMS*, to its familiar clicking and whirring.

"Book, I need your help," Billy entered. "I would like to determine which files a process has open at any given point in time. By determining which processes are issuing the most direct I/Os, I could then find out which files they have open and move them around the available disk spindles, balancing the I/O load.

"Can you help me out?"

The *Guide* responded, "Sure, I would be glad to help you out."

"What information is available to tell me which file a process has open?" Billy asked.

"When a file is opened by a process, there is a channel assignment associated with the file. You can distinguish the channels assigned for files, with those associated for other devices by the fact that there is an associated window control block (WCB)," the *Guide* replied.

"When a channel is assigned, a data structure called a channel control block (CCB) is constructed in P1 space. The channel control block is a 16-byte data structure that contains, among other things, a pointer to the unit control block (UCB) of the device unit. This pointer is stored in the field CCB$L_UCB. The UCB is the data structure that you used in the I/O interceptor program you just wrote. (See Figure 20.)

"The WCB address is stored in the field CCB$L_WIND. If the channel does not have a file associated with it, the CCB$L_WIND field typically contains 0. Note that this does not hold true on a remote terminal. DECnet uses the WCB to point to its own network data structure, describing the incoming link."

"How would I differentiate a WCB associated with a file from one associated with a network device?" Billy interrupted.

"Because you have the pointer to the UCB, you could check the device class to determine whether the device associated with the channel is a disk. If it is a disk, the field UCB$B_DEVCLASS will contain the constant DC$_DISK," the *Guide* answered.

"So, I could locate the channel control blocks and examine each CCB to determine which channels are assigned. The channels with WCB pointers that are also disks will tell me that there is a file associated with the channel. How do I locate the CCBs for a process?" Billy queried.

"The CCBs are contained in the channel control block table, which is pointed to by the location CTL$GL_CCBBASE. The CCBs are stored in the table, growing toward lower addresses. So, you could start at the base of the table, grabbing each CCB. After you are done with a given CCB, you can back through the table by 16 bytes, until you have hit the maximum channel index for this process, which is stored in the location CTL$GW_CHINDX."

"Is this 16-byte index the same as the number returned by the SYS$ASSIGN system service?" Billy asked.

"Yes, it is," the *Guide* answered.

"Now that I will have identified the files associated with the process, how do I determine the file names associated with the channels?" Billy queried.

"The file name is not stored in memory. However, the WCB points to the file control block (FCB), which contains the file ID of the open file in the six bytes starting at the offset defined by FCB$W_FID," the *Guide* started.

"So, I can pass the file ID to the routine LIB$FID_TO_NAME that I used with the blocking_lock program," (see Figure 15). "But to use the routine, I will also need the device name that file resides on. How can I determine the device name associated with the file?"

The *Guide* responded, "If you had paid attention when we discussed the data structures used in channel assignment, you would not be asking me this question now." (See Episode 8.)

"Great," thought Billy. "A book that talks to me like my seventh grade English teacher!"

"You simply have to back track through the data structures used in channel assignment and construct the device name. You have the UCB address from CCB$L_UCB. The UCB contains a binary representation of the unit number of the device, in the field UCB$W_UNIT.

"From the UCB, you can locate the device data block (DDB). The DDB may be located through the field UCB$L_DDB. The DDB is a controller data structure and contains the device name through the controller designation in the field DDB$T_NAME. The device name is in this field stored as an ASCII counted string.

"While you are pointing to the DDB, you can pull out the field DDB$L_ALLOCLS. This field contains the allocation class, if any, of the device in binary.

"In the case where there is no allocation class, you will want to determine whether there is a system communication services (SCS) node name associated with the device name. The DDB contains a pointer to the system block (SB) in the field DDB$L_SB.

"The SB contains the name of the node serving the disk, if any, in the field SB$T_NODENAME. This field is also represented as an ASCII counted string."

"Sorry for not paying closer attention earlier," Billy apologized. "So, it sounds like that's all the information that I'll need to determine which files are open by a process. Am I missing anything?"

"Yes," the *Guide* replied. "One anomaly associated with the WCB pointer is that it may contain a non-zero value which is not an address. If the high word of the CCB$L_WIND field contains a 0, and the low word is not 0, the window field contains a process section table index."

"The process section table index is a negative index into the process section table, used to locate the process section table entry.

"The process section table entry (PSTE) is a 32-byte data structure used to locate a section of code or data in the image file when resolving a hard page fault. The PTE contains a pointer to the WCB describing the open image file. The pointer is stored in the field SEC$L_WINDOW."

"How do I locate the process section table?" asked Billy.

The *Guide* responded, "The process section table is stored in the process header (PHD) of the process. The PHD may be located by the pointer CTL$GL_PHD. The PHD contains a field, PHD$L_PSTBASOFF, which is a byte offset to the end of the process section table.

"The sign extended process section table index is a negative longword index from the end of the section table to the PTE."

"Okay, I have that down, I think," Billy mused.

"Why do you want to determine the files that a process has open?" the *Guide* asked.

"For performance reasons," Billy replied. "I want to be able to move hot files to lightly loaded disks."

"Then, you might want to know that the WCB contains a count of the reads and writes issued on the file since it was opened by the process," offered the *Guide*. "This might be useful in determining which files are indeed hot."

"That would be great information," Billy acknowledged. "Which fields contain the read and write counts?"

"The field WCB$L_READS contains the count of reads, and WCB$L_WRITES contains the count of writes," the *Guide* replied.

"Are these fields valid?" Billy asked.

"Yes," responded the *Guide*. "They are updated prior to SYS$QIO dispatching to the driver start I/O routine. The only potentially misleading information would be if the process continually opens and closes the file: the counts are only meaningful since the last open."

"I can live with that," Billy responded.

Billy thought for a moment and observed, "I just realized that the CCBs are stored in P1 space. Process virtual address space is private to that process. How do I go about accessing the other process' P1 space?"

"You could queue an asynchronous system trap (AST) to the process, as you did in the WSBLASTER program," the *Guide* responded (see Figure 8). "After you have forced the target process to become current, you can touch its P1 space.

"You might also want to check to determine whether the target process is suspended or has a delete pending. If it is suspended in kernel mode, the AST will be blocked. If there is a delete pending, the AST will never get there. To perform these checks, you can examine the bits PCB$V_SUSPEN and PCB$V_DELPEN in the field PCB$L_STS."

"Okay, now how do I get the information back to my original process?" Billy requested.

"Prior to queueing the AST, you could save your process ID. After you have found the file information, you could save it in a buffer in non-paged pool. Then, you could queue another AST back to the originating process and copy the data back to your P0 space for local processing," answered the *Guide*.

"So," proposed Billy, "I can get his PID, using EXE$NAMPID. Then I can use EXE$ALONONPAGED to allocate non-paged pool for my AST control block (ACB) and code and also for my information buffer. How do I know the upper bound on how many channels the process could be using?"

"The upper bound on channel assignment is defined by the special SYSGEN parameter CHANNELCNT," the *Guide* replied. "Its parameter value is stored in the location SGN$GW_PCHANCNT. The typical setting for the parameter is 127 channels."

"So, I could allocate a buffer large enough to hold as many of my structures as CHANNELCNT. What type should I place in the type field?" Billy asked.

"It really does not matter," the *Guide* answered, "as long as it is a positive byte value. The values 120 through 127 are reserved for users. But you could just as easily use an existing type, such as DYN$C_BUFIO."

Billy thought at the terminal, "After I have allocated the buffer and built the ACB, I can use SCH$QAST to queue the AST to the target process.

"What about the fact that the AST delivery will occur asynchronously from the execution of my program? If I queue the AST and return, couldn't the program run down before the return AST is executed?"

"Yes, it is possible for the program to run down prior to the return AST," the *Guide* concurred. "To prevent this situation from causing the potential problem of attempting to write to a nonexistent buffer, you should probably wait for an event flag to be set when you return from the SYS$CMKRNL system service call.

"To set the event flag in the return AST routine, you may use the JSB instruction to call the subroutine SCH$POSTEF. The inputs to the routine require that you put the value for the event flag to be set in register R3. R1 should contain your process identification, and R2 should contain the priority boost class, if any boost is to be requested."

"What if the process aborts the program while the target process is executing its AST?" Billy inquired. "Maybe the user, running the program, has entered a Ctrl-Y to abort the program. How do you guarantee that he is still running the same program and,when you are copying the buffer, that you are not trashing the P0 space of a different program being run?"

"What? Have you been eating your Wheaties?" the *Guide* teased. "Good thought.

"To guarantee that you are still running the same program, you could save the PHD$L_IMGCNT location from the PHD. This location contains a count of the images that have run down since the process was created.

"If you save this location, then upon execution of the return AST, you could check to make sure that the image count has not changed. If the value in the image count field has not changed, you can be positive that the same image is executing."

"What if the originating process went away before the delivery of the return AST?" queried Billy.

"Prior to turning around the AST," the *Guide* replied, "you could check to make sure that the process that initiated the original AST is still operating on the system. Remember from our original discussion of the EXE$NAMPID routine, the process control block (PCB) of the target process was located using the low word of the internal process ID as an index into the PCB vector table?" (See Episode 2.)

"The PID of the original process must be saved to turn around the AST anyway," the *Guide* went on. "So, you could get the address of the PCB vector table from the contents of the location SCH$GL_PCBVEC and index into it, using the low word of the saved PID. After you have located the PCB, you can check the internal PID, stored in the field PCB$L_PID, against the saved PID. If they match, the original process is still on the system. The process is the same because the sequence number, in the high word of the PID, has not changed."

"How do you know that the entry in the PCB vector table points to a valid PCB?" asked Billy.

The *Guide* answered, "If the slot in the PCB vector table is not in use, it points to the null PCB. Note that even though the null process no longer appears on the system, its PCB serves as a place holder for unused entries in the PCB vector table."

"It appears that I am about done with the detail information. Now all I have to do is write the code to go around these details. You know, Book, the methodology of system programming under VMS seems to be getting almost easy," Billy noted. "Before I start writing this code, I have one more question. What type of synchronization is required in this program?"

"The routine EXE$NAMPID will take out a scheduling spinlock," began the *Guide*. "You may hold this spinlock until you queue the AST, guaranteeing that the target process does not get deleted from the system, prior to actually queueing the AST.

"In your AST routine, you should take out a mutex on the I/O database. The mutex is located at IOC$GL_MUTEX. This will guarantee that data structures like the UCB, DDB, and SB will not go away, until you are done looking at them and have released the mutex.

"While accessing structures like the WCB and the FCB, you could take out the file system spinlock, FILSYS. This should not be necessary, because the structures are created from your process context by the extended QIO procedures (XQP). If you choose to use a special kernel AST, and you should, you will be blocking the XQP, as it is activated by a normal kernel AST.

"I mentioned that you should use a special kernel AST. Actually, it is required because your code will be allocating non-paged pool and you will want to block process deletion until after you have returned the pool.

"Also, note that, because you are operating in a special kernel AST routine, you should not lower the interrupt priority level (IPL) below 2. The special kernel AST is delivered at IPL 2. By keeping IPL at 2 or greater, you will be blocking any ASTs from being delivered, including the process deletion AST."

"Sounds good to me," Billy noted. "Let me try this out. Thanks again, Book."

"No problem," the *Guide* responded.

Billy spent some time planning the code. He wrote the program with a separate routine to spill the file information (see Figure 24 and Figure 25). They worked (see Figure 26).

Billy was incredibly happy. Now he had the tools that he required to help resolve his disk I/O bottlenecks. He also had a boss whom he respected and enjoyed working for. He was going out with the girl he had met at school. The Bulls were winning. The Cubs ... well, there was always next year.

The only thing that was still giving him some trouble was a little program that he was using to track and trend the Massachusetts' lotteries. With a little work, he might be able to even get this program working. Unfortunately, the *Guide* could not help him out with this program.

WILL BILLY CONTINUE to date the girl? How long can Billy's luck stay up? Does the girl have a name? What progress will Billy make with the lottery? Where will he delve next into VMS?

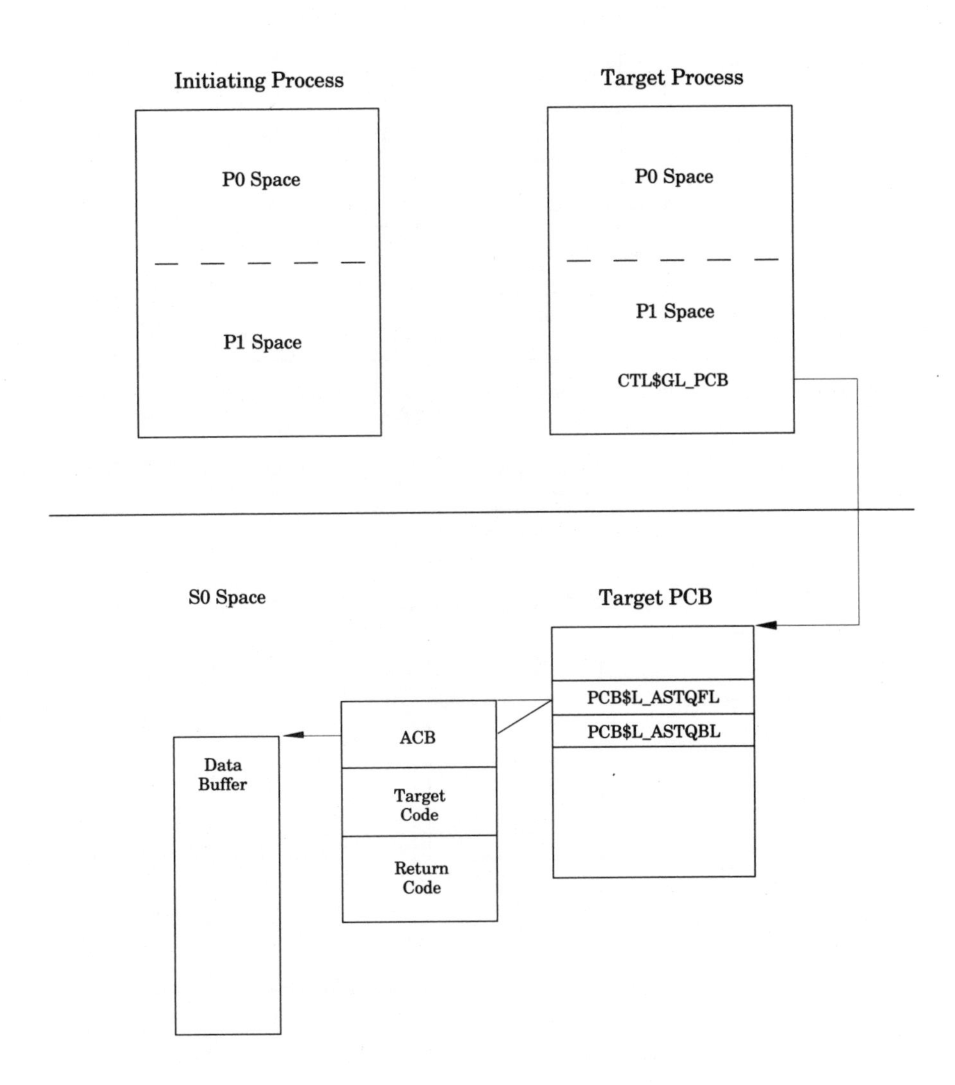

AST mechanism for SHOW_PROC_FILES.MAR

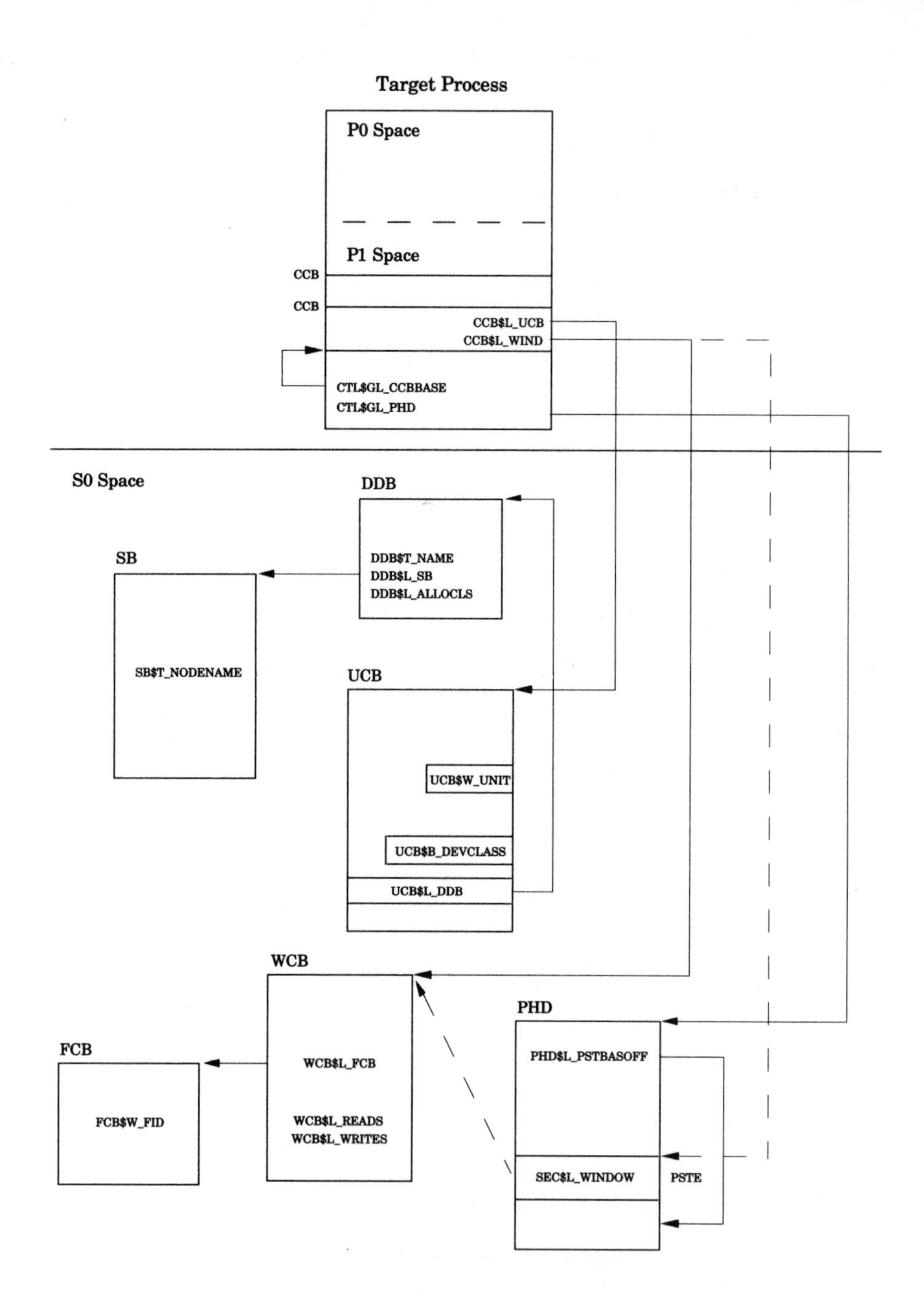

Structures used to determine open files by SHOW_PROC_FILES.MAR

Figure 24.

```
;********************************************************
;Program:        show_proc_files
;Author:         Billy Bitsenbites (Bruce Ellis)
;Synopsis:       This program displays the files currently
;                open to the specified process.  Along with
;                each file, the number of mapping pointers
;                that map the file is displayed, as well as
;                the reads/writes on this open.
;
;
;********************************************************

;Macro definitions
        .macro  check ?lab
        blbs    r0,lab
        $exit_s r0
lab:
        .endm   check
;Macro library includes
        .library        /sys$library:lib/
        .link   /sys$system:sys.stb/
        $dcdef          ;Device classes
        $pcbdef
        $phddef
        $pridef
        $ipldef
        $acbdef
        $ccbdef
        $wcbdef
        $fcbdef
        $ucbdef
        $secdef
        $sbdef
        $ddbdef
        $dyndef
ef=32
;data area
pid_asc:
        .long   8
        .address        10$
10$:    .blkb   8
pid:    .blkl   1
prompt: .ascid  /Pid?/

lock_adr:
        .address        lock1
        .address        lock2

;^^^^^^^^^^^^^^^^^^^^^^^^^^^^^
;Allocate header for file information buffer
;Note: Position dependence is crucial.
;^^^^^^^^^^^^^^^^^^^^^^^^^^^^^
proc_files:
        .blkb   12              ;reserved space for pool header info
header1=0                       ;;offset to the first longword (unused)
header2=4                       ;offset to second longword (unused)
block_size=8                    ;size of pool allocated to the block
block_type=10                   ;type of dynamic structure
prc_name:
        .blkb   16              ;process name
prcnam=prc_name-proc_files      ;offset to process name in block
pid_other:                      ;returned pid
        .long   0
pid_other_off=pid_other-proc_files              ;offset to pid in block
count:  .long   0               ;count of number of files open by the process
ret_count=count-proc_files      ;offset to the returned count
file_buffer_loc:                ;location of the file buffers
file_buffer_max=256             ;philosophically we should not even allow for
                                ; this many concurrent files
file_buffers=file_buffer_loc-proc_files    ;offset to file buffers
header=file_buffers
node=0                  ;offset within buffer to scs nodename
devnam=8                ;offset to device name (NOTE: This program assumes
```

Figure 24 contd.

```
                        ; that precedent has not been broken with three
                        ; character device names.  If it is, the area for
                        ; device names will have to be increased in size.
unit=12                 ;offset within buffer to the unit
fid=14                  ;offset within buffer to the file id
fid_rvn=18              ;offset within the buffer to the the rvn of file
reads=20                ;offset into buffer to locate the count of reads
writes=24               ;offset within buffer to locate the count of writes
file_buffer_size=28     ;size of each file buffer
;^^^^^^^^^^^^^^^^^^^^^^^^^^^^^^^^^^^^
; Allocate space for per file information buffers
;^^^^^^^^^^^^^^^^^^^^^^^^^^^^^^^^^^^^
        .rept   file_buffer_max
        .blkb   8               ;node name
        .blkb   4               ;device name
        .blkb   6               ;file id
        .blkl   2               ;count of reads and writes
        .endr
prc_args:
        .long   2
        .address        pid
        .long   0

fmt:    .ascid  /Process: !15AC with pid !8XL has the following files open:/
out_buf:
        .long   80
        .address        10$
10$:    .blkb   80
no_file_msg:
        .ascid  /This process has no files open. /
;Code
        .psect  code    shr,nowrt,pic,exe
        .entry  show_proc_files,^m<>
        $lkwset_s       inadr=lock_adr   ;No page faults at high ipl
        check
        pushal  pid_asc                 ;Determine which process we
        pushal  prompt                  ;   are supposed to get the info
        pushal  pid_asc                 ;   from.
        calls   #3,g^lib$get_input
        check
        pushal  pid                     ;Convert pid from ascii to binary
        pushal  pid_asc                 ;
        calls   #2,g^ots$cvt_tz_l       ;
        check
        $clref_s        efn=#ef         ;clear event flag we are going to wait
        check                           ;   on for completion of kast
        $cmkrnl_s       routin=get_file,arglst=prc_args
                                        ;Queue a special kernel ast to the
        check                           ;process to obtain the needed info
        $waitfr_s       efn=#ef         ;wait until sp kast sets efn for
        check                           ; asynchronous completion
;*************************************************
;Format and spill the process name and PID
;*************************************************
        $fao_s  ctrstr=fmt,outbuf=out_buf,outlen=out_buf,p1=#prc_name,-
                p2=pid_other
        check
        pushal  out_buf
        calls   #1,g^lib$put_output
        movl    count,r6                ;How many open files
        beql    no_files_open
        moval   proc_files+file_buffers,-  ;locate the beginning of file buffers
                r7
10$:    pushl   r7                      ;dump the file information 1 file at
        calls   #1,spill_file_info      ; a time

        addl    #<file_buffer_size>,r7  ;point to next file buffer
        sobgtr  r6,10$                  ;loop till all files processed
over_and_out:
        ret                             ;Auf Wiedersehen!
no_files_open:
        pushal  no_file_msg
        calls   #1,g^lib$put_output
```

Figure 24 contd.

```
        brb     over_and_out

;**************************************************
;       Special kast setup
;**************************************************
lockl:
        .entry  get_file,^m<r2,r3,r4,r5,r6,r7,r8,r9,r10,r11>
;**************************************************
;       Get process PCB address
;**************************************************
;       Inputs: 4(ap)  - pidadr/ 8(ap) - prcnam desc adr / r4 - PCB
        jsb     g^exe$nampid
;       Outputs:
;               r0      -       status
;               r1      -       ipid of the other guy
;               r4      -       pcb of the other guy
;               ipl is at synch, with sched spinlock
        blbs    r0,ok2
        setipl  #0
        ret
;**************************************************
;       Allocate pool for ACB
;**************************************************
ok2:                                    ; by exe$nampid
        movl    r4,r10                  ;save his pcb
        moval   acb,r6                  ;set up acb
        movl    g^ctl$gl_pcb,r4         ;Save my
        movl    pcb$l_pid(r4),acb_l_mypid       ;pid for return sp kast
        bbc     #pcb$v_suspen,pcb$l_sts(r10),hes_ok1
        setipl  #0
        movl    #ss$_suspended,r0
        brw     err_ret
hes_ok1:
        bbc     #pcb$v_delpen,pcb$l_sts(r10),hes_ok2
        movl    #ss$_nonexpr,r0
        brw     err_ret
hes_ok2:
        movl    @#ctl$gl_phd,r9         ;get phd address
        movl    phd$l_imgcnt(r9),imgcnt ;Save the image count so return AST
                                        ;knows whether we are in same image or
                                        ;not
        moval   proc_files,file_ret_adr ;save return address from p0 space
        moval   count,count_ret_adr     ;save return count address from p0
        movl    #size_of_pool,r1        ;Set up for allocating pool
        jsb     g^exe$alononpaged       ;get it
        blbs    r0,ok3                  ;continue if all is cool
        brw     err_ret                 ;else get out
ok3:    pushr   #^m<r0,r1,r2,r3,r4,r5>  ;save regs from movc3
        movc3   #size_of_pool,acb,(r2)  ;copy acb and routines to pool
        popr    #^m<r0,r1,r2,r3,r4,r5>  ;restore regs
        movw    r1,acb$w_size(r2)       ;save size of pool
        movb    #dyn$c_acb,acb$b_type(r2)       ;setup type
        movb    #<1@acb$v_kast>,acb$b_rmod(r2)  ;set up for sp kast
        movl    pcb$l_pid(r10),acb$l_pid(r2)    ;define acb of process to get ast
        moval   <copy_file-acb>(r2),acb$l_kast(r2)  ;set ast address for kast
        movl    r2,r5                   ;set up r5 for sch$qast
;**************************************************
;       Allocate pool for channel info
;**************************************************
        movzwl  g^sgn$gw_pchancnt,r1    ;get channelcnt sysgen parameter
        cmpl    #file_buffer_max,r1     ;too many channels?
        bgtr    channcnt_ok             ; branch if not
        movl    #file_buffer_max,r1     ;else reset to max (sorry, charlie!)
channcnt_ok:
        mull2   #file_buffer_size,r1    ;calculate max buffer size needed
        addl2   #header,r1              ;add on header
        movl    r1,r6                   ;save pool size requested
        jsb     g^exe$alononpaged       ;get the pool for the buffer
        blbs    r0,still_cool           ;continue if sufficient pool
        brw     err_ret_deallo          ;cannot continue/not enough pool
still_cool:
        pushr   #^m<r0,r1,r2,r3,r4,r5>  ;save regs for movc5
        movc5   #0,,#0,r6,(r2)          ;zero the buffer
```

Figure 24 contd.

```
        popr    #^m<r0,r1,r2,r3,r4,r5>    ;restore regs
        movw    r1,block_size(r2)         ;save the size of pool
        movb    #dyn$c_bufio,block_type(r2)
        movl    r2,file_info_buffer(r5)   ;save the buffer pointer
;****************************************************
;       Queue the ast
;****************************************************
;lockl: setipl  #ipl$_synch               ;synch w/sched db
        movzwl  acb$l_pid(r5),r4          ;retrieve the pid of the process we want
        movl    #pri$_ticom,r2            ;give him a boost
        movl    g^ctl$gl_pcb,r4           ;restore our pcb address
        jsb     g^sch$qast                ;queue an ast to the process
        unlock  lockname=SCHED,newipl=#0  ;lower ipl from synch implied
        movl    #ss$_normal,r0            ;Get outta here
        ret
err_ret_deallo:
        movl    file_info_buffer(r5),r0   ;get pool buffer address
        beql    no_buffer_to_deallo       ;
        jsb     g^exe$deanonpaged         ;deallocate the buffer
no_buffer_to_deallo:
        movl    r5,r0                     ;r0 points to the pool to return
        jsb     g^exe$deanonpaged
        movl    #ss$_insfmem,r0
err_ret:unlock  lockname=SCHED,newipl=#0
        ret
        .psect  data_and_code   wrt,exe
acb:    .blkb   acb$l_kast+4              ;allocate space for the acb portion
acb_l_mypid:
        .blkl   1               ;My pid for return ast
ret_ast_adr:
        .blkl   1               ;return ast address
file_info_buffer=.-acb
        .blkl   1               ;location of file info buffer in pool
count_ret:
        .long   0               ;return count of files processed
file_ret_adr:
        .blkl   1               ;P0 buffer address
count_ret_adr:
        .blkl   1               ;return location for count
imgcnt: .blkl   1               ;count of images run
;****************************************************
;       AST get file/channel info
;****************************************************

;****************************************************
;Special kernel ast code
;****************************************************
copy_file:
        pushr   #^m<r0,r1,r2,r3,r4,r5,r6,r7,r8,r9,r10,r11>
        movl    acb_l_mypid,acb$l_pid(r5)         ;reset pid for return trip
        moval   ret_ast,acb$l_kast(r5)            ;set return ast address
        bisb2   #<1@acb$v_kast>,acb$b_rmod(r5)    ;set up for sp kast
        movl    file_info_buffer(r5),r11          ;locate the buffer
        movl    g^ctl$gl_pcb,r10                  ;get this guy's pcb address
        movq    pcb$t_lname(r10),prcnam(r11)      ;copy the process name
        movq    <pcb$t_lname+8>(r10),<prcnam+8>(r11)      ;copy the rest
        movl    pcb$l_epid(r10),pid_other_off(r11)        ;get his pid
        moval   file_buffers(r11),r9              ;locate the file buffers
        clrl    ret_count(r11)                    ;zero counter of file names
        movl    @#ctl$gl_ccbbase,r10              ;set up link to fix up vectors
        clrl    r6
        movl    g^ctl$gl_pcb,r4
        moval   g^ioc$gl_mutex,r0
        jsb     g^sch$lockr
nxt_ccb:                                          ;Index from base back
        subl    #16,r10                           ;  1 CCB at a time
        addl    #16,r6                            ;keep track of current chan #
        cmpw    r6,g^ctl$gw_chindx                ;if past max scram
        bgtr    done
        movl    ccb$l_ucb(r10),r7                 ;get ucb
        beql    all_donel
        cmpb    #dc$_disk,ucb$b_devclass(r7)      ;if not a disk skip it
        bneq    not_a_file
```

Figure 24 contd.

```
        movl    ccb$l_wind(r10),r8              ;get wcb
        beql    not_a_file
        blss    not_a_section_file
        cvtwl   ccb$l_wind(r10),r2              ;get negative pstx out of ccb
        movl    g^ctl$gl_phd,r1                 ;get the phd address
        addl2   phd$l_pstbasoff(r1),r1          ;locate the end of the pst
        movl    sec$l_window(r1)[r2],r8         ;get the wcb pointer
not_a_section_file:
        movl    wcb$l_reads(r8),reads(r9)       ;get reads since open
        movl    wcb$l_writes(r8),writes(r9)     ;get writes since open
        movl    wcb$l_fcb(r8),r8                ;get fcb
        movl    fcb$w_fid(r8),fid(r9)           ;get file id
        movw    fcb$w_fid_rvn(r8),fid_rvn(r9)   ;get rest of fid
        movw    ucb$w_unit(r7),unit(r9)         ;get unit number
        movl    ucb$l_ddb(r7),r7                ;get the device name
        movl    ddb$t_name(r7),devnam(r9)
        movl    ddb$l_allocls(r7),<node+2>(r9)  ;get allo class if any
        beql    no_alloclass                    ;  branch if none
        movw    #-1,node(r9)                    ;mark that alloclass exists
        brb     skip_name                       ;don't need name
no_alloclass:
        movl    ddb$l_sb(r7),r7                 ;get the node name
        movl    sb$t_nodename(r7),node(r9)      ;
        movl    sb$t_nodename+4(r7),<node+4>(r9)
skip_name:
        incl    ret_count(r11)                  ;count fo files +=1
        cmpw    #file_buffer_max,ret_count(r11) ;too many?
        blss    all_done1
        addl2   #file_buffer_size,r9            ;point to next buffer
not_a_file:
all_done2:
        brw     nxt_ccb                         ;get the next file
done:
all_done1:
;**************************************************
;       AST return file/channel info
;**************************************************
;**************************************************
;We have the info now let us send it back to the
;original process.
;**************************************************
        movl    g^ctl$gl_pcb,r4
        moval   g^ioc$gl_mutex,r0
        jsb     g^sch$unlock
        lock    lockname=SCHED,lockipl=#ipl$_sched
        movzwl  acb$l_pid(r5),r1                ;set up return pid for astdel
        movl    g^sch$gl_pcbvec,r2              ;get at pcb vector table
        movl    (r2)[r1],r1                     ;get our pcb address
                                                ;Who are we anyway? (Zelig)
        cmpl    pcb$l_pid(r1),acb$l_pid(r5)     ;are we still around or are we
                                                ;  The Ghost in the Machine
        bneq    err_ast_exit                    ;if initial process is not
                                                ;here exit
        unlock  lockname=SCHED,newipl=#ipl$_astdel
        clrl    r2                              ;no boost for the ast
        jsb     g^sch$qast                      ;return to home
        setipl  #ipl$_astdel                    ;return to initial ipl
        popr    #^m<r0,r1,r2,r3,r4,r5,r6,r7,r8,r9,r10,r11>
        rsb                                     ;back to astdel
err_ast_exit:
        unlock  lockname=SCHED,newipl=#ipl$_astdel
        popr    #^m<r0,r1,r2,r3,r4,r5,r6,r7,r8,r9,r10,r11>
        movl    file_info_buffer(r5),r0         ;return file info buffer to
                                                ;pool
        jsb     g^exe$deanonpaged               ;
        movl    r5,r0                           ;deallocate ourselves
        jmp     g^exe$deanonpaged               ;and don't come back here
                                                ;instead go directly back to
                                                ;astdel and do not collect $200
;*************************************************************
;We are back home now so lets put the info at his
;doorstep, ring the doorbell, and disappear
;*************************************************************
```

Figure 24 contd.

```
ret_ast:
        pushr   #^m<r0,r1,r2,r3,r4,r5,r6,r7,r8,r9,r10,r11>
        movl    pcb$l_phd(r4),r3                ;get our process header
        cmpl    phd$l_imgcnt(r3),imgcnt         ;are we still in the same
                                                ;image? If not get out.
        bneq    exit                            ;
        movl    file_info_buffer(r5),r6         ;locate the file info buffer

        mull3   #<file_buffer_size>,-           ;
                ret_count(r6),r2                ;how much to return?
        addl2   #header,r2                      ;return header info
        pushr   #^m<r0,r1,r2,r3,r4,r5>
        movc3   r2,(r6),-                       ;
                @file_ret_adr                   ;return the goods
        popr    #^m<r0,r1,r2,r3,r4,r5>
        movl    ret_count(r6),@count_ret_adr    ;return the count
        movl    #ef,r3                          ;set efn ef
        movl    pcb$l_pid(r4),r1                ;for ourselves
        clrl    r2                              ;no boost
        jsb     g^sch$postef                    ; set it
exit:   popr    #^m<r0,r1,r2,r3,r4,r5,r6,r7,r8,r9,r10,r11>
        movl    file_info_buffer(r5),r0         ;return file info buffer to
                                                ;pool
        jsb     g^exe$deanonpaged               ;
        movl    r5,r0
        jmp     g^exe$deanonpaged               ;become a nonentity
size_of_pool = .-acb
lock2:
        .end    show_proc_files
```

Figure 25.

```
;*****************************************************
;       Subroutine - Spill_File_Info
;       Author: Billy Bitsenbites (Bruce Ellis)
;       Synopsis:       This subroutine is called to
;               format and display the Device name, file
;               name, file id, reads and writes on the
;               file since opened, and the number of mapping
;               pointers in the file header(s).
;       Inputs: address of a block of the following form:
;               8 bytes containing the scsnode
;               4 bytes containing the device name
;               2 bytes containing the unit number of the device
;               6 bytes containing the file id of the file
;               4 bytes containing the count of reads on the window
;               4 bytes containing the count of writes on the window
;
;*****************************************************


;Macros
        .macro  check ?1
        blbs    r0,1
        $exit_s r0
1:
        .endm   check
;Data
dev:    .long   15                      ;Descriptor holding the device name
        .address        dev_a
dev_a:  .blkb   15
out_string:                             ;Output string buffer
        .long   256
        .address        10$
10$:    .blkb   256

;formats
file_dev:
        .ascid  <10><13>/File:/
fid_fmt:.ascid  /File id: (!UW,!UW,!UW)/
fmt_rw: .ascid  /Reads on window: !10UL         Writes on window: !10UL/
```

Figure 25 contd.

```
out_ptr:                                ;Output buffer
        .long   80
        .address        10$
10$:    .blkb   80
ptr_count:                              ;Count of the number of mapping pointers
        .blkl   1
file_buffer:                            ;Local copy of the passed file buffer
node:   .blkb   8
devnam: .blkb   4
unit:   .blkw   1
fid:    .blkb   6
reads:  .long   0
writes: .long   0
buffer_size=.-file_buffer
allo:   .long   3                       ;Allocation class descriptor
        .address        allo_a
allo_a_prefix:
        .ascii  /$/
allo_a: .blkb   3
allo_f: .ascid  /!UB/
unit_f: .ascid  /!UW/
unit_d: .long   5
        .address        unit_a
unit_a: .blkb   5

;Code

        .entry  spill_file_info,^m<>
        movc3   #buffer_size,@4(ap),file_buffer ;Copy the buffer to local
                                                ; storage
        cmpw    node,#-1                        ;Alloclass?
        bneq    no_alloclass                    ;branch if not
;^^^^^^^^^^^^
;Format the allocation class to ascii
;^^^^^^^^^^^^
        $fao_s  ctrstr=allo_f,outbuf=allo,outlen=allo,p1=node+2
        check
        incl    allo                            ;increment to include
                                                ; last '$' sign
        movc3   allo,allo_a_prefix,dev_a
        brb     finish_node                     ;skip to rest of devnam
no_alloclass:
        movzbl  node,r0                         ;Get node name size
        bneq    got_node                        ;Process the node name
        moval   dev_a,r3                        ;no node so skip it
        brb     skip_node                       ;
got_node:
        movc3   r0,<node+1>,dev_a               ;Copy node name
finish_node:
        movb    #^a/$/,(r3)+            ;Plug in a $ after node name
skip_node:
        movw    devnam+1,(r3)+          ; Get device and controller
        movb    devnam+3,(r3)+          ; portion of the device name
        movl    #5,unit_d               ;Format the unit #
        $fao_s  ctrstr=unit_f,outbuf=unit_d,outlen=unit_d,p1=unit
        check
        movc3   unit_d,unit_a,(r3)      ;Append unit (in ascii) to devnam
        movb    #^a/:/,(r3)+            ;Append ':'
        subl3   #dev_a,r3,dev           ;Calculate size of device name
        pushal  file_dev                ;Spill header
        calls   #1,g^lib$put_output
        movl    #256,out_string         ;Allow for a large file name
        pushal  out_string              ;Pass location to return size
                                        ; of file name string
        pushal  out_string              ;Pass file spec descriptor
        pushal  fid                     ;Pass the file id
        pushal  dev                     ;Pass the device name
        calls   #4,g^lib$fid_to_name    ;Convert the fid to file name
        check
        pushal  out_string              ;spill the file name
        calls   #1,g^lib$put_output
;^^^^^^^^^^^^^^^^^^^^^^^^^^^^^^^^^^^^^^^^
;Format the file id
```

Figure 25 contd.

```
;^^^^^^^^^^^^^^^^^^^^^^^^^^^^^^^^^^^^^^^^^
        movl    #80,out_ptr
        $fao_s  ctrstr=fid_fmt,outbuf=out_ptr,outlen=out_ptr,-
                p1=fid,p2=fid+2,p3=fid+4
        check
        pushal  out_ptr
        calls   #1,g^lib$put_output   ;Spill the file id
;^^^^^^^^^^^^^^^^^^^^^^^^^^^^^^^^^^^^^^^^^
;format the count of reads/writes
;^^^^^^^^^^^^^^^^^^^^^^^^^^^^^^^^^^^^^^^^^
        movl    #80,out_ptr
        $fao_s  ctrstr=fmt_rw,outbuf=out_ptr,outlen=out_ptr,p1=reads,-
                p2=writes
        check
        pushal  out_ptr                       ;Spill the count
        calls   #1,g^lib$put_output
        ret                                   ;Sayonara
        .end
```

Figure 26. Output from SHOW_PROC_FILES and SPILL_FILE_INFO.

```
$mac show_proc_files
$mac spill_file_info
$
$link show_proc_files,spill_file_info
$
$sh sys
VAX/VMS V5.3  on node LABDOG   5-JUN-1990  04:58:19.26   Uptime  0 00:22:02
   Pid    Process Name    State  Pri      I/O       CPU        Page flts  Ph.Mem
00000021 SWAPPER          HIB     16        0   0 00:00:01.98          0       0
00000025 ERRFMT           HIB      9       44   0 00:00:00.41         82     116
00000026 OPCOM            HIB     10       37   0 00:00:00.77        207      77
00000027 AUDIT_SERVER     HIB     10       27   0 00:00:01.58       1281     198
00000028 JOB_CONTROL      HIB      9      200   0 00:00:01.60        181     329
00000029 CONFIGURE        HIB      8        9   0 00:00:00.30         93     135
0000002A NETACP           HIB     10       55   0 00:00:01.57        208     348
0000002B EVL              HIB      5       52   0 00:00:01.45        608      35  N
0000002C REMACP           HIB      9       12   0 00:00:00.18         77      44
0000002D SYMBIONT_0001    HIB      4       24   0 00:00:00.90        223     113
0000002E MULTINET_SERVER HIB       6      201   0 00:00:06.19        414      93
0000002F SMTP_SYMBIONT    HIB      4       18   0 00:00:01.25        354      41
00000030 R7_DETACHED_01   LEF      3     8404   0 00:01:04.34       2603     957
00000033 ELLISB           CUR      4      361   0 00:01:06.61       3089     286
$
$set proc/priv=(cmkrnl,readall,world)
$
$r show_proc_files
Pid?28
Process: JOB_CONTROL     with pid 00000028 has the following files open:

File:
DISK$LABSYSRL5:[VMS$COMMON.SYSEXE]JOBCTL.EXE;1
File id: (358,3,0)
Reads on window:          18         Writes on window:          0

File:
DISK$LABSYSRL5:[VMS$COMMON.SYSEXE]JBCSYSQUE.DAT;1
File id: (55,19,0)
Reads on window:          56         Writes on window:         65
$
```

Episode 10

Stuck Inside a Page File with the Dismount Blues Again

Billy's mouth throbbed, as he sat staring at the terminal. Last night, he took his girlfriend to a movie on their second date.

While watching the movie, they shared a box of popcorn. Billy bit into a handful of popcorn and found new meaning in the phrase, kernel mode protection. One of his molars cracked, sending a shot of pain through his head.

His mouth probably would not have been used extensively for kissing that night anyway. Perhaps "Teenage Mutant Ninja Turtles" was not the most romantic selection for a movie date. But, it was a fun movie, as Billy visualized Dennis Cutlery in the role of the evil Shredder and Dr. Albino as the wizened rat, Splinter. He saw himself in the role of Casey Jones. A bat-wielding software engineer seemed a marvelous thought.

Between the pain in his mouth and the fact that his beloved Chicago Bulls had folded in game seven of the playoffs, his week was not going well.

Work was not going much better, as he was going to perform an image backup and restore on a disk that he had determined was rather fragmented. However, when he attempted to dismount the disk, he received the following error messages:

```
%DISM-W-CANNOTDMT, DUA2: cannot be dismounted

%DISM-W-USERFILES, 1 user file open on the volume
```

He issued a $SHOW DEVICE/FILES command on DUA2: and noticed that there was a page file installed from the volume. This was somewhat perturbing as he noticed, using $SHOW MEMORY/FILES, that there were indeed four equal size page files installed from various disks as well as two swap files. They were not particularly large, so disk space did not seem to be a reason for having so many page files installed. Also, because VMS did not pre-reserve swap slots in the swap files under version 5 and they never swapped, there was no need for swap files at all.

He had monitored the paging statistics and noticed that the hard fault rate, or the READ I/O rate, never seemed to exceed three per second and averaged less than one. In addition, the modified page list was rarely being written. So, having so many page files seemed to provide no benefit.

It appeared that Dennis Cutlery had heard that having multiple page files might improve performance and randomly installed page files on multiple disks. He also chose the most heavily accessed disks, so that the small amount of hard paging and modified page list writing I/O would be processed more slowly when it did occur. Dennis Cutlery was living proof that a little knowledge can be dangerous.

Because he was running version 5.3 of VMS, he could deinstall the page file. He got into the SYSGEN utility, issued the following command:

```
DEINSTALL DUA2:[SYSEXE]PAGEFILE.SYS/PAGEFILE
```

and received the message:

```
%SYSGEN-I-FILNOTDINS, file not deinstalled - process(es)
actively using file
```

He issued a $SHOW MEMORY/FILE/FULL command and noticed that, indeed, there was a process usage count greater than 0. He had no clue, however, which processes might be using this page file. Had it been swapping usage, his job would be much easier as processes, which were swapped, showed up in an outswapped state. He would know immediately which processes might be using the swapping space in the page or swap files. There was no similar indicator associated with page file use.

Because his mouth was in pain and his mood was pretty foul already, he decided to skip any preliminary research and go directly to the *Guide*. He opened the grey tome to its familiar clicking and whirring.

He entered, "Hey Guide. What can you tell me about page files and page file use by processes?"

The *Guide* replied, "Prior to version 5.0 of VMS, when a process was created, it was assigned to use the page file with the largest number of free blocks. This technique was an attempt to balance the I/O load and general use across the available page files on the system.

"Load balancing based on the number of free blocks had its drawbacks, however. If several processes were to be created at roughly the same time and all were fairly inactive, they might use little or no actual space in the first page file that they came across. This situation could cause all or most of the processes to be assigned to the same page file.

"If the processes were using the same page file, they could all become active simultaneously. This activity would force more paging I/O to the assigned page file, while the other page files remained relatively inactive. A page file is more likely to become full, as well, if the majority of processes were using the same one.

"To correct the problem, processes in version 5 are assigned to the page file with the largest number of reservable blocks. At installation of the page file, the number of reservable blocks is assigned to be equal to the actual number of blocks in the page file.

"After the process has been assigned to a page file, at process creation, roughly 128 blocks are reserved for the process, initially. After the initial reservation, blocks are reserved based on the number of writable pages that the process has assigned to its virtual address space. The number of blocks reserved is defined in multiples of the special SYSGEN parameter RSRVPAGCNT. If the process has more writable pages than RSRVPAGCNT, additional RSRVPAGCNT blocks will be reserved, until the process has reserved enough blocks to hold all writable pages. The default setting for RSRVPAGCNT is 2048 blocks.

"This reservation of blocks makes the distribution of processes between page files more sensitive to potential use of the blocks. This distribution makes it more likely that with N relatively quiescent processes being created simultaneously, N/2 will be using each page file, where the system supports two page files of equal size.

"The dynamics of page file block reservation occurs, typically, at image activation of programs that have fairly large data areas. To make the balancing characteristics more sensitive to changing demand, VMS reclaims 30 of the reserved blocks on image rundown. Therefore, processes running small programs will be continually returning reservable blocks to correspond with the likelihood that they will not be using all the reserved space."

"What if they run out of reservable blocks?" Billy asked.

"As soon as they have more writable space than reserved blocks, they will reserve an additional RSRVPAGCNT block," answered the *Guide*.

"I have noticed that the number of reservable blocks in a given page file might become negative. Does this indicate a problem?" queried Billy.

"This should be treated as a yellow light type indication," the *Guide* answered, "Proceed with caution. Basically, processes have reserved more space than exists in the page file. If the space is never used, you will have no problem. If all the processes become active at the same time, there is a chance that you will run out of space in the page file and processes will hang in a resource wait modified page writer busy (RWMPB) state.

"It is best to monitor the page file use, when the page file shows negative reservable blocks. If you never use more than 50 percent of the page file, you probably will not experience any problems."

"If a process has reserved space in a page file, is this considered paging use by a process?" Billy inquired.

"Yes," the *Guide* replied. "Reserved space in the page file does imply that the process has paging use."

"So," Billy questioned, "Reserved space in the page file will block deinstallation, even if there is no actual space in use?"

"Yes," the *Guide* responded.

"That seems awfully stupid to me," Billy noted.

"Reserved space blocks the deinstallation because the pages that the process has on the modified page list are marked to be written to the current page file in the page frame number (PFN) database," the *Guide* went on (see Episode 4). "The PFN database has an array, called the backing store (BAK) array. The BAK array describes the current disk location of a page, if the representation of the page is lost from memory. The BAK array is used to update the page table entry of a page that has been taken off the free page list by another process, which is uninterested in the original contents of the page. This updating allows us to locate a disk representation of the page if the original process becomes interested in the page again.

"Pages on the modified page list have not been written to disk yet, and therefore have no disk representation. In this case, the BAK array simply describes to which page file the page is to be written. This page file corresponds to the one in which the process last reserved space.

"If VMS were to allow the deinstallation of a page file, in which one or more processes had reserved but not used space, the deinstallation procedure would have to scan the modified page list, redirecting the pages that were targeted for that page file to one of the remaining page files. Although this procedure could be done, it would be non-trivial.

"What if I were to delete the process or processes with reserved space in the page file that I want to deinstall?" Billy inquired.

"In this case, the modified pages could be freed, in a somewhat trivial fashion, as the process would no longer be interested in the pages, targeted for the page file," the *Guide* replied.

"So, all that I would have to do is determine which processes are using the page file that I want to deinstall and delete them. Does that sound correct?" asked Billy.

"Yes," replied the *Guide*.

"VMS must keep track of which page files are assigned to a process in some data cell, in some data structure. Which one?" requested Billy.

"The process header (PHD) keeps track of which page files have been assigned to a process," the *Guide* responded.

"Hold on," interrupted Billy. "Are you telling me that a process can use more than one page file?"

"Yes," the *Guide* answered. "With the advent of version 5 of VMS, a process can use up to four page files simultaneously. This change facilitates two behaviors that may have minimized the negative effects of multiple page files in pre-version 5 releases of VMS.

"In terms of balancing the I/O load, in pre-version 5 systems, a process could use only one page file. This means that a process would be limited to using one spindle to maintain the I/O workload, if the process was data intensive. Now, the paging I/Os from the page file may be spread over multiple spindles for a single process. This improvement may be minimized by the fact that a hard page fault is a synchronous operation for a single process.

"The load balancing between spindles is also facilitated by the fact that the version 5 modified page writer is multithreaded. It can issue multiple concurrent writes up to a limit defined by the SYSGEN parameter MPW_IOLIMIT. With one large process, there might be balancing of write operations.

"Also, prior to version 5 of VMS, if a process filled a page file, the process would hang in a resource wait state named RWMPB. This hang would occur even though there might be a large amount of free space in another page file.

"In version 5, there is a good chance that the process can move to a page file with more available space, because the check for balancing the reserved space occurs on each reservation. This is not guaranteed, however, because a system, with a fair amount of activity and a large process running, might block the running process from reserving space in an alternate page file. If existing pages are targeted to a page file that is already full, the process will still hang in RWMPB state, until space is freed in the page file by a process running down an image or until a reboot occurs."

"Okay, let's get back to determining which page files are being used by a process," Billy requested.

"The field PHD$B_PGFLCNT in the PHD contains a count of the number of page files that are in use by the process. The field PHD$B_PRCPGFL is a four-byte array that contains the page file numbers of the page files that the process is currently using."

"I have noticed the page file numbers when I issued a $SHOW MEMORY/FILE/FULL command. What are they used for?" Billy inquired.

"When VMS boots, a table is allocated out of non-paged pool," started the *Guide*. "The size of the table is set to be one longword, plus the SYSGEN parameter SWPFILCNT longwords, plus PAGFILCNT longwords. The table is pointed to by the location MMG$GL_PAGSWPVC.

"Initially, all entries in the table point to the null page file control block, which is also pointed to by the location MMG$AR_NULLPFL. When a swap file is installed, a page file control block is allocated from non-paged pool and pointed to by one of the longwords in the table. The swap file entries would have an index in the range of 1 to SWPFILCNT.

"Control blocks for page files are allocated in the same fashion, but the range of indexes are from SWPFILCNT + 1 to SWPFILCNT + PAGFILCNT."

"Do the page file control blocks differentiate types of control blocks as being page files or swap files?" asked Billy.

"No," answered the *Guide*. "The only differentiation is the order in which they appear in the table."

The *Guide* continued, "The page file control blocks describe how to perform I/O operations to the page or swap file. They maintain a pointer to the window control block for the opened page or swap files. They also maintain the same information that you would see in the $SHOW

MEMORY/FILES/FULL display.

"The control blocks maintain a bitmap describing which blocks are in use and which are available. One other field of interest is the minimum free page count, PFL$L_MINFREPAGCNT. This field contains the lower bound on free space in the page file."

"So, this would be a good field to examine, if the page file showed negative reservable space. How can I determine the contents of this field?" Billy asked.

"You could examine the field using SDA, or use AUTOGEN and obtain this information through feedback," answered the *Guide*. In SDA, you would use the command:

```
FORMAT @(@MMG$GL_PAGSWPVC+N*4)
```

where N is the page file number of the page file in which you are interested. The command will format the page file control block. You may locate the PFL$L_MINFREPAGCNT field within the formatted structure."

"If page and swap files use the same control blocks, how are they differentiated functionally?" Billy questioned.

"The only difference functionally is that you can only swap to a swap file, whereas you can page or swap to page files," the *Guide* responded.

"So, an outswap could block deinstallation of a page file as well. How do I know which swap or page file a process has been swapped to?" asked Billy.

"If a process is swapped to a contiguous swap slot, the field PCB$L_WSSWP describes in the high byte the file to which the process was swapped. If the process is not outswapped, the field contains 0.

"If the process is swapped to multiple swap slots, in the same or multiple files, the field PCB$L_WSSWP contains a pointer to a structure called a page file mapping window (PFLMAP). The PFLMAP structure contains quadword pointers starting at the offset PFLMAP$Q_PTR, which describe the starting virtual block number, swap file number, and size of the slot for each contiguous piece of the process working set swapped.

"The list can contain multiple pointers. You know that you have exhausted the list of pointers when the most significant bit is set in the first longword of the pointer. You can distinguish a PFLMAP pointer from a contiguous swap slot by testing the high bit of the PCB$L_WSSWP field. If this bit is set, you have a pointer to a PFLMAP structure. (All system space addresses have the most significant bit of the address set.) The highest page file number would not cause this bit to be set."

"Okay, I think that I have the program worked out. Let me bounce my plan off you," Billy proposed. "I can acquire the scheduling spinlock and chain through the PCB vector table, which is located through the pointer SCH$GL_PCBVEC. If the slot does not point to the null PCB, I know that I have a valid process. How do I know where the null PCB is located?" asked Billy.

"The null PCB is pointed to by the location SCH$AR_NULLPCB," answered the *Guide*.

"Okay, then I can go from the PCB to the PHD, through PCB$L_PHD, and get the process header," Billy continued.

"Hold your horses," the *Guide* interrupted. "Three states could be true here. The process could be memory resident, in which case you could go directly to the PHD and obtain the page file number list. The process' body could be swapped, and the PHD could be resident, in which case you would want to obtain both the page and swap file information. Or the PHD and body could be swapped, in which case you would want the swap file number from the PCB."

"Okay," Billy agreed. "How do I know whether the process body and the PHD are swapped?"

"The bit PCB$V_RES, if clear, defines that the process body is swapped. The bit PCB$V_PHDRES, if clear, defines that the process header has been swapped. These bits are maintained in the field PCB$L_STS of the process control block," replied the *Guide*.

"So," Billy resumed, "I could obtain this information on each process. I will print the page file numbers which are in use. I will only print the swap file number if the process has been swapped contiguously. If the process has been swapped to discontiguous slots, I will print that the process is PFLMAPED. This technique will save me from having to deal with the potentially difficult case of processing the PFLMAP structures. Basically, the saving of data and later presentation will be simpler. I will also have enough information to know where to look later for the PFLMAP structure.

"How do I know whether I have examined all the entries in the PCB vector table?" he asked.

"The largest index is stored in the location SCH$GL_MAXPIX," answered the *Guide*. "You will also want to skip the swapper process. Its

PID is stored in SCH$GL_SWPPID."

"Am I missing anything else?" Billy asked.

"One other thing to keep in mind is that the system has a header, and it may page. You should also list any page file used by the system. Unfortunately, you will be stuck, if the system is using the page file that you are trying to deinstall," answered the *Guide*. "The system header is pointed to by the location MMG$GL_SYSPHD."

"Let me try this out," entered Billy. "Thanks again, Book."

Billy wrote and tested the program. (See Figure 27.) He was reasonably satisfied that it worked (see Figure 28) and packed to head home and then to the dentist to have his molar repaired.

On his way out, Dr. Albino stopped him.

"Billy," Dr. Albino started, "because of budget cuts and the fact that the company is being directed by the whims of Wall Street investors, we are undergoing another reorganization. I was asked to take another position within the company.

"This will personally be my last reorganization within this company. I have accepted an offer from another company.

"I have enjoyed working with you. If you are ever interested in leaving, give me a call and I am sure that I can get you a job.

"When I gave notice, they asked me to leave immediately. Keep in touch."

A shocked Billy replied, "Well, it was nice working for you. By the way, do you know who will be taking your place?"

"I am not privy to that information," answered the Doctor. "But rumor has it that Dennis Cutlery is moving back to his old position."

"Great," thought Billy.

"Well, take care," said Billy. "I may take you up on your offer."

Dr. Albino left, and Billy headed home to drop off his things before heading to the dentist.

When Billy arrived home, he found a note tacked to the door. It read,

Dear Billy,

I was granted a fellowship at the University of California. I had to leave in a hurry. Keep in touch.

Gwen

"Keep in touch," thought Billy painfully. "Dr. Albino is gone. My girlfriend has gone 3,000 miles to Berzerkley to be tempted by the UNIX faction, worshipers of a system with no balls. The Bulls are out of the playoffs. I have to spend Friday night at the dentist, after waiting the better part of a day trying to deinstall a page file. What else could go wrong?"

Billy forgot to run his lotto number program before leaving work. Following the logic that you can't win if you don't play, he stopped at a convenience store on the way to the dentist and picked up a couple of bucks worth of quick-picks.

Later, Billy sat in the dentist's chair, letting the novacaine take its effect. The rest of his body was already numb.

WILL BILLY SURVIVE his bout with the dentist? Where will he go for support, now that the Doctor is out and Gwen has left? How will he operate again under the domain of Dennis Cutlery? Will Billy win the lottery before the Cubs win the pennant? Where will Billy go next into VMS?

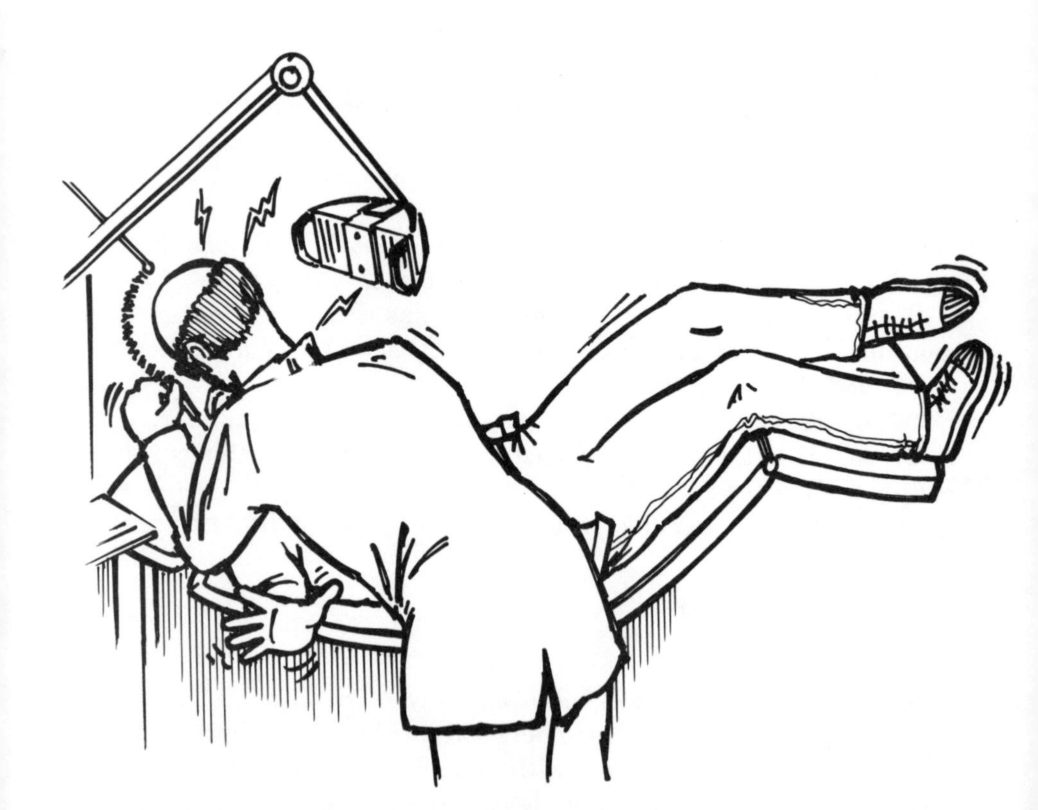

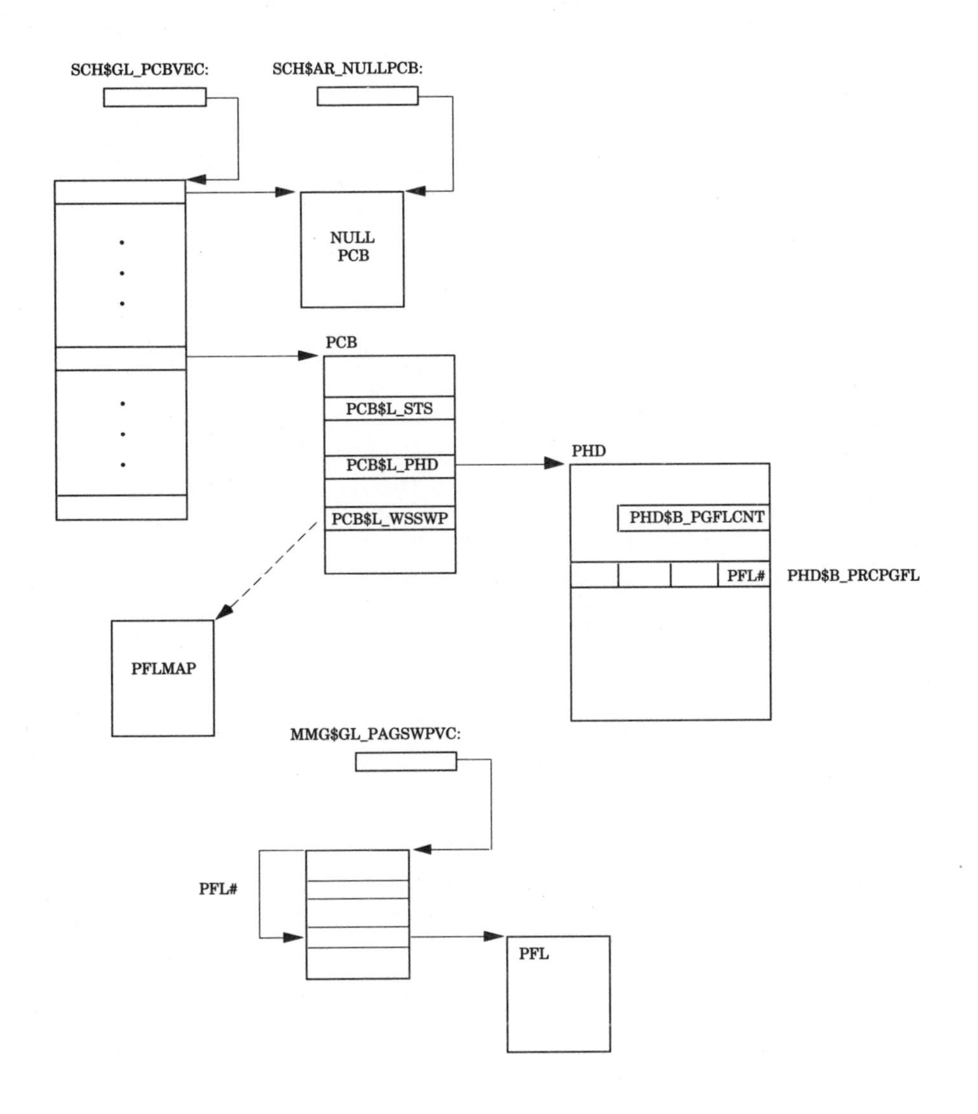

Structures used to determine page file assignments by SHOW_PROC_PAGE.MAR

Figure 27.

```
;**************************************************
;       Program:        show_proc_page
;       Author:         Billy Bitsenbites (Bruce Ellis)
;       Function:       This program will determine and
;                       display the page and swap file
;                       usage by page file number, per
;                       process
;       Date written:   6/2/90
;**************************************************
;Macro to check status
        .macro  check   ?1
        blbs    r0,1
        $exit_s r0
1:
        .endm   check
;Include system definitions
        .library        /sys$library:lib.mlb/
        .link           /sys$system:sys.stb/
        $pcbdef         ;Process control block definitions
        $phddef         ;Process header definitions
;Define offsets into information buffer structure
long_size=4
name_size=16
flags=0
prcpgfl=flags+long_size
pgflcnt=prcpgfl+long_size
wsswp=pgflcnt+long_size
epid=wsswp+long_size
prcnam=epid+long_size
align_skip=prcnam+long_size
buf_size=align_skip+name_size

;address range to lock for code
code_lock:
        .address        code_lock_start
        .address        code_lock_end
;P0 expand region and address range to lock for data
p0_exp:
        .address        512
        .address        512
;Argument list for SYS$CMKRNL
kargs:  .long   2
buffer_loc:
        .long   0
        .address        proc_cnt
proc_cnt:
        .long   0
disp_buffer:
        .long   80                      ;Display buffer
        .address        10$
10$:    .blkb   80
post_size=8
slot_desc:
        .long   post_size
        .address        post
swap_str:
        .long   pre_size+post_size      ;total buffer size
        .address        prefix          ;swap file prefix
prefix: .ascii  /Swap slot: /
        pre_size=.-prefix
post:   .blkb   post_size               ;storage for string or swap file #
none:   .ascii  /None/
none_size=.-none
pfl:    .ascii  /PFLMAPed/
pfl_size=.-pfl
prc_fmt:
        .ascid  $!/Process name: !15AC   Pid: !8XL$
pag_fmt:
        .ascid  /Number of page files: !2UB  Page file #s: !2UB,!2UB,!2UB,!2UB/
sys_pfl:
        .blkl   1
sys_pfl_cnt:
        .blkl   1
```

Figure 27 contd.

```
sys_pfl_hdr:
        .ascid  <10><13>/System header/
page_size=512                           ;Avoid assumptions
;^^^^^^^^^^^^^^^^^^^^^^^^^^^^^^^^^^^^^^^^
;       Main program
;       Flow:
;       Allocate a buffer large enough to hold MAXPROCESSCNT
;               structures
;       Lock code and buffer accessed at ipl>2
;       Get into kernel mode and grab data
;       Spill the info
;^^^^^^^^^^^^^^^^^^^^^^^^^^^^^^^^^^^^^^^^
        .entry  show_proc_page,^m<r2,r3,r5,r6,r7,r8,r9,r10,r11>
        movzwl  g^sgn$gw_maxprcct,r3    ;get MAXPROCESSCNT setting
        mull3   #buf_size,-             ;size the buffer to hold
                r3,r2                   ;info on all possible processes
        divl2   #page_size,r2           ;calculate number of pages for buffer
        incl    r2                      ;allow for truncation
;^^^^^^^^^^^^^^^^
;allocate a buffer
;^^^^^^^^^^^^^^^^
        $expreg_s       inadr=p0_exp,retadr=p0_exp,pagcnt=r2
        check
;^^^^^^^^^^^^^^^^
;Lock code and data accessed at High IPL
;^^^^^^^^^^^^^^^^
        $lkwset_s       inadr=p0_exp    ;lock the buffer
        check
        $lkwset_s       inadr=code_lock ;lock the code
        check
        movl    p0_exp,buffer_loc       ;set data buffer address
;^^^^^^^^^^^^^^^^
;Get the info
;^^^^^^^^^^^^^^^^
        $cmkrnl_s       routin=get_pfl_info,arglst=kargs
        check
        movl    p0_exp,r11              ;Get address of data buffer
        movl    proc_cnt,r6             ;Get process count
display:
        moval   prcnam(r11),r3          ;get address of process name string
;^^^^^^^^^^^^^^^^^^^^^^^^^^^^^^^^
;Format and display Process name and Pid
;^^^^^^^^^^^^^^^^^^^^^^^^^^^^^^^^
        $fao_s  ctrstr=prc_fmt,outbuf=disp_buffer,outlen=disp_buffer,-
                p1=r3 ,p2=epid(r11)
        pushal  disp_buffer             ;Spill the display buffer
        calls   #1,g^lib$put_output
        movl    #80,disp_buffer         ;Reset buffer size
        movl    pgflcnt(r11),r5         ;get count of page files
        movzbl  prcpgfl(r11),r7         ;get 1st page file number
        movzbl  <prcpgfl+1>(r11),r8     ;get 2nd page file number
        movzbl  <prcpgfl+2>(r11),r9     ;get 3rd page file number
        movzbl  <prcpgfl+3>(r11),r10    ;get 4th page file number
;^^^^^^^^^^^^^^^^^^^^^^^^^^^^^^^^
;Format and display page file info
;^^^^^^^^^^^^^^^^^^^^^^^^^^^^^^^^
        $fao_s  ctrstr=pag_fmt,outbuf=disp_buffer,outlen=disp_buffer,-
                p1=r5,p2=r7,p3=r8,p4=r9,p5=r10
        pushal  disp_buffer             ;spill the display buffer
        calls   #1,g^lib$put_output
        movl    #80,disp_buffer         ;reset buffer size
        tstb    wsswp(r11)              ;check swap slot number
        beql    no_swapfile             ;if=0, print none
        bgtr    swap_slot               ;if high bit clear, process slot number
        movc5   #pfl_size,pfl,#^a/ /,-  ;append 'PFLMAPed' on prefix
                #post_size,post
        brb     done_w_swap             ;done with swap file string
no_swapfile:
        movc5   #none_size,none,#^a/ /,- ;append 'None' on prefix
                #post_size,post
        brb     done_w_swap             ;done with swap file string
swap_slot:
        pushal  slot_desc               ;format the slot number
        pushal  wsswp(r11)
```

Figure 27 contd.

```
        calls   #2,g^ots$cvt_l_ti          ;format to decimal
        check
done_w_swap:
        pushal  swap_str                   ;Spill swap file info string
        calls   #1,g^lib$put_output
        addl    #buf_size,r11              ;get next process structure
        sobgtr  r6,br_display              ;Continue until out of processes
        brb     done_display
br_display:
        brw     display
done_display:
        pushal  sys_pfl_hdr                ;Display header for system header
        calls   #1,g^lib$put_output
        movl    #80,disp_buffer            ;Reset buffer size
        movl    sys_pfl_cnt,r5             ;get count of page files
        movzbl  sys_pfl,r7                 ;get 1st page file number
        movzbl  sys_pfl+1,r8               ;get 2nd page file number
        movzbl  sys_pfl+2,r9               ;get 3rd page file number
        movzbl  sys_pfl+3,r10              ;get 4th page file number
;^^^^^^^^^^^^^^^^^^^^^^^^^^^^^^^^^
;Format and display page file info
;^^^^^^^^^^^^^^^^^^^^^^^^^^^^^^^^^
        $fao_s  ctrstr=pag_fmt,outbuf=disp_buffer,outlen=disp_buffer,-
                p1=r5,p2=r7,p3=r8,p4=r9,p5=r10
        pushal  disp_buffer                ;spill the display buffer
        calls   #1,g^lib$put_output

        ret

;^^^^^^^^^^^^^^^^^^^^^^^^^^^^^^^^^^^^^^^^^^^^^^^^^^^^^^^^^^^^
;       Routine:        get_pfl_info
;       function:       Returns page file count, page file #s
;                       swap file #s, process name, and epid for
;                       each process on the system.
;       inputs:         4(ap) -> buffer of per process structures
;                       whose format is described at the beginning of the
;                       program.
;                       8(ap) -> address of longword to receive
;                       the count of actual process on the system
;       outputs:        buffer filled in.
;                       process count returned in @8(ap)
;                       r0 <- ss$_normal
;^^^^^^^^^^^^^^^^^^^^^^^^^^^^^^^^^^^^^^^^^^^^^^^^^^^^^^^^^^^^
buffer=4
prccnt=8
        .entry  get_pfl_info,^m<r6,r7,r8,r9,r10,r11>
        movl    buffer(ap),r6              ;Get address of data buffer
        movl    g^sch$gl_pcbvec,r7         ;get the address of PCB vector table
        movl    g^sch$gl_maxpix,r8         ;get the maximum process index
code_lock_start:
        lock    lockname=SCHED,lockipl=#ipl$_sched  ;lock the scheduling db
pixloop:
        movl    (r7)[r8],r9                ;get the next pcb address
        decl    r8                         ;use next proces index
        cmpl    pcb$l_pid(r9),-            ;If we are at the SWAPPER, we are done
                g^sch$gl_swppid
        bneq    process_process            ;else process the process
        brw     done_with_procs            ;if done, scram
process_process:
        cmpl    r9,g^sch$ar_nullpcb        ;if the slot is empty, skip it
        beql    pixloop                    ;get next pcb
        movl    pcb$l_sts(r9),flags(r6)    ;copy status flags
        bbc     #pcb$v_phdres,-            ;if PHD swapped, skip it
                pcb$l_sts(r9),phd_swapped
        movl    pcb$l_phd(r9),r10          ;get the PHD of this process
        movl    phd$b_prcpgfl(r10),-       ;copy page file array
                prcpgfl(r6)
        movzbl  phd$b_pgflcnt(r10),-       ;copy the count of page files
                pgflcnt(r6)
        bbs     #pcb$v_res,-               ;if Process body res, skip swap file
                pcb$l_sts(r9),body_res
phd_swapped:
        movzbl  <pcb$l_wsswp+3>(r9),-      ;get swap slot info
                wsswp(r6)
```

Figure 27 contd.

```
body_res:
        movl    pcb$l_epid(r9),epid(r6)  ;get process id (extended)
        movq    pcb$t_lname(r9),-        ;copy the process name (1st half)
                prcnam(r6)
        movq    <pcb$t_lname+8>(r9),-    ;copy the process name (2nd half)
                <prcnam+8>(r6)
        incl    @prccnt(ap)              ;bump the count of processes
        addl    #buf_size,r6             ;point to next buffer structure
        brw     pixloop                  ;get next process
done_with_procs:
        unlock  lockname=SCHED,newipl=#0 ;unlock sched db
code_lock_end:
        movl    g^mmg$gl_sysphd,r6       ;locate the system header
        movl    phd$b_prcpgfl(r6),-      ;get the page file array
                sys_pfl
        movzbl  phd$b_pgflcnt(r6),-      ;get count of page files
                sys_pfl_cnt
        movl    #ss$_normal,r0           ;return success, no chance for failure
        ret
        .end    show_proc_page
```

Figure 28. *Output from running SHOW_PROC_PAGE.MAR.*

```
$sh mem/fil/full
              System Memory Resources on 10-JUL-1990 01:35:34.48
DISK$LABSYSRL5:[SYS0.SYSEXE]SWAPFILE.SYS
    Free Blocks                 25360     Reservable Blocks       25360
    Total Size (blocks)         25600     Paging File Number          1
    Swap Usage (processes)          1     Paging Usage (processes)    0
  This file is used exclusively for swapping.
DISK$LABSYSRL5:[SYS0.SYSEXE]PAGEFILE.SYS
    Free Blocks                302009     Reservable Blocks      281604
    Total Size (blocks)        304640     Paging File Number          3
    Swap Usage (processes)          0     Paging Usage (processes)   13
  This file can be used for either paging or swapping.
LABUSER:[USERS.ELLISB]PAGEFILE.SYS;1
    Free Blocks                299992     Reservable Blocks      296185
    Total Size (blocks)        299992     Paging File Number          4
    Swap Usage (processes)          0     Paging Usage (processes)    2
  This file can be used for either paging or swapping.
$sh sys
VAX/VMS V5.3-1  on node LABDOG  10-JUL-1990 01:35:42.56   Uptime  7 16:24:28
  Pid    Process Name    State  Pri      I/O        CPU       Page flts  Ph.Mem
00000021 SWAPPER         HIB     16        0   0 00:00:07.06         0       0
000000C4 ELLISB          HIB      8      672   0 00:00:15.58      2389     302
00000025 ERRFMT          HIB      7     5483   0 00:01:11.52        82     116
00000026 OPCOM           HIB      8      312   0 00:00:03.40       375     137
00000027 AUDIT_SERVER    HIB     10      108   0 00:00:02.74      1345     214
00000028 JOB_CONTROL     HIB      9     1320   0 00:00:05.71       195     355
00000029 CONFIGURE       HIBO     8        -  swapped  out  -              135
0000002A NETACP          HIB     10      291   0 00:02:05.46       210     349
0000002B EVL             HIB      6      127   0 00:00:55.63    159075      46  N
0000002C REMACP          HIB      9      112   0 00:00:00.63        78      45
0000002D SYMBIONT_0001   HIB      4       24   0 00:00:01.03       223     113
0000002E MULTINET_SERVER HIB      6      691   0 00:00:26.72       719     508
0000002F SMTP_SYMBIONT   HIB      4       19   0 00:00:01.31       354      41
00000030 R7_DETACHED_01  HIB      2   101080   0 00:15:32.54     29015     162
000000F1 _RTA1:          CUR      4      148   0 00:00:03.26       576     320
$
$mac show_proc_page
$link show_proc_page
$
$r show_proc_page
%SYSTEM-F-NOPRIV, no privilege for attempted operation
$set proc/priv=cmkrnl
$
$r show_proc_page

Process name: _RTA1:              Pid: 000000F1
Number of page files:  1  Page file #s:  4, 0, 0, 0
Swap slot: None
```

Figure 28 contd.

```
Process name: R7_DETACHED_01     Pid: 00000030
Number of page files:  1  Page file #s:  3, 0, 0, 0
Swap slot: None

Process name: SMTP_SYMBIONT      Pid: 0000002F
Number of page files:  1  Page file #s:  3, 0, 0, 0
Swap slot: None

Process name: MULTINET_SERVER    Pid: 0000002E
Number of page files:  1  Page file #s:  3, 0, 0, 0
Swap slot: None

Process name: SYMBIONT_0001      Pid: 0000002D
Number of page files:  1  Page file #s:  3, 0, 0, 0
Swap slot: None

Process name: REMACP             Pid: 0000002C
Number of page files:  1  Page file #s:  3, 0, 0, 0
Swap slot: None

Process name: EVL                Pid: 0000002B
Number of page files:  1  Page file #s:  3, 0, 0, 0
Swap slot: None

Process name: NETACP             Pid: 0000002A
Number of page files:  1  Page file #s:  3, 0, 0, 0
Swap slot: None

Process name: CONFIGURE          Pid: 00000029
Number of page files:  0  Page file #s:  0, 0, 0, 0
Swap slot:        1

Process name: JOB_CONTROL        Pid: 00000028
Number of page files:  1  Page file #s:  3, 0, 0, 0
Swap slot: None

Process name: AUDIT_SERVER       Pid: 00000027
Number of page files:  1  Page file #s:  3, 0, 0, 0
Swap slot: None

Process name: OPCOM              Pid: 00000026
Number of page files:  1  Page file #s:  3, 0, 0, 0
Swap slot: None

Process name: ERRFMT             Pid: 00000025
Number of page files:  1  Page file #s:  3, 0, 0, 0
Swap slot: None

Process name: ELLISB             Pid: 000000C4
Number of page files:  1  Page file #s:  4, 0, 0, 0
Swap slot: None

System header
Number of page files:  1  Page file #s:  3, 0, 0, 0
$
```

Episode 11

To Be Or Not To Be

Billy came to work Monday morning filled with trepidation over which boss he would be facing. He unpacked his backpack and logged into the system. The new mail count appeared on his screen with a non-zero value. It was the first non-zero value that he had seen in a long time.

Billy was naturally curious to discover who was sending him mail and issued a READ command in the mail utility. The message was listed as being sent from DCUTLERY. The message read:

Billy,

I have moved back into my previous system management position. It appears that you will be reporting to me, again. My predecessor has informed me that you have become fairly adept at system programming. I have a new task for you.

The operators are running a program at night, on behalf of the users. Billing is becoming confused, as the program they are running has several phases, and even with image accounting enabled, only one user is being charged in the accounting file record. I would like you to change the behavior, so that the accounting records are forced out during the run of the program and that they reflect the user for whom the operator is running the program.

D. Cutlery

P.S. It would also be nice if the files that they created for the users were indeed owned by the users.

Billy thought about the mail message. It seemed funny to him that he was now forced to talk to his boss in the same fashion that he talked to the *Guide*, through a keyboard. Perhaps, as you escalate (and de-escalate) in position, it is easier and faster to talk to someone through a computer than it is to use the telephone or walk down the hall.

Billy was not really that interested in the task, as he viewed it as a

potential security hole. He was more interested in writing performance tools than in straightening out the beans for the bean counters.

He was still working for the company, however, and had to meet his responsibilities. He thought about the problem. Basically, he had to change the user name, the account name, write an accounting record, and clear the accounting statistics. He should probably change the user identification code (UIC), the group logical name table, and ideally add any identifiers associated with the user. To do all this, he needed help from the *Guide* to work out the details.

Billy opened the grey tome to the overly familiar clicking and whirring.

"*Guide*, I need your help again," entered Billy.

The *Guide*, always willing to be helpful, politely responded, "With what do you need my help?"

"I need to become someone else," Billy entered.

"Who are you, Zelig?" asked the *Guide*.

"No," Billy typed. "I need to make my process look like it is actually running under someone else's account."

"User name, account name, quotas, priority, privileges, the whole shooting match?" asked the *Guide*.

"No, we can work on the bells and whistles later," Billy replied. "For now, I would like to write an accounting record, clear the current accounting counters, and change the user name, account name, and the UIC. It might also be nice to redirect the group logical name table and add any identifiers associated with the user."

"To approach this step-by-step, you will probably want to obtain the user name. Assuming your users do not know their numeric UIC, you can call the system service, SYS$ASCTOID, to convert the ASCII user name to its numeric identifier equivalent, which corresponds to the user's UIC. If the user name is not represented in the user authorization file, error status will be returned. The routine is documented in the *System Services Reference Manual*.

"You might want to note that, if you are running in kernel mode, this routine should not be called. The routine uses the record management services (RMS) to access the RIGHTSLIST.DAT file, which is an indexed file.

"RMS runs in executive mode. If you called the routine from kernel mode, you would, eventually, attempt to return from the change mode to executive exception, through a return from exception instruction (REI).

This return would attempt to place you in a more privileged access mode, which would be a security breach. To prevent this situation, the REI microcode will trigger a reserved operand exception, when the REI attempts to place the processor in a more privileged access mode."

"How would this be a security breach?" asked Billy.

"You could push a processor status longword (PSL) onto the stack that marked the previous access mode as being kernel mode. Then, you could push a program counter pointing to your code. If the REI microcode allowed you to, which it does not, you could then return to yourself, except that now, the current mode would be kernel," replied the *Guide*.

"Okay," Billy acknowledged. "That will validate the user name and give me the UIC. Now, how do I go about writing the accounting record and clearing the counters?"

"The accounting record can be forced to the job controller process, which writes the accounting record, by issuing a jump to subroutine (JSB) instruction to the routine EXE$PRCPURMSG," responded the *Guide*. "Before writing the accounting record, you might want to place the value SS$_NORMAL into the location CTL$GL_FINALSTS, marking normal completion.

"EXE$PRCPURMSG sends a process purge accounting message to the job controller process via a mailbox message. The routine may be called as a special kernel AST routine. If it is called in this fashion, you may pass the address of the AST control block in R5 for automatic deallocation and dismissal of the AST. The routine requires that R4 point to the PCB of the current process. The routines EXE$PRCDELMSG, EXE$IMGPURMSG, and EXE$IMGDELMSG may also be called to send process deletion, image purge and image rundown messages to the job controller. These routines are listed in the ACCOUNTING module of the source listings.

"The accounting counters are stored in process P1 space and in the process header (PHD). In P1 space, you will have to clear the data cells for the number of volumes mounted (CTL$GL_VOLUMES), the peak working set size (CTL$GL_WPEAK), and the peak virtual address set size (CTL$GL_VIRTPEAK). Also, you will have to copy the current time (SYS$GQ_SYSTIME) into the connect time (CTL$GQ_LOGIN).

"In the PHD, you will have to clear the fields for the charged CPU time (PHD$L_CPUTIM), the total page faults (PHD$L_PAGEFAULTS), the count of hard faults (PHD$L_PGFLTIO), the count of buffered I/Os (PHD$L_BIOCNT), the count of direct I/Os (PHD$L_DIOCNT), and the count of images run down (PHD$L_IMGCNT). The PHD can be located through CTL$GL_PHD."

"That sounds good," Billy entered. "Now, how do I redirect the group logical name table?"

"The group logical name table is defined by the logical name LNM$GROUP," the *Guide* responded. "This logical name is defined in the logical name table LNM$PROCESS_DIRECTORY. The logical name LNM$GROUP is assigned to the LNM$GROUP_XXXXXX equivalence name, where the XXXXXX corresponds to the octal representation of the group number of the UIC of the process. The group number of the UIC is stored in the high word of the UIC.

"You could format the group number into ASCII by using the formatted ASCII output system service SYS$FAO and create the logical name LNM$GROUP, using the create logical name system service, SYS$CRELNM. These services are documented in the *System Services Reference Manual*."

"We are really moving along," noted Billy. "Now how do I change the UIC, user name, and account name?"

"The UIC," answered the *Guide*, "is stored in the field PCB$L_UIC of the process control block. The account and user names are stored in two places, the job information block (JIB) and in P1 space. The fields in the JIB that you would have to change are JIB$T_ACCOUNT and JIB$T_USERNAME. These fields are left-justified space-filled strings. The account name is currently an eight-byte field and the user name is 12 bytes. To minimize the effects of potential future changes in the size of these fields, you can use the constant symbols, JIB$S_ACCOUNT and JIB$S_USERNAME, to define the size of the fields.

"In P1 space, you will have to change the fields CTL$T_ACCOUNT and CTL$T_USERNAME. These fields are also maintained as left-justified space-filled strings."

"I have two questions," Billy interjected. "I know, from the STEALTH program, that I can locate the JIB, using the field PCB$L_JIB, in the PCB." (See Figure 5.) "What base address do I use for the symbols CTL$T_ACCOUNT and CTL$T_USERNAME?"

"You do not use any base address," replied the *Guide*. "These are not offsets but symbols for virtual addresses."

"Shouldn't the symbols have a 'GT' following the dollar sign?" Billy demanded.

"Yes," responded the *Guide*. "Remember, though, that the symbol naming conventions are just that, conventions. You had another question?"

"Why are the account and user names stored in two locations?" Billy asked.

The *Guide* answered, "It sells more memory. Just kidding. Actually, the advantage of storing the information in the JIB is that it is easily accessible for systemwide utilities such as $SHOW USERS.

"The disadvantage of storing them in the JIB is that the JIB is allocated out of non-paged pool. Non-paged pool is readable from executive mode. So, it requires privileged code to read the locations. Because the user and account names are also stored in P1 space, the pages are protected to allow user mode read access and kernel mode write access."

"It looks like I am about done," entered Billy. "What if I wanted to add any user specific identifiers?"

"You could call SYS$FIND_HELD, passing the original UIC, repeatedly, revoking each identifier previously held by calling SYS$REVOKID. You would repeat the calls until SYS$FIND_HELD returns a status value of SS$_NOSUCHID.

"You could do the same activity, using the new UIC. In this case, however, you would want to call SYS$GRANTID to grant the identifiers held by the given UIC," responded the *Guide*.

"I suppose that I could call SYS$GETUAI to get the default directory and reset it, using SYS$SETDDIR," Billy entered into the keyboard, thinking aloud with his fingers. "In fact, I am quite sure that I could get really carried away with the user authorization parameters. But, I was not asked to go that far. A project for another time, perhaps.

"How would I go about allowing a non-privileged or a partially privileged user to run this code? Operators would be running this code. They usually are not running around with change mode to kernel privilege."

"You could use the install utility and install the code, using the /PRIVILEGE qualifier. The qualifier could be used to grant change mode to kernel (CMKRNL) privilege, while the program is being run," answered the *Guide*.

"What is to prevent the user from aborting the program, using a Ctrl-Y and entering the DEBUG command? This would allow the user to patch the virtual address space of the running program. He could then add his own code, which would run with the elevated privilege," pondered Billy.

"An image installed with privileges must be linked with the

/NOTRACE qualifier," replied the *Guide*. "This prevents the traceback handler from being included at the run of the image, which in turn prevents the use of the debugger," the *Guide* responded.

"How do I make sure that only the operators run this program? It could become pretty dangerous if any user could run under any UIC and user name," requested Billy.

The *Guide* replied, "You could check to determine whether the privilege bit PCB$V_OPER is set in the privilege mask, stored in the process control block. The mask is stored in the quadword field PCB$Q_PRIV. To perform the checking, you could use a VMS supplied macro named IFNPRIV or IFPRIV. The macros both use the following format:

```
IFNPRIV    OPER,label
```

"The macro will branch to the label, if the process does not have OPER privilege. The macro assumes that R4 points to the PCB. If R4 does not point to the PCB, you can pass the register which does contain the PCB address in the PCBREG argument to the macro.

"If the process does not have OPER privilege, you could abort, returning the status SS$_NOOPER."

"It looks as if I have all the information that I need," entered Billy. "Thanks."

Billy went off and started to work on the code. He wrote a prototype program to perform the functions required (see Figure 29 and Figure 30), but he ran into a stumbling block. "How do I get this program to run while the operator is still in the other program?" he wondered. He thought about spawning a subprocess to run the program. This would not work easily, because the program had to access P1 space and the spawned subprocess would now be running in a new process context.

He could add the code to the program that the operators were running. That would present a more severe problem, as the entire program would be running with CMKRNL privilege. This was totally unacceptable. He decided to go back to the *Guide*.

"Hey Book," Billy entered, "I have a problem with the program."

"What is that?" asked the *Guide*.

"I want to be able to run the code while I am running another program, but I cannot seem to figure out how to do that easily," Billy responded.

"Why not write a user-written system service?" the *Guide* proposed.

"Because I do not have a clue on how to write one," Billy banged into the keyboard. "Can you help me out?"

"Sure," the *Guide* responded. "To start, let us review the general mechanisms involved in system service dispatching.

"When you call a system service, you really call a vector for the system service. The system service vectors that you call are located in P1 space and are doubly mapped from S0 space. The vector contains a register save mask, corresponding to the VAX calling procedure standard.

"Following the register save mask, there will be a jump (JMP) instruction for system services that execute in the mode of the caller, such as SYS$FAO. For services that will start execution in a more privileged access mode than the caller, there will be a change mode to kernel or executive (CHMK or CHME) instruction. The vector also typically includes a return (RET) instruction following the CHMK or CHME.

"The CHMK and CHME instructions have one operand, which is a value, describing which system service is being called. The instructions, when executed, cause a trap to occur. Processing the trap causes the stack to switch to the stack corresponding to the mode of the instruction. In addition, the processor status longword (PSL) and the program counter (PC) are pushed on the stack, as in any exception, and the code associated with the instruction is placed on the stack.

"Control is transferred to an instruction whose address is located through the system control block (SCB). The instruction is at the beginning of the change mode dispatcher, corresponding with the given mode. The entry points are at EXE$CMODKRNL for kernel mode and EXE$CMODEXEC for executive mode. The symbols are not carried through to the system map.

"The dispatchers have three primary responsibilities; building a psuedo call frame on the stack, checking the argument list for accessibility, and dispatching to the system service corresponding to the change mode code, through a jump instruction.

"The pseudo call frame allows the services to be written following the VAX calling procedure standard. It also allows for a central location to receive control and perform any required post-processing, such as generating a system service exception on error, if the SYS$SETSFM service were previously called. The common exit code also contains the REI instruction required to return to the mode of execution of the caller.

"Checking the argument list for readability allows the services to immediately access the argument list safely. An access violation detected in kernel mode will typically cause a system to crash. Note that the argument list has been checked, but the actual arguments have not been checked for accessibility. This responsibility falls on the system service itself.

"The service is then dispatched to, in the elevated access mode. Prior to performing any actual processing, the system service must check the accessibility of the arguments and must check that the process has any required privileges. Note that no privilege checking is performed prior to entry of the system service.

"One side effect of system service dispatching, for kernel mode services, is that the PCB address is stored in R4, prior to entering the system service.

"After the service has completed its functional processing, it places a success status in register R0 and returns through a RET instruction. This causes the pseudo call frame to be popped off the stack and control to be passed to the common service exit. The common service exit issues an REI instruction, which pops the PC and PSL pair off the stack and returns control to, typically, the RET instruction in the system service vector. The RET in the vector then returns control to the caller.

"The addresses of system service vectors, which were once described in the system map, are now defined in the module SYS$P1_VECTOR, in the object library SYS$SHARE:STARLET.OLB.

"Note that this is a somewhat simplified view of system service dispatching. Keep in mind that some of the system services, such as SYS$FIND_HELD, are implemented through the user-written system service mechanism that you're going to write.

"The key to VMS support for user-written system services is based on issuing the change mode instructions with unused codes. If the code used with the change mode instruction does not match any of the valid VMS system services, we fall through the jump to the system service and perform two additional checks.

"The first check determines whether there is a per process user written system service dispatcher, by checking in the location CTL$GL_USRCHMK for kernel mode services. If this location contains a non-zero value, we issue a JSB instruction to jump to a table, which contains one JSB instruction for every privileged shareable image mapped for the current image.

"The dispatchers are responsible for checking the change mode code, which is stored in R0, and determining whether this code corresponds to a service supported by the dispatcher. If it does not correspond, we return to the table, through a return from subroutine (RSB) instruction, and continue processing dispatchers, until one can handle this code or we exhaust the JSB instructions. If the JSB instructions are exhausted, we will return to an RSB instruction, which will return us to the change mode dispatcher.

"Besides checking the code, the user-written dispatcher in the privileged shareable image is responsible for checking the accessibility of the argument list and dispatching to the user-written system service."

"What is a privileged shareable image?" interrupted Billy.

"For now, assume that there is such a thing as a privileged shareable image, and we will define exactly what it is in a few moments," the *Guide* deferred. "If the user provided dispatcher can handle the code, a user-written system service will be entered.

"The user written system service, like a VMS service, is responsible for checking privileges and checking the accessibility of the actual arguments. Checking accessibility can be performed by using the IFRD, IFNORD, IFWRT, and IFNOWRT macros, documented in the *VMS Device Support Manual*. The macros use the PROBER and PROBEW instructions to check readability or writability of memory locations. They have the following general format:

```
IFNORD  siz,adr,dest,mode
```

"The macro will check 'siz' bytes, starting at 'adr' for readability. If, in the case of IFNORD, the bytes are not readable, in the mode described by the 'mode' argument, which defaults to 0 (or kernel) mode, control will be passed to the location 'dest'.

"If there were no per process dispatchers or if they could not handle the code passed to them, VMS checks for a systemwide user-written system service dispatcher, by examining EXE$GL_USRCHMK. If one exists, control is passed to it through a JSB instruction. It must operate in a similar fashion to the per process dispatcher. However, VMS provides no support for a systemwide dispatcher other than checking the location EXE$GL_USRCHMK.

"To implement a systemwide dispatcher, you would have to copy code into system space and perform all the associated checking in that code.

"If no dispatcher can handle this code, VMS returns an error status, describing this as an invalid system service request.

"The per process dispatcher is implemented by writing a privileged shareable image. A privileged shareable image is similar to a shareable image, with three major exceptions. It must contain a program section marked with the VEC attribute. It must be linked with the /SHARE and /PROTECT qualifiers and must be installed using the same qualifiers.

"If a program is linked against a privileged shareable image, at image activation, the image activator determines whether the image was installed with the /PROTECT qualifier. If it was, the image activator locates the section of the image with the VEC attributes and uses it to construct the table of JSB instructions.

"The section with VEC attributes must be organized with the following longwords, in order:

```
vector type (set to PLV$C_TYP_CMOD)
Reserved
Offset to kernel mode dispatcher or 0
Offset to executive mode dispatcher or 0
Offset to user rundown service or 0
Reserved
Offset to RMS dispatcher or 0
Reserved address check
```

"The privileged shareable image must contain this section. It typically also contains the user-written system service vectors (using negative change mode codes, which are reserved for user services), the dispatcher code, and the user-written system services."

Billy interrupted, "This code is going to be running in kernel or executive mode with potentially no privilege checks. What prevents any user from writing a privileged shareable image and compromising system security?"

The *Guide* responded, "The privileged shareable image must be installed with the /PROTECT and /SHARE qualifiers. To perform this installation requires CMKRNL, PRMGBL, and SYSGBL privileges. After the image is installed, anyone with read access to the image file may use it. So, great caution should be taken to perform proper privilege checking in the user-written system services.

"Would you prefer to write a privileged shareable image or a systemwide system service dispatcher?" queried the *Guide*.

"Which is easier?" Billy countered.

"The privileged shareable image," the *Guide* replied.

"I will choose the privileged shareable image, for now," Billy entered.

"A good place to start with the privileged shareable image would be copying the template, SYS$EXAMPLES:USSDISP.MAR and modifying it. The template provides the code to check the change mode code and argument list. It also supports the dispatching to the services.

"The dispatcher template provides a macro that can be used to build your transfer vectors. The program section with VEC attributes is also contained in the template.

"If you choose to use the template, the only major modifications that you will have to make are invoking a macro named DEFINE_SERVICE, once per service, and writing the system services.

"The DEFINE_SERVICE macro is invoked as follows:

```
DEFINE_SERVICE name,number_of_argumnts,mode
```

"The 'name' argument allows the macro to construct the system service vector. The macro uses a .TRANSFER directive to create a universal symbol for the service name. Universal symbols are not used as references when compiling or linking the privileged shareable image. Any references to the symbols within the context of the privilege shareable image will refer to the original symbol location.

"The universal symbols, however, will be described in the image file that you create. Any references to the universal symbols by programs, linking against the privileged shareable image, will refer to the location of the .TRANSFER directive.

"The .MASK directive is used to copy the register save mask. If the mode argument is passed as KERNEL, a CHMK instruction is generated following the mask. Otherwise, a CHME instruction is generated.

"The codes start at the value defined by the symbols KCODE_BASE and ECODE_BASE. They are set to -1024 in the template. You might want to change them to prevent conflict with change mode codes already in use by other user-written dispatchers. It is the responsibility of the site to prevent conflicting codes.

"The codes are incremented every time the macro is invoked."

"What if conflicting codes do exist?" Billy asked.

The *Guide* answered, "Then the first dispatcher to field the call is the one whose service will be called."

"That stinks," remarked Billy.

"Sorry," the *Guide* responded. "Not my job, man."

"The 'number_of_arguments' argument is used to build a table for checking the argument list in the code generated by the template. The macro also constructs a case table for dispatching to the user-written system services."

"Now, I have the fundamentals down for writing the privileged shareable image. How do I link it and use it?" inquired Billy.

The *Guide* replied, "After you have written and assembled the code, you can link it using the following command:

```
$LINK/PROTECT/SHARE=become_serv/MAP=become_serv/FULL SYS$INPUT/OPT
SYS$SYSTEM:SYS.STB/SELECTIVE
CLUSTER=TRANSFER_VECTOR,,,dev:[]become_serv.obj GSMATCH=LEQUAL,1,1
^Z
$
```

"We already discussed the /PROTECT qualifier, so let's move on. The /SHARE qualifier makes it a shareable image, allowing the sharing of sections which are read-only or marked with the SHR attribute. It also defines the shareable image as being named BECOME_SERV.EXE.

"The /NOSYSSHR qualifier tells the linker that any references should be resolved using STARLET.OLB, the system object library, and not by using any other shareable images. This is required to prevent potential security problems of the shareable image making an outbound call to an unprotected area.

"The sections for the privileged shareable image are marked as being protected. This means that the image activator will create page table entries for the privileged shareable image which are protected in executive mode, preventing the user from using the debugger to modify the routines in the privileged shareable image.

"The enforcement of preventing outbound calls is made by the image activator. This will preclude you from using the call to SYS$FIND_HELD, as this routine is implemented as a part of the shareable image SYS$SHARE:SECURSHR.EXE. The SECURESHR image calls routines in a privileged shareable image SYS$SHARE:SECURSHRP.EXE to perform privileged functions."

"Well, I will drop that piece for now," Billy remarked. "Isn't there a SECURSHR.OLB?"

“No,” the *Guide* answered, “and it would not help you anyway, as you would still have to deal with the calls to SECURSHRP.”

“That stinks, too,” Billy entered.

“You seem to be confusing me with someone who has control over the implementation of VMS,” the *Guide* lectured. “Remember that I am just a book.

“The CLUSTER= option groups the pages to be protected together and may be used to force the transfer vectors to the beginning of the privileged shareable image to allow upgrades to occur without relinking the main program, as in shareable images.

“The GSMATCH option allows for the upgrading of the privileged shareable image without relinking. The 1,1 piece effectively applies a version number to the image. You can think of it as version 1 and release 1. If you made a minor change to the image, you can increase the second number to 2. Because of the LEQUAL option, as long as the release number that the main program linked against is less than or equal to the current release number, the program may be run without relinking, assuming the version number has not been changed. Any changes to the version number will force a relink.

“It is important to specify the GSMATCH option. If you do not, the version and release number come from the time-of-day register and the match criterion is EQUAL. This implies that you will not have an upgradable privileged shareable image.

“As soon as you have linked the privileged shareable image, you will have to assign a logical name, corresponding to the image name, to be the full file specification of the image. This is required since, at image activation time, all that we know in the image file is the name portion of the file specification of the privileged shareable image.

“You could, instead, copy the image to the directory SYS$SHARE:. At image activation, all that the image activator knows about the privileged shareable image is its file name. It translates the file name as a logical name. If the logical name exists, we open the file corresponding to the equivalence name. Otherwise, we look for the image file in the directory SYS$SHARE:. Copying the image to SYS$SHARE: is a more unstructured approach, as you are modifying the contents of a VMS reserved directory.

“After you have performed these steps, you may install the privileged shareable image, using the following command:

```
$INSTALL ADD become_serv/SHARE/PROTECT
```

"Then all that you will have to do is modify the program to call your service. You can link the main program against the privileged shareable image as you would link against any shareable image. A sample link follows:

```
$LINK main,SYS$INPUT/OPT
become_serv/SHARE
^Z
$
```

"Do you have any questions?"

"A few," replied Billy. "First, can I get the linker to automatically locate my privileged shareable image?"

"Yes," responded the *Guide*. "You can create a shareable image object library and insert references to your privileged shareable image. This can be done with the following command:

```
$LIBRARY/SHARE/CREATE BECOME_LIB.OLB BECOME_SERV
```

"The linker will automatically search object and shareable image object libraries, using logical names. The linker will translate LNK$LIBRARY, looking for an object library. If the logical name is defined, the linker will open the library and use it. It will next translate LNK$LIBRARY_1. This procedure will be repeated, with the number being incremented up to 999, until the logical name it is using is not defined.

"So, you would simply define one of the next available logical names in the list to correspond to your shareable image object library.

You could also insert the reference to the privileged shareable image into the library SYS$LIBRARY:IMAGELIB.OLB, which is automatically searched by the linker during a link operation. This file, however, is reserved for VMS, and it is generally considered to be highly unstructured for a user to make entries in this file."

"The other question that I have is based on the fact that," Billy entered, "the code with the call to SYS$ASCTOID must be implemented as an executive mode service. If I incorporate the kernel mode service in the same file, because of the implementation of universal symbol, my call will be a direct call in executive mode to the routine that I want to be running in kernel mode. How can I force the transfer vector to be called, instead of the routine?"

"You could redefine the program section, used in the macro DEFINE_SERVICE, prior to the first invocation of the macro. Then you could define another label and call this new label. You would now be calling the transfer vector, instead of the routine directly.

"If you have no other usage planned for the kernel mode service than local support for the executive mode system service, you could implement it using the SYS$CMKRNL system service. CMKRNL privilege would not be required here as you would be calling the routine from executive mode," offered the *Guide*.

The *Guide* continued, "Since you are now writing an accounting record from within an image, you will have to also clear image accounting fields in P1 space: CTL$GL_IVOLUMES, CTL$GL_IWSPEAK, CTL$GL_ICPUTIM, CTL$GL_IFAULTS, CTL$GL_IFAULTIO, CTL$GL_IBIOCNT, CTL$GL_IDIOCNT, and CTL$GL_IPAGEFL. These fields correspond to the other fields that you cleared, except at image activation time. You will also want to reset the image activation time in the field CTL$GQ_ISTART."

"Okay, that should do it for now. Thanks again, Book," Billy entered. He then went off to code the privileged shareable image. (See Figure 31.) He tested it out (see Figure 32), and it worked fine (see Figure 33).

He then sent a mail message to Dennis Cutlery, stating that the code was written and that he had incorporated it into the program that the operators were running on behalf of the users.

He thought about the new work environment. If Dennis Cutlery were to leave him alone and allow him to code, Billy might be able to coexist with him as a manager.

HOW LONG will Billy be able to coexist with his new/old boss? Should he have left with Dr. Albino? Has Billy given up forever the revenge factor in system programming? Where will Billy delve next into the world of VMS?

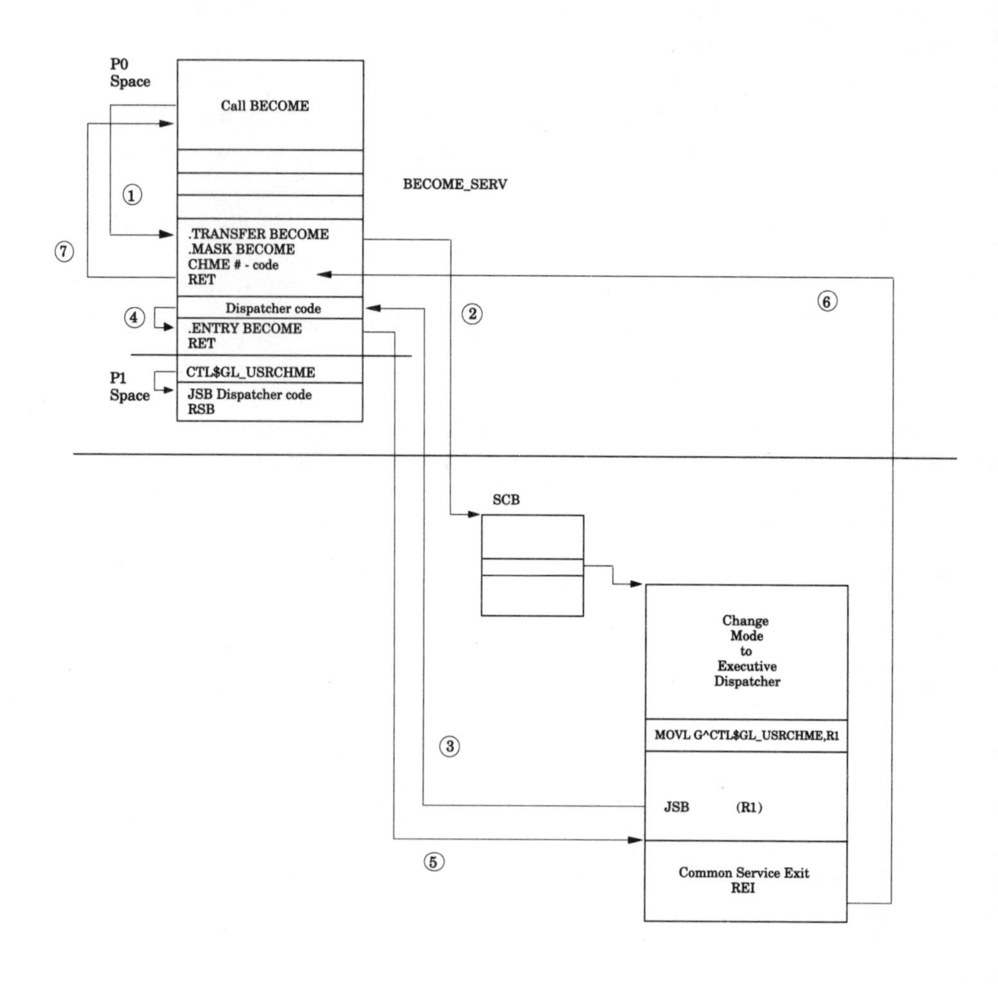

Steps involved in user-written system service dispatching (executive mode case; kernal case similar)

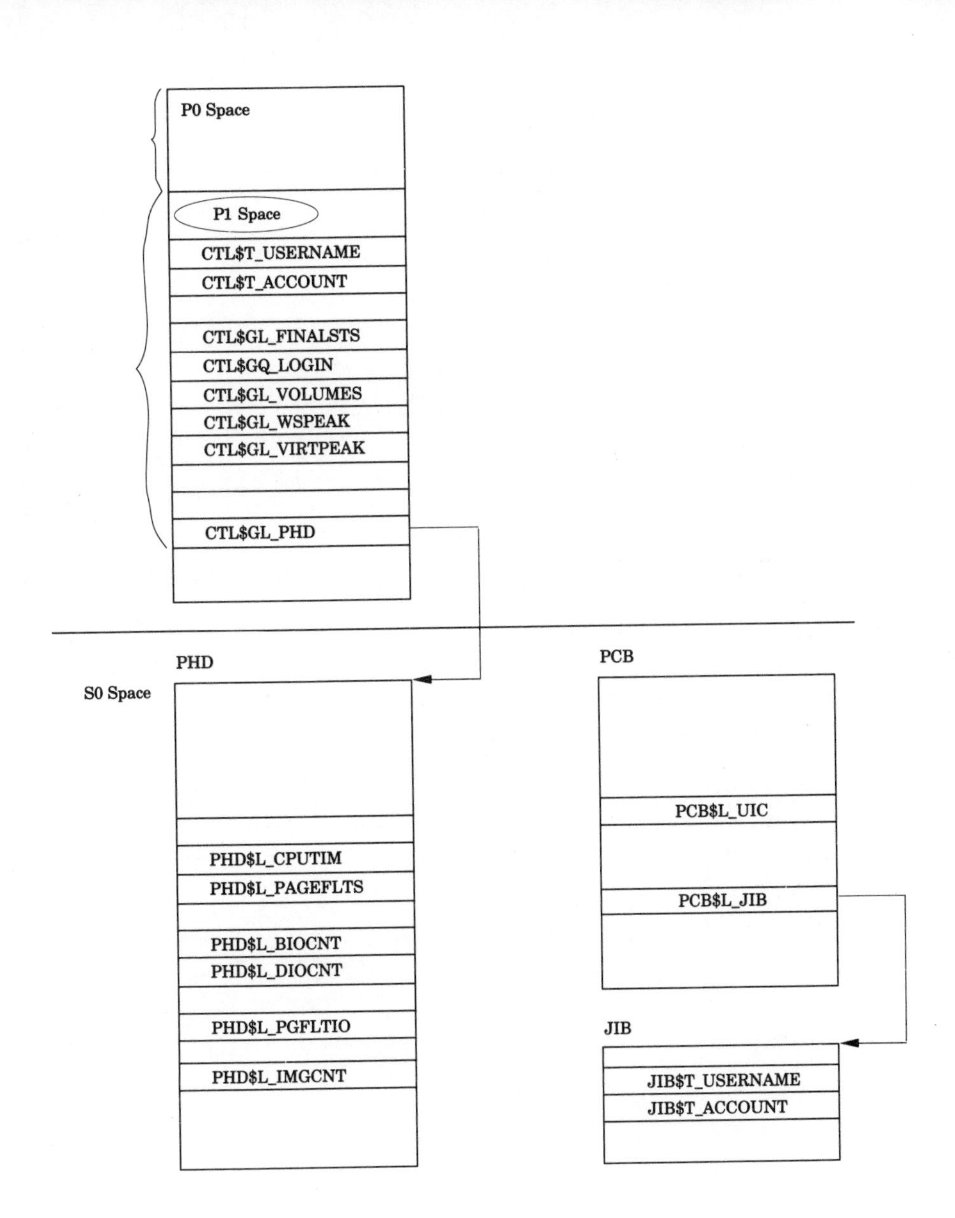

Structures affected by BECOME.MAR and BECOME_SERV.MAR

Figure 29.

```
;^^^^^^^^^^^^^^^^^^^^^^^^^^^^^^^^^^^^^^^^^^^^^^^^^^
;       Program:        BECOME
;       Author:         Billy Bitsenbites (Bruce Ellis)
;       Function:       become pretty much like the
;                       specified user name.
;^^^^^^^^^^^^^^^^^^^^^^^^^^^^^^^^^^^^^^^^^^^^^^^^^^
        .library        /sys$library:lib.mlb/
        .link           /sys$system:sys.stb/
        .macro  check   ?1
        blbs    r0,1
        $exit_s r0
1:
        .endm   check
        $jibdef         ;Job Information Block definitions
        $phddef         ;Process Header definitions
        $pcbdef         ;Process Control Block definitions
        $prvdef         ;Define privilege bits
in_user:
        .long   jib$s_username
        .address        user
user:   .blkb   jib$s_username
in_acct:
        .long   jib$s_account
        .address        account
account:
        .blkb   jib$s_account
user_pmt:
        .ascid  /New username>/
acct_pmt:
        .ascid  /New account>/
        .entry  change_acct,^m<>
        pushal  in_user                 ;Issue a read with
        pushal  user_pmt                ; prompt to obtain the new
        pushal  in_user                 ; User name
        calls   #3,g^lib$get_input
        check
        pushal  in_acct                 ;Issue a read with prompt
        pushal  acct_pmt                ; to obtain the new
        pushal  in_acct                 ; account name
        calls   #3,g^lib$get_input
        check
        $cmexec_s       routin=get_id           ;Convert user name to UIC
        check
        $cmkrnl_s       routin=blast_it         ;Write accounting record
        check                                   ; and become new user
        $cmexec_s       routin=set_rights       ;Acquire new rights
        check
        ret                                     ;Beat it

;^^^^^^^^^^^^^^^^^^^^^^^^^^^^^^^^^^^^^^^^^^^^^^^^^^^^^^^^
;       Routine:        Get_ID
;       Function:       Converts username to UIC
;       Implied inputs: the location in_user is the
;                       address of a descriptor for new user name
;       Implied outputs: UIC contains the binary UIC
;                        corresponding to the new user name.
;^^^^^^^^^^^^^^^^^^^^^^^^^^^^^^^^^^^^^^^^^^^^^^^^^^^^^^^^
;Data area
uic:    .blkl   1
        .long   0

        .entry  get_id,^m<>
        $ASCTOID_S      name=in_user,id=uic
        ret
;^^^^^^^^^^^^^^^^^^^^^^^^^^^^^^^^^^^^^^^^^^^^^^^^^^^^^^^^
;       Routine blast_it
;       Function:       Writes an accounting record,
;                       clears accounting data cells,
;                       changes UIC, user name, account name
;                       the logical LNM$GROUP
;       Implied inputs: in_user -> descriptor for new user name
;                       in_acc -> descriptor for new account name
;                       uic -> new uic
```

Figure 29 contd.

```
;^^^^^^^^^^^^^^^^^^^^^^^^^^^^^^^^^^^^^^^^^^^^^^^^^^^^^^^^

        $LNMDEF                                 ;Logical name defintions
        $PSLDEF                                 ;Processor status longword bit settings
grp_fmt: .ascid  /!60W/
group_desc:
        .long   6
        .address         group_num
group_val:
        .long   16
        .address         group_str
group_str:
        .ascii  /LNM$GROUP_/
group_num:
        .blkb   6
proc_table:
.ascid  /LNM$PROCESS_DIRECTORY/
group:  .ascid  /LNM$GROUP/
log_items:
        .word   16,LNM$_STRING
        .address         group_str
        .long   0,0
err_out_krnl:
        movl    #ss$_nooper,r0                      ;exit if no oper privilege
        ret
        .entry  blast_it,^m<r2>
        ifnpriv OPER,err_out_krnl
        movl    #ss$_normal,g^ctl$gl_finalsts       ;Set success status
        clrl    r5                                  ;not a special kast
        jsb     g^exe$prcpurmsg                     ;write an accounting record
        movl    #ss$_normal,g^ctl$gl_finalsts       ;reset status
        movq    g^exe$gq_systime,g^ctl$gq_login     ;reset connect time
        clrl    g^ctl$gl_volumes                    ;reset count of mounted volumes
        clrl    g^ctl$gl_wspeak                     ;reset peak working set size
        movl    g^ctl$gl_phd,r2                     ;Get P1 window to process header
        clrl    g^ctl$gl_virtpeak                   ;reset peak virtual addr. space
        clrl    phd$l_cputim(r2)                    ;reset cpu time
        clrl    phd$l_pageflts(r2)                  ;reset total faults
        clrl    phd$l_pgfltio(r2)                   ;reset total hard faults
        clrl    phd$l_biocnt(r2)                    ;reset buffered I/O count
        clrl    phd$l_diocnt(r2)                    ;reset direct I/O count
        clrl    phd$l_imgcnt(r2)                    ;reset number/image activations
;^^^^^^^^^^^^^^^^^^^^^^^^
;Format equivalence for LNM$GROUP
;^^^^^^^^^^^^^^^^^^^^^^^^
        $fao_s  ctrstr=grp_fmt,outbuf=group_desc,p1=<<uic+2>>
        blbs    r0,30$
        ret
;^^^^^^^^^^^^^^^^^^^^^^^^
;Reset logical for LNM$GROUP
;^^^^^^^^^^^^^^^^^^^^^^^^
30$:    $crelnm_s       tabnam=proc_table,-
                        lognam=group,-
                        acmode=#psl$c_super,-
                        itmlst=log_items
        blbs    r0,20$
        ret
20$:    movl    pcb$l_uic(r4),old_uic     ;Save old UIC
        movl    uic,pcb$l_uic(r4)         ;Set to new UIC
        movl    pcb$l_jib(r4),r6          ;Get address of Job Info Blk
;^^^^^^^^^^^^^^^^^^^^^^^
;Reset user and account names
;^^^^^^^^^^^^^^^^^^^^^^^
        pushr   #^m<r0,r1,r2,r3,r4,r5>
        movc5   in_user,user,#^a/ /,#jib$s_username,jib$t_username(r6)
        movc5   in_user,user,#^a/ /,#jib$s_username,g^ctl$t_username
        movc5   in_acct,account,#^a/ /,#jib$s_account,jib$t_account(r6)
        movc5   in_acct,account,#^a/ /,#jib$s_account,g^ctl$t_account
        popr    #^m<r0,r1,r2,r3,r4,r5>
        ret
;^^^^^^^^^^^^^^^^^^^^^^^^^^^^^^^^^^^^^^^^^^^^^^^
;       Routine:        SET_RIGHTS
;       Function:       revokes old user specific rights
```

Figure 29 contd.

```
;                         and adds new corresponding to new UIC
;^^^^^^^^^^^^^^^^^^^^^^^^^^^^^^^^^^^^^^^^^^^^^^^^^^^^
old_uic:
        .blkl   1
        .long   0
ident:  .blkl   1
ctx:    .long   0
        .entry  set_rights,^m<>
        clrl    ctx                     ;Clear context for rights db access
next_old:
;^^^^^^^^^^^^^^^^^^^^^^^^^^^^^^^^^^^^^^^^
; Determine all identifiers held by old user name and revoke them
;^^^^^^^^^^^^^^^^^^^^^^^^^^^^^^^^^^^^^^^^
        $find_held_s     holder=old_uic,id=ident,-
                         contxt=ctx
        cmpl    #ss$_nosuchid,r0
        beql    done_old
        blbs    r0,10$
        ret
10$:    $revokid_s       id=ident
        blbs    r0,next_old
        ret
done_old:
;^^^^^^^^^^^^^^^^^^^^^^^^^^^^^^^^^^^^^^^^
; Determine all identifiers held by new user name and grant them
;^^^^^^^^^^^^^^^^^^^^^^^^^^^^^^^^^^^^^^^^
next_new:
        $find_held_s     holder=uic,id=ident,-
                         contxt=ctx
        cmpl    #ss$_nosuchid,r0
        beql    done_new
        blbs    r0,10$
        ret
10$:    $grantid_s       id=ident
        blbs    r0,next_new
        ret
done_new:
        movl    #ss$_normal,r0
        ret                                     ;Beat it
        .end    change_acct
```

Figure 30. Output from running BECOME.

```
$set proc/priv=all
$
$mac become
$link/notrace become
$
$install add sys$login:become/priv=(cmkrnl,cmexec)
$
$set proc/priv=noall
$
$sh proc

 1-JUL-1990 09:31:24.35   User: ELLISB            Process ID:   00000052
                                                   Process name: "ELLISB"

Terminal:            RTA1:  (THORIN::ELLISB)
User Identifier:     [VPRB,ELLISB]
Base priority:       4
Default file spec:   DUB1:[USERS.ELLISB]

Devices allocated:   RTA1:
$sh proc/priv

 1-JUL-1990 09:31:28.21   User: ELLISB            Process ID:   00000052
                                                   Process name: "ELLISB"

Process privileges:

Process rights identifiers:
```

Figure 30 contd.

```
 INTERACTIVE
 REMOTE
 BRUCE
$sh log/group

(LNM$GROUP_000030)
%SHOW-S-NOTRAN, no translation for logical name *
$
$r become
New username>SYSTEM
New account>bits
%SYSTEM-F-NOOPER, operation requires OPER privilege
$set proc/priv=oper
$
$r become
New username>SYSTEM
New account>bits
$
$sh proc

 1-JUL-1990 09:32:19.18   User: SYSTEM          Process ID:   00000052
                                                 Process name: "ELLISB"

Terminal:           RTA1:  (THORIN::ELLISB)
User Identifier:    [SYSTEM]
Base priority:      4
Default file spec:  DUB1:[USERS.ELLISB]

Devices allocated:  RTA1:
$sh proc/priv

 1-JUL-1990 09:32:27.27   User: SYSTEM          Process ID:   00000052
                                                 Process name: "ELLISB"

Process privileges:
 OPER                   operator privilege

Process rights identifiers:
 INTERACTIVE
 REMOTE
$sh log/group

(LNM$GROUP_000001)

  "CLU$CONFIGURE_MBX" = "MBA8:"
$
```

Figure 31.

```
;^^^^^^^^^^^^^^^^^^^^^^^^^^^^^^^^^^^^^^^^^^^^^^^^^^^^^^^^^^^^^^^^^^^^^^^^^^^
;       User written system service dispatcher for the
;       become routines
;
;       Author: Billy Bitsenbites (Bruce Ellis)
;       Function:       These services will receive a user name and
;       account name and write an accounting record, clear
;       the accounting data cells, change the user name, account
;       name, the UIC, redirect LNM$GROUP to the new group #,
;       and add any rights associated with the new UIC.
;       Note:  This code is a modification of the Digital supplied
;       User-written system service dipatcher.  In the interest of
;       brevity and saving a few trees, several comments were removed
;       from the original.  The reader is directed to the file
;       SYS$EXAMPLES:USSDISP.MAR for a completely documented version
;       of the system service dispatcher.
;
;^^^^^^^^^^^^^^^^^^^^^^^^^^^^^^^^^^^^^^^^^^^^^^^^^^^^^^^^^^^^^^^^^^^^^^^^^^^

;

        .LIBRARY "SYS$LIBRARY:LIB.MLB"          ; Macro library for system structure
```

Figure 31 contd.

```
                                                    ;  definitions
;
;       Macro Definitions
;
;
;       DEFINE_SERVICE -   A macro to make the appropriate entries in several
;                          different PSECTs required to define an EXEC or KERNEL
;                          mode service.  These include the transfer vector,
;                          the case table for dispatching, and a table containing
;                          the number of required arguments.
;
;       DEFINE_SERVICE Name,Number_of_Arguments,Mode
;
        .MACRO  DEFINE_SERVICE,NAME,NARG=0,MODE=KERNEL
        .PSECT  $$$TRANSFER_VECTOR,PAGE,NOWRT,EXE,PIC
        .ALIGN  QUAD                        ; Align entry points for speed and style
        .TRANSFER       NAME                ; Define name as universal sym for ent
        .MASK   NAME                        ; Use entry mask defined in main routine
        .IF     IDN MODE,KERNEL
        CHMK    #<KCODE_BASE+KERNEL_COUNTER> ; Change to kernel mode and execute
        RET                                 ; Return
        KERNEL_COUNTER=KERNEL_COUNTER+1     ; Advance counter

        .PSECT  KERNEL_NARG,BYTE,NOWRT,EXE,PIC
        .BYTE   NARG                        ; Define number of required arguments

        .PSECT  USER_KERNEL_DISP1,BYTE,NOWRT,EXE,PIC
        .SIGNED_WORD    2+NAME-KCASE_BASE           ; Make entry in krnl mode CASE
                                                    ; table

        .IFF
        CHME    #<ECODE_BASE+EXEC_COUNTER> ; Change to executive mode
        RET                                 ; Return
        EXEC_COUNTER=EXEC_COUNTER+1         ; Advance counter

        .PSECT  EXEC_NARG,BYTE,NOWRT,EXE,PIC
        .BYTE   NARG                        ; Define number of required arguments

        .PSECT  USER_EXEC_DISP1,BYTE,NOWRT,EXE,PIC
        .SIGNED_WORD    2+NAME-ECASE_BASE           ; Make entry in exec mode CASE
                                                    ; table
        .ENDC                               ;
        .ENDM   DEFINE_SERVICE              ;
;
;       Equated Symbols
;

        $prvdef                             ; privilege symbols
        $pcbdef                             ; process control block offsets
        $jibdef                             ; job information block offsets
        $lnmdef                             ; logical name symbols
        $psldef                             ; Processor status longword symbols
        $PHDDEF                             ; Define process header offsets
        $PLVDEF                             ; Define PLV offsets and values
        $SSDEF                              ; Define system status codes
;
;       Initialize counters for change mode dispatching codes
;
KERNEL_COUNTER=0                            ; Kernel code counter
EXEC_COUNTER=0                              ; Exec code counter

;
;       Own Storage
;
        .PSECT  KERNEL_NARG,BYTE,NOWRT,EXE,PIC
KERNEL_NARG:                                ; Base of byte table containing the
                                            ;  number of required arguments.
        .PSECT  EXEC_NARG,BYTE,NOWRT,EXE,PIC
EXEC_NARG:                                  ; Base of byte table containing the
                                            ;  number of required arguments.
        .PAGE
        .SBTTL  Transfer Vector and Service Definitions
;Note: this a kludge to allow us to be able
;to access the local transfer vector for our
```

Figure 31 contd.

```
;kernel mode service, as internally we would go directly
;to the routine in exec mode.
        .PSECT  $$$TRANSFER_VECTOR,PAGE,NOWRT,EXE,PIC
become_blast_it_vec:
        DEFINE_SERVICE   become_blast_it,4,KERNEL  ; Service to write acc record
                                                    ;  and reset user and acct name
                                                    ;  UIC and LNM$GROUP
        DEFINE_SERVICE   become,2,EXEC  ; Exec mode shell which gets UIC
                                        ; from user name, calls become_blast_it
                                        ; and revokes old idents and adds
                                        ;idents for the new UIC.


;
KCODE_BASE= -1024               ; Base CHMK code value for these services
ECODE_BASE= -1024               ; Base CHME code value for these services
        .PAGE
        .SBTTL  Change Mode Dispatcher Vector Block
;
;
;
        .PSECT  USER_SERVICES,PAGE,VEC,PIC,NOWRT,EXE

        .LONG   PLV$C_TYP_CMOD          ; Set type of vec to change mode disp
        .LONG   0                       ; Reserved
        .LONG   KERNEL_DISPATCH-.       ; Offset to kernel mode dispatcher
        .LONG   EXEC_DISPATCH-.         ; Offset to executive mode dispatcher
        .LONG   0                       ; No user rundown service
        .LONG   0                       ; Reserved.
        .LONG   0                       ; No RMS dispatcher
        .LONG   0                       ; Address check - PIC image
        .PAGE
        .SBTTL  Kernel Mode Dispatcher
;++
; Input Parameters:
;
;       (SP) - Return address if bad change mode value
;
;        R0  - Change mode argument value.
;
;        R4  - Current PCB Address. (Therefore R4 must be specified in all
;                register save masks for kernel routines.)
;
;        AP  - Argument pointer existing when the change
;              mode instruction was executed.
;
;        FP  - Address of minimal call frame to exit
;              the change mode dispatcher and return to
;              the original mode.
;--
        .PSECT  USER_KERNEL_DISP0,BYTE,NOWRT,EXE,PIC
KACCVIO:                                ; Kernel access violation
        MOVZWL  #SS$_ACCVIO,R0          ; Set access violation status code
        RET                             ;  and return
KINSFARG:                               ; Kernel insufficient arguments.
        MOVZWL  #SS$_INSFARG,R0         ; Set status code and
        RET                             ;  return
KNOTME: RSB                             ; RSB to forward request

KERNEL_DISPATCH::                       ; Entry to dispatcher
        MOVAB   W^-KCODE_BASE(R0),R1    ; Normalize dispatch code value
        BLSS    KNOTME                  ; Branch if code value too low
        CMPW    R1,#KERNEL_COUNTER      ; Check high limit
        BGEQU   KNOTME                  ; Branch if out of range
;
; The dispatch code has now been verified as being handled by this dispatcher,
; now the argument list will be probed and the required number of arguments
; verified.
;
        MOVZBL  W^KERNEL_NARG[R1],R1    ; Get required argument count
        MOVAL   @#4[R1],R1              ; Compute byte count including arg count
        IFNORD  R1,(AP),KACCVIO         ; Branch if arglist not readable
        CMPB    (AP),W^<KERNEL_NARG-KCODE_BASE>[R0] ; Check for required number
        BLSSU   KINSFARG                ;  of arguments
```

Figure 31 contd.

```
        MOVL    FP,SP                   ; Reset stack for service routine
        CASEW   R0,-                    ; Case on change mode
                -                       ; argument value
                #KCODE_BASE,-           ; Base value
                #<KERNEL_COUNTER-1>     ; Limit value (number of entries)
KCASE_BASE:                             ; Case table base address for
                                        ; DEFINE_SERVICE
;
;       Case table entries are made in the PSECT USER_KERNEL_DISP1 by
;       invocations of the DEFINE_SERVICE macro.  The three PSECTS,
;       USER_KERNEL_DISP0,1,2 will be abutted in lexical order at link-time.
;
        .PSECT  USER_KERNEL_DISP2,BYTE,NOWRT,EXE,PIC
        BUG_CHECK IVSSRVRQST,FATAL      ; Since the change mode code is valid
                                        ; above, we should never get here
        .PAGE
        .SBTTL  Executive Mode Dispatcher
;++
; Input Parameters:
;
;       (SP) - Return address if bad change mode value
;
;        R0  - Change mode argument value.
;
;        AP  - Argument pointer existing when the change
;              mode instruction was executed.
;
;        FP  - Address of minimal call frame to exit
;              the change mode dispatcher and return to
;              the original mode.
;--
        .PSECT  USER_EXEC_DISP0,BYTE,NOWRT,EXE,PIC
EACCVIO:                                ; Exec access violation
        MOVZWL  #SS$_ACCVIO,R0          ; Set access violation status code
        RET                             ;  and return
EINSFARG:                               ; Exec insufficient arguments.
        MOVZWL  #SS$_INSFARG,R0         ; Set status code and
        RET                             ;  return
ENOTME: RSB                             ; RSB to forward request

EXEC_DISPATCH::                         ; Entry to dispatcher
        MOVAB   W^-ECODE_BASE(R0),R1    ; Normalize dispatch code value
        BLSS    ENOTME                  ; Branch if code value too low
        CMPW    R1,#EXEC_COUNTER        ; Check high limit
        BGEQU   ENOTME                  ; Branch if out of range
;
; The dispatch code has now been verified as being handled by this dispatcher,
; now the argument list will be probed and the required number of arguments
; verified.
;
        MOVZBL  W^EXEC_NARG[R1],R1      ; Get required argument count
        MOVAL   @#4[R1],R1              ; Compute byte count including arg count
        IFNORD  R1,(AP),EACCVIO         ; Branch if arglist not readable
        CMPB    (AP),W^<EXEC_NARG-ECODE_BASE>[R0] ; Check for required number
        BLSSU   EINSFARG                ;  of arguments
        MOVL    FP,SP                   ; Reset stack for service routine
        CASEW   R0,-                    ; Case on change mode
                -                       ; argument value
                #ECODE_BASE,-           ; Base value
                #<EXEC_COUNTER-1>       ; Limit value (number of entries)
ECASE_BASE:                             ; Case table base address for
                                        ; DEFINE_SERVICE
;
;       Case table entries are made in the PSECT USER_EXEC_DISP1 by
;       invocations of the DEFINE_SERVICE macro.  The three PSECTS,
;       USER_EXEC_DISP0,1,2 will be abutted in lexical order at link-time.
;
        .PSECT  USER_EXEC_DISP2,BYTE,NOWRT,EXE,PIC
        BUG_CHECK IVSSRVRQST,FATAL      ; Since the change mode code is valid
                                        ; above, we should never get here
        .SBTTL  Blast username, acct name, UIC, and LNM$GROUP
;++
; Functional Description:
```

Figure 31 contd.

```
;       This routine receives the user name, account name, uic
;       and resets them.  It also resets LNM$GROUP to
;       correspond to the new group and returns the old uic.
;
;
; Input Parameters:
;       4(AP) - Address of descriptor containing user name
;       8(AP) - Address of descriptor containing new account name
;       12(ap) -  Address of uic
;       16(ap) - Address to receive old UIC
;       R4 - Address of current PCB
;
; Output Parameters:
;       16(AP) - gets old UIC.
;       R0 - Completion Status Code
;--
        .psect  zzzkernel_data,byte,wrt,noexe,noshr
grp_fmt:
        .ascid  /!6OW/
group_desc:
        .long   6
        .address        group_num
group_val:
        .long   16
        .address        group_str
group_str:
        .ascii  /LNM$GROUP_/
group_num:
        .blkb   6
proc_table:
        .ascid  /LNM$PROCESS_DIRECTORY/
group:  .ascid  /LNM$GROUP/
log_items:
        .word   16,LNM$_STRING
        .address        group_str
        .long   0,0
        .psect  user_code,byte,nowrt,exe,pic
kr_accvio:
        movl    #ss$_accvio,r0     ;Return access violation
        ret
kr_nopriv:
        movl    #ss$_nooper,r0     ;Return no oper privilege
        ret



        .entry  become_blast_it,^m<r2,r4,r6,r7,r8,r9,r10>
        ifnpriv OPER,kr_nopriv             ;No OPER, no can do
        movl    4(ap),r8                   ;get username descriptor address
        ifnord  #8,(r8),kr_accvio          ;if can't touch desc. error out
        movzwl  (r8),r7                    ;get size of string (user)
        movl    4(r8),r8                   ;get address of string (user)
        ifnord  r7,(r8),kr_accvio          ;if can't touch string error out
        movl    8(ap),r9                   ;get acct name descriptor address
        ifnord  #8,(r9),kr_accvio          ;if can't touch desc. error out
        movzwl  (r9),r10                   ;get size of string (acct)
        movl    4(r9),r9                   ;get address of string (acct)
        ifnord  r10,(r9),kr_accvio         ;if can't touch string error out
        ifnord  #4,@12(ap),kr_accvio       ;if can't read UIC error out
        ifnowrt #4,@16(ap),kr_accvio       ;if can't write return UIC error out
        movl    #ss$_normal,g^ctl$gl_finalsts      ;set succuss for acct rec.
        clrl    r5                         ;not a special kast
        jsb     g^exe$prcpurmsg            ;write acct record
        movl    #ss$_normal,g^ctl$gl_finalsts      ;set new success status
        movq    g^exe$gq_systime,g^ctl$gq_login    ;reset connect time
        clrl    g^ctl$gl_volumes           ;clear number of volumes mounted
        clrl    g^ctl$gl_wspeak            ;clear peak working set size
        movl    g^ctl$gl_phd,r2            ;get P1 window to phd
        clrl    g^ctl$gl_virtpeak          ;clear peak virtual adddress space size
        clrl    phd$l_cputim(r2)           ;clear cputime
        clrl    phd$l_pageflts(r2)         ;clear count of page faults
        clrl    phd$l_pgfltio(r2)          ;clear count of "hard" faults
        clrl    phd$l_biocnt(r2)           ;clear count of buffered I/Os
        clrl    phd$l_diocnt(r2)           ;clear count of direct I/Os
```

Figure 31 contd.

```
        clrl    phd$l_imgcnt(r2)          ;clear count of images run
        movq    g^exe$gq_systime,g^ctl$gq_istart  ;reset imgact time
        clrl    g^ctl$gl_ivolumes         ;clear image volume count
        clrl    g^ctl$gl_iwspeak          ;clear image working set peak
        clrl    g^ctl$gl_icputim          ;clear image cpu time
        clrl    g^ctl$gl_ifaults          ;clear image faults
        clrl    g^ctl$gl_ifaultio         ;clear image hard faults
        clrl    g^ctl$gl_ibiocnt          ;clear image buffered I/Os
        clrl    g^ctl$gl_idiocnt          ;clear image direct I/Os
        clrl    g^ctl$gl_ipagefl          ;clear image page file usage
;Format the group number to octal ascii
        $fao_s  ctrstr=grp_fmt,outbuf=group_desc,p1=<<uic+2>>
        blbs    r0,30$
        ret
;Reset LNM$GROUP to correspond to new group #
30$:    $crelnm_s          tabnam=proc_table,-
                           lognam=group,-
                           acmode=#psl$c_super,-
                           itmlst=log_items
        blbs    r0,20$
        ret
20$:    movl    pcb$l_uic(r4),@16(ap)     ;Return old UIC
        movl    @12(ap),pcb$l_uic(r4)     ;Reset to new UIC
        movl    pcb$l_jib(r4),r6          ;Get the JIB
        pushr   #^m<r0,r1,r2,r3,r4,r5>
;Reset the user name
        movc5   r7,(r8),#^a/ /,#jib$s_username,jib$t_username(r6)
        movc5   r7,(r8),#^a/ /,#jib$s_username,g^ctl$t_username
;Reset the account name
        movc5   r10,(r9),#^a/ /,#jib$s_account,jib$t_account(r6)
        movc5   r10,(r9),#^a/ /,#jib$s_account,g^ctl$t_account
        popr    #^m<r0,r1,r2,r3,r4,r5>
        movl    #ss$_normal,r0            ;success
        ret



        .PAGE
        .SBTTL  become another user
;++
; Functional Description:
;       This routine allows the calling program to operate
;       under the general environment of the passed user
;       name
;
; Input Parameters:
;       04(AP) - address of new user name
;       08(AP) - address of new account name
;
; Output Parameters:
;       R0 - Completion Status code
;       resets username, account name, UIC, LNM$GROUP, identifiers
;       writes accounting record under old username.
;--
        .psect  zzzexec_data,byte,wrt,noexe,noshr

old_uic:
        .blkl   1               ;storage for old uic
        .long   0               ;set valid identifier format
uic:    .blkl   1               ;storage for new UIC
        .long   0               ;set valid identifier format
ident:  .blkl   1
ctx:    .long   0               ;context for Rightslist DataBase access
        .psect  user_code,byte,nowrt,exe,pic
er_accvio:
        movl    #ss$_accvio,r0            ;return access violation
        ret
        .entry  become,^m<r7,r8>
        movl    4(ap),r8                  ;get username descriptor address
        ifnord  #8,(r8),er_accvio         ;if can't touch desc. error out
        movzwl  (r8),r7                   ;get size of string (user)
        movl    4(r8),r8                  ;get address of string (user)
        ifnord  r7,(r8),er_accvio         ;if can't touch string error out
```

Figure 31 contd.

```
        $asctoid_s      name=@4(ap),-   ;convert the username to UIC
                        id=uic
        blbs    r0,10$
        ret
10$:    pushal  old_uic                 ;pass return address for old uic
        pushal  uic                     ;pass uic
        pushl   8(ap)                   ;pass account name
        pushl   4(ap)                   ;pass user name
        calls   #4,g^become_blast_it_vec        ;blast the stuff
        blbs    r0,20$
        ret
20$:
        movl    #ss$_normal,r0
        ret
        .END
```

Figure 32.

```
;*************************************************************
;       Program:  become_test
;       Author:   Billy Bitsenbites (Bruce Ellis)
;       Function: Sample call to the become system service
;
;*************************************************************

        .library        /sys$library:lib.mlb/
        .macro  check   ?1
        blbs    r0,1
        $exit_s r0
1:
        .endm   check
        $jibdef
in_user:
        .long   jib$s_username
        .address        user
user:   .blkb   jib$s_username
in_acct:
        .long   jib$s_account
        .address        account
account:
        .blkb   jib$s_account
user_pmt:
        .ascid  /New username>/
acct_pmt:
        .ascid  /New account>/
        .entry  change_acct,^m<>
        pushal  in_user                         ;Read in a new user name
        pushal  user_pmt
        pushal  in_user
        calls   #3,g^lib$get_input
        check
        pushal  in_acct                         ;Read in a new user name
        pushal  acct_pmt
        pushal  in_acct
        calls   #3,g^lib$get_input
        check
        pushal  in_acct                         ;become that user
        pushal  in_user
        calls   #2,g^become
        ret

        .end    change_acct
```

Figure 33. Output from running BECOME_TEST.

```
$set proc/priv=(cmkrnl,sysgbl,prmgbl,sysnam,sysprv)
$!
$!assemble the source
$macro  become_serv.mar
$!      Command file to link User System Service example.
$!
```

Figure 33 contd.

```
$ LINK/PROTECT/NOSYSSHR/SHARE=become_serv/MAP=become_serv/FULL SYS$INPUT/OPTIONS
!
!       Options file for the link of User System Service example.
!
        SYS$SYSTEM:SYS.STB/SELECTIVE
!
!       Create a separate cluster for the transfer vector.
!
CLUSTER=TRANSTER_VECTOR,,,dubl:[]become_serv.OBJ
!
GSMATCH=LEQUAL,1,1
$define/sys/executive become_serv dubl:[users.ellisb.guide]become_serv.exe
$install add become_serv/share/protect
$library/creat/share become_lib.olb become_serv
$define lnk$library dubl:[users.ellisb.guide]become_lib.olb
$
$!assemble the test program
$mac become_test
$link become_test
$r become_test
New username>SYSTEM
New account>edgar
%SYSTEM-F-NOOPER, operation requires OPER privilege
$set proc/priv=oper
$
$r become_test
New username>SYSTEM
New account>edgar
$
$sh proc/priv

16-JUN-1990 19:57:32.26   User: SYSTEM           Process ID:   00000036
                                                  Process name: "ELLISB"

Process privileges:
 CMKRNL               may change mode to kernel
 SYSNAM               may insert in system logical name table
 SETPRV               may set any privilege bit
 TMPMBX               may create temporary mailbox
 OPER                 operator privilege
 NETMBX               may create network device
 PRMGBL               may create permanent global sections
 SYSGBL               may create system wide global sections
 SYSPRV               may access objects via system protection
Process rights identifiers:
 INTERACTIVE
 REMOTE
 BRUCE
$sh proc/acco

16-JUN-1990 19:57:44.90   User: SYSTEM           Process ID:   00000036
                                                  Process name: "ELLISB"

Accounting information:
 Buffered I/O count:        33  Peak working set size:        411
 Direct I/O count:           4  Peak virtual size:           2210
 Page faults:               57  Mounted volumes:                0
 Images activated:           2
 Elapsed CPU time:      0 00:00:00.68
 Connect time:          0 00:00:19.33
$
$set proc/priv=(noall,oper,readall)
$
$r become_test
New username>ELLISB
New account>bruce
$
$sh proc/priv

16-JUN-1990 19:58:31.62   User: ELLISB           Process ID:   00000036
                                                  Process name: "ELLISB"

Process privileges:
```

Figure 33 contd.

```
 OPER                     operator privilege
 READALL                  may read anything as the owner

Process rights identifiers:
 INTERACTIVE
 REMOTE
 BRUCE
$sh proc/acco

16-JUN-1990 19:58:37.46   User: ELLISB           Process ID:   00000036
                                                  Process name: "ELLISB"

Accounting information:
 Buffered I/O count:          26  Peak working set size:        341
 Direct I/O count:             4  Peak virtual size:           2210
 Page faults:                 74  Mounted volumes:                0
 Images activated:             2
 Elapsed CPU time:      0 00:00:00.64
 Connect time:          0 00:00:17.73
$
```

Episode 12

The Ghost in the Machine

Billy arrived at work, ready to start the day with a bang. He unpacked his backpack and logged into the system. The new mail count was again non-zero.

"I guess I had better take the time to familiarize myself with the mail utility," Billy thought. "This is becoming a regular occurrence."

He entered the mail utility and read the first message, which as expected was from DCUTLERY. The message read:

```
Billy,
    I understand that you were enrolled in a VMS internals course. We will
have to cancel this enrollment because of budget cuts. As we are not a
software company, I see no reason for you to learn this information anyway.
System programming is the responsibility of Digital.
    Besides, you already seem to have a good handle on VMS internals.
    D. Cutlery
```

Billy sat in disbelief. The VMS internals training was required to expose him to the general relationships and structures of VMS. He needed a big picture of the system to be able to address problems more quickly. Dr. Albino understood this.

The knowledge of the internals of any operating system is tantamount to being able to troubleshoot effectively. This is true even if no system programming is performed. Disgruntled, Billy fell into a funk.

"Why not read the rest of the messages?" thought Billy. "What else can go wrong?"

The next message was not addressed specifically to Billy but was a general announcement. Billy figured that it was junk mail, but he read it anyway. It said:

```
To All Staff,
    All nonessential privileges have been revoked, effective immediately.
```

```
This has been done to guarantee that proper security controls remain in
place.
    D. Cutlery
```

Billy passed the stage of disbelief and moved into a mood of hostility. He wanted to strangle Cutlery. He knew that something had to be done before the system became messed up again, like it was when he began working on it. It was obvious from the tone of Cutlery's mail messages that Dennis would simply blame DEC for his own mismanagement.

Billy issued a $SHOW PROCESS/PRIVILEGES command and noticed that he was left with temporary mailbox (TMPMBX), network mailbox (NETMBX), and operator (OPER) privileges. Apparently, Billy's new responsibilities would include mounting tapes for users and performing backups.

He did have an in, however, and it was left there thanks to the BECOME user-written system service that Dennis Cutlery had asked him to write (see Figure 31). With OPER privilege, he could write a program to become another user. If he were to become SYSTEM, the options would become limitless.

Under the SYSTEM user identification code (UIC), he would own the user authorization file (UAF). However, changes to the UAF would be traced by the AUDIT_SERVER. An even simpler solution would be to submit a batch job running the program that he wanted to be executed with privilege. Because the job controller process uses the user name to determine under which account to create the batch job, he would then be running with all privileges.

One of the beauties of this solution would be that the program would be run from an account other than his own. Prior to running the program and in batch mode, he would have to be careful to disable accounting for his process. But the solution seemed elegant. He would nail Cutlery with the stupid code that Dennis had asked Billy to write.

Billy did not want to be malicious; however, he did want his privileges returned. Perhaps he could fool Cutlery into giving back his privileges legitimately. His code would have to become part of the system to guarantee that Cutlery would not simply blame some privileged user for Billy's planned annoyance. He would have to produce the ghost in the machine.

To get this code to run, he would have to check out some details with the *Guide*. He opened the gray tome to the now pleasant clicking and whirring.

"Book, I need your help," Billy entered. "I want to use the system to get even and, for that matter, to get my privileges back."

"Back to revenge, are we?" the *Guide* inquired.

"Well, kind of," Billy replied. "Actually, I just want to have a little fun and get my privileges back. So, I want to fool my boss into thinking that there is a problem with the system that he can't resolve. He, in turn, will ask me for help with the problem. Of course, I will not be able to look into this problem without sufficient privileges."

"Well," the *Guide* lectured, "I want to inform you that hacking, per se, is no longer fashionable."

"I realize that," Billy retorted. "But don't worry. The Feds aren't going to send a book to jail. And if we do it right, no one will know."

Billy was too upset with the current situation to let an old bitty book talk him out of writing this code.

"I already have an idea on how to attack the problem," Billy proposed. "I would simply like you to listen to the proposal and answer a few questions along the way."

"Okay," the *Guide* agreed. "But don't say that I didn't warn you."

"I want my code to be buried inside VMS," Billy started. "I figure that I can allocate a chunk of non-paged pool by issuing a jump to subroutine (JSB) to EXE$ALONONPAGED. Then, I can copy my code into pool using a MOVC3 instruction.

"I need a way to activate the code, though, without having a process on the system. I am kind of stumped here. Do you have any suggestions?"

"You could use the timer code," offered the *Guide*. "VMS has an interrupt service routine called the hardware clock interrupt service routine. This piece of code runs every 10 milliseconds and performs several functions. These functions include re-enabling the clock interrupt, updating the system time if we are in process context charging quantum and CPU time, and checking the timer queue.

"If a process has run to quantum end or a timer has expired, the clock interrupt service routine requests an interrupt at interrupt priority level (IPL) 7. This interrupt activates the software timer code.

"The software timer code raises IPL to 8 and acquires a timer spinlock. It performs quantum end processing, if necessary and rechecks the timer queue.

"The timer queue is located at the address EXE$GL_TQFL. The time of expiration of the first timer queue entry is stored in the location EXE$GQ_1ST_TIME. The timer code compares this value against the system time stored in the location EXE$GQ_SYSTIME. If the timer has expired, it rips its timer queue entry (TQE) off the queue and activates the code associated with the TQE.

"There are three general ways to request a TQE be set. The most common ways are to call the scheduled wake up system service (SYS$SCHDWK) or to request a timer by calling SYS$SETIMR. It will cause an event flag to be set or an asynchronous system trap (AST) to be delivered, by calling SYS$SETIMR. These timers are differentiated in the TQE by checking bits in the field TQE$B_RQTYPE.

"If one of these types of process timers is requested, the timer code will use the TQE to queue an AST to the process. The process is identified by the field TQE$L_PID. If a process-requested AST is associated with the timer, it's address will be stored in the field TQE$L_AST.

"The other type of timer queue entry is for a system subroutine. This may be requested by placing either the value TQE$C_SSNGL or TQE$C_SSREPT into the TQE$B_RQTYPE field. The TQE$C_SSNGL value indentifies that this is a one-time timer request. When this timer expires, VMS will, after releasing all owned spinlocks, issue a JSB to the location stored in the field TQE$L_FPC of the TQE. The code will be entered at IPL 8.

"When the value TQE$C_SSREPT is placed in the field TQE$L_RQTYPE, you are also asking for a system subroutine to be executed when the timer expires. Again, the software timer will issue a JSB to the location stored in the field TQE$L_FPC. The difference is that this timer will be repeated, by taking the value in the field TQE$Q_DELTA and adding it to the contents of the expiration time in the field TQE$Q_TIME. The TQE will then be requeued based on the newly calculated expiration time.

"Also, note that the field TQE$L_FPC overlays the field TQE$L_PID, as a TQE describes either a process requested timer or a system subroutine.

"VMS uses a system subroutine, triggered by a TQE, to perform functions that must be checked on a regular basis. The routine is named EXE$TIMEOUT, and it runs once per second. This routine checks to determine whether the swapper or ERRFMT processes need to be awakened and wakes them if necessary, checks for device and controller timeouts, checks for deadlocks with the lock management services, updates the up time in the field EXE$GL_ABSTIM, declares resources available, and guarantees that CPU starved processes eventually get the

CPU using the PIXSCAN SYSGEN parameter."

"So, I could have my code activated on a regular basis, using this system subroutine mechanism," Billy entered, "and there would be no process context associated with the code whatsoever?"

"Yes," confirmed the *Guide*.

"I like that," Billy noted. "Do I have to do all the work, allocating the TQE and inserting it into the timer queue?"

"No," the *Guide* replied. "VMS can help you out on three points. The routine EXE$ALLOCTQE may be used to allocate non-paged pool of the form of a timer queue entry. There are no inputs to the routine, and the outputs have R0 containing status, R1 containing the size of the pool, and R2 containing the address of the pool allocated.

"After you have allocated the TQE and filled in the appropriate fields, you can have it inserted into the timer queue by issuing a JSB to the routine EXE$INSTIMQ. The inputs to this routine are that R5 should contain the address of the initialized TQE, and registers R0 and R1 should contain the time of expiration of the TQE. The routine performs any required synchronization."

"I assume that the time is defined in 10-millisecond intervals, as this is the granularity of the hardware clock," Billy speculated.

"No," the *Guide* informed, "the units are defined in 100-nanosecond intervals."

"What about the absolute time of expiration?" Billy asked.

"It is defined as the number of 100-nanosecond intervals since November 17, 1858," the *Guide* replied. "This corresponds to Smithsonian base date zero."

"Why is that date used?" Billy asked.

"The *Guide* once asked someone from the Smithsonian the importance of the date," the *Guide* responded. When he did not know this bit of esoterica, the following entry was made into the *Guide*: *Who cares?*"

"Assuming that I would want to stop this timer at some point, will VMS support the removal of a TQE?" Billy asked.

"Yes," the *Guide* answered. "To have a TQE removed, the routine EXE$RMVTIMQ may be called through a JSB instruction.

"So, I could save the address of the TQE in the site specific longword, EXE$GL_SITESPEC. Then, if I wanted to shut down the code, I could JSB to EXE$RMVTIMQ, use the TQE$L_FPC field to locate the code in pool, deallocate the pool, and finally deallocate the TQE," Billy proposed.

"Yes," the *Guide* concurred.

"Now," Billy continued, "I will have to determine whether Cutlery has a process on the system. To do this, I could walk through each entry in the process control block (PCB) vector table, looking for his PCB.

"I can locate the PCB vector table through the location SCH$GL_PCBVEC. The greatest index may be obtained by getting the contents of the location SCH$GL_MAXPIX. Then, I would simply loop, processing PCBs, until I found his PCB or ran out of entries in the table.

"Where is the process name stored?"

The *Guide* responded, "The field PCB$T_LNAME contains the process name of the process, stored as an ASCII counted string."

"After I find his PCB, I can blast a message to his terminal. I could assign a channel to his terminal and issue a $QIO to send the message," Billy proposed.

The *Guide* interrupted, "No, you cannot."

"Why not?" questioned Billy.

"Because issuing a $QIO requires process context," the *Guide* informed. "Remember that the code that you are executing is not running in any process context."

"Well, how can I get a message out to his terminal?" Billy asked.

"You have two options," the *Guide* offered. "You could scan the I/O database, looking for the unit control block (UCB) address that corresponds to his terminal. After you have the UCB address, you could JSB to the subroutine IOC$BROADCAST, which allows you to broadcast a terminal I/O with no process context required on the caller's behalf.

"The other option is to queue an AST to his process, because you already have the address of the PCB. In the AST routine, you can assign a channel to his terminal and perform the $QIO, as you are now running in his process context."

"I like the second technique," Billy noted. "The beauty of that technique is that, in effect, he would be sending the message to himself and not even realize that he is doing it. I could obtain the terminal name from the field PCB$T_TERMINAL. I remember that from our first discussions."

"Yes, you could," the *Guide* added. "However, there is a chance that the actual terminal name size is larger than the seven-character size that the terminal name field will hold. If you are using a terminal server or virtual terminals, the unit number could grow to a five-digit length. You might be better off simply checking whether a terminal is associated with the process by using the field. Then, you can use the SYS$OUTPUT logical name on the channel assignment.

"Be careful when using string descriptors in data stored in non-paged pool. The address of the string locations must be computed at run time for the descriptors to point to the correct place. The .ASCID directive is only position-independent in programs and shareable images. Your code in non-paged pool must be written in a position-independent fashion, independent of any support from the image activator."

"I will keep that in mind," Billy responded, "but our systems never stay up long enough for the terminal unit number to become too large.

"Before queueing the AST, I should check to make sure that there is not a delete pending on the process and that the process is not suspended. I can do this by checking to determine whether the bits PCB$V_DELPEN and PCB$V_SUSPEN are set in the field PCB$L_STS. If the process is soft suspended, it will not block our AST from being delivered, so I will not have to check for this situation.

"So, should I use a special kernel AST?"

"No," the *Guide* replied. "If you issued a $QIO from a special kernel AST routine, the I/O you initiated would never complete."

"Why not?" asked Billy.

"Because I/O completes through a special kernel AST. If you are already in one, you would be blocking the delivery of the completion AST," the *Guide* answered.

"I can use a normal kernel mode AST then," Billy entered. "So, now all that I would need to do is allocate the pool for the AST control block, fill in his process ID and queue the AST. I could queue the AST by placing a priority boost class in R2, putting the address of the AST control block in R5, and issuing a JSB to SCH$QAST.

"I will also need to acquire the scheduling spinlock in the code that accesses the PCB vector table. Am I missing anything else?"

"No, it does not appear that you are missing anything, other than morals," concurred the *Guide*.

"Cut me some slack, Book.

"I can input a message to display on his terminal every 10 seconds. I will use:

```
FATAL MACHINE CHECK, Please logout and use another terminal.
```

"That should keep him going for awhile," Billy smirked, "Well, thanks again, Book."

Billy then entered the code. (See Figures 34 and 35.) He created a command procedure that would run the program ZAPPER. He wrote a program to call the BECOME user-written system service he had written earlier (see Figure 31). He submitted the command procedure.

Using the $SHOW SYSTEM/BATCH command, he watched until the command procedure had completed its execution. He issued a $DELETE/ERASE command, deleting the command procedure, its log file and the original program. He then logged off.

Billy wandered through the halls, occasionally passing by Dennis Cutlery's office. He noticed Cutlery moving from terminal to terminal and had to keep himself from laughing out loud.

Cutlery came out of his office and asked an operator for the telephone number for Digital Support in Colorado Springs. Later, Billy walked by his office and overheard Cutlery saying:

"What do you mean, you have never heard of this problem before? Why is it that I am always the first person who seems to experience these problems? Who is your boss, anyway?"

Billy felt sorry for the poor guy on the other end of the phone. He went back to his office. He realized that he would have to work up a credible solution, should Cutlery actually ask for his help. He opened the *Guide*.

"What's up, Doc?" the *Guide* asked.

"Are there any SYSGEN parameters that are no longer used?" Billy entered.

"Yes," the *Guide* responded. "The first that comes to mind is KFILSTCNT, which used to limit the number of known file descriptors. It no longer has any meaning. Why?"

"Just call it no risc insurance. Thanks," entered Billy.

Billy avoided logging into the system, for fear that the blame might be arbitrarily laid on his shoulders, should he be found at the sight of the crime. He wondered how he would explain that only terminals Dennis Cutlery was logged into were receiving these messages.

Billy heard the door open and turned to see who was entering without knocking. Dennis Cutlery stood before him.

"Billy, what have you been doing?" Cutlery demanded. "I've been sending you mail for the last 15 minutes."

"Well, I ..." Billy started.

"Forget it," Cutlery interrupted. "I'm having a problem with the system, and I'd like you to look into it. It appears to be some kind of machine check from the terminal driver."

"Well, I'll need some privileges to investigate the situation," Billy noted.

"What kind of privileges?" Cutlery inquired.

"Well, at a minimum, change mode to kernel," Billy replied.

"You can have it for now," Cutlery responded.

"Okay, I'll look into it," Billy offered. "Give me a call after the privilege has been enabled."

Billy breathed a sigh of relief, realizing that Cutlery was probably too embarrassed to ask whether other users were having the same problems.

Billy logged in and fooled around in the system dump analyzer, trying to look busy. He then got into SYSGEN and changed the parameter KFILSTCNT to 42. He next issued a WRITE CURRENT command to change the parameter on reboot.

He walked down the hall to Dennis Cutlery's office and said,

"Dennis, I had to change the parameter KFILSTCNT to a higher value. It was causing a pool conflict with the terminal driver, which was in turn causing storms on the Ethernet.

"If you reboot the system, the change will take effect and the problem should go away."

Billy hoped that this contrived solution would sound plausible.

"Thanks, I'll give it a try," Cutlery responded and left.

Billy walked back to his desk and pondered the situation. He had originally taken the privileges that he needed to do his job. Then, he received them from Dr. Albino by earning his boss' respect. Now, he was deceiving Dennis Cutlery into giving his privileges back. He wondered whether it was really worth it.

He also struggled over the question of whether you could know too much about a given subject. He had learned a lot about VMS since receiving the *Guide*. He still had a great deal more to learn. However, he would be continually fighting to keep the system in shape. As he made improvements, new fourth-generation languages and database products would arrive to sop up any spare resource. He was tired of playing the role of a software Sisyphus.

He logged into the system and entered the mail utility. He sent the following short message to the user DCUTLERY:

```
Dennis,
I quit.
Sincerely,
Billy Bitsenbites
```

Billy grabbed a box and cleaned out his desk. He thought about where he would go and what he would do. After he packed the box, he sat back and perused the newspaper.

He looked at the sports section, checking out the Cubs' box score.

"If kids like Boskie and Harkey come along, the Cubs might have a chance. Next year," he thought.

He turned to the lottery section and pulled the crumpled lottery ticket from his pocket. Checking the numbers, he matched 9, 10, 14, 18, 26, and 42. Gradually, it dawned on him that he matched all six numbers. He won the lotto jackpot of about $2 million in the Mass Millions. Even after Taxachusetts got its share, he'd have a decent chunk of change.

Billy made up his mind. He was finished working with computers. He would make his mark on society by selling Frosty Malts at Wrigley Field. That way, when the Cubs did win the World Series, he would be there.

The Datsun B210 could not hold much, so he limited the things that he took from work to Cubs pennants from the 1984 and 1989 division championship seasons, a coffee mug from DECUS, a picture of Gwen, and a bag of peanuts autographed by Douglas Adams.

The rest of the stuff, he jammed into trash cans throughout the office. He held *The Hitchhiker's Guide to VMS* in his hands and looked at it. He opened the gray tome and listened to a final clicking and whirring.

He entered, "Well, Book, so long and thanks for all the fiche."

"Sayonara," the *Guide* responded.

Billy looked at the back of the book and saw a label stating, "Made in Japan." He shook his head and gently placed the book in the trash.

He ran into Dennis Cutlery on his way out and Cutlery said, "You know that you will have to leave immediately because of security reasons and that you will not be allowed to remove any technical documentation?"

"No problem," Billy acknowledged.

"Well, I am sorry that you made this decision," Cutlery said, "We would have made a great combination."

"Yeah, like gasoline and a match," thought Billy.

"It's been a slice," said Billy. "Sayonara."

BILLY CASHED IN his lottery ticket and was on his way to Chicago, when a young programmer leaned over Billy's trash can and pulled out a fairly large, somewhat heavy gray book. He opened the gray tome to an unfamiliar clicking and whirring....

THE END

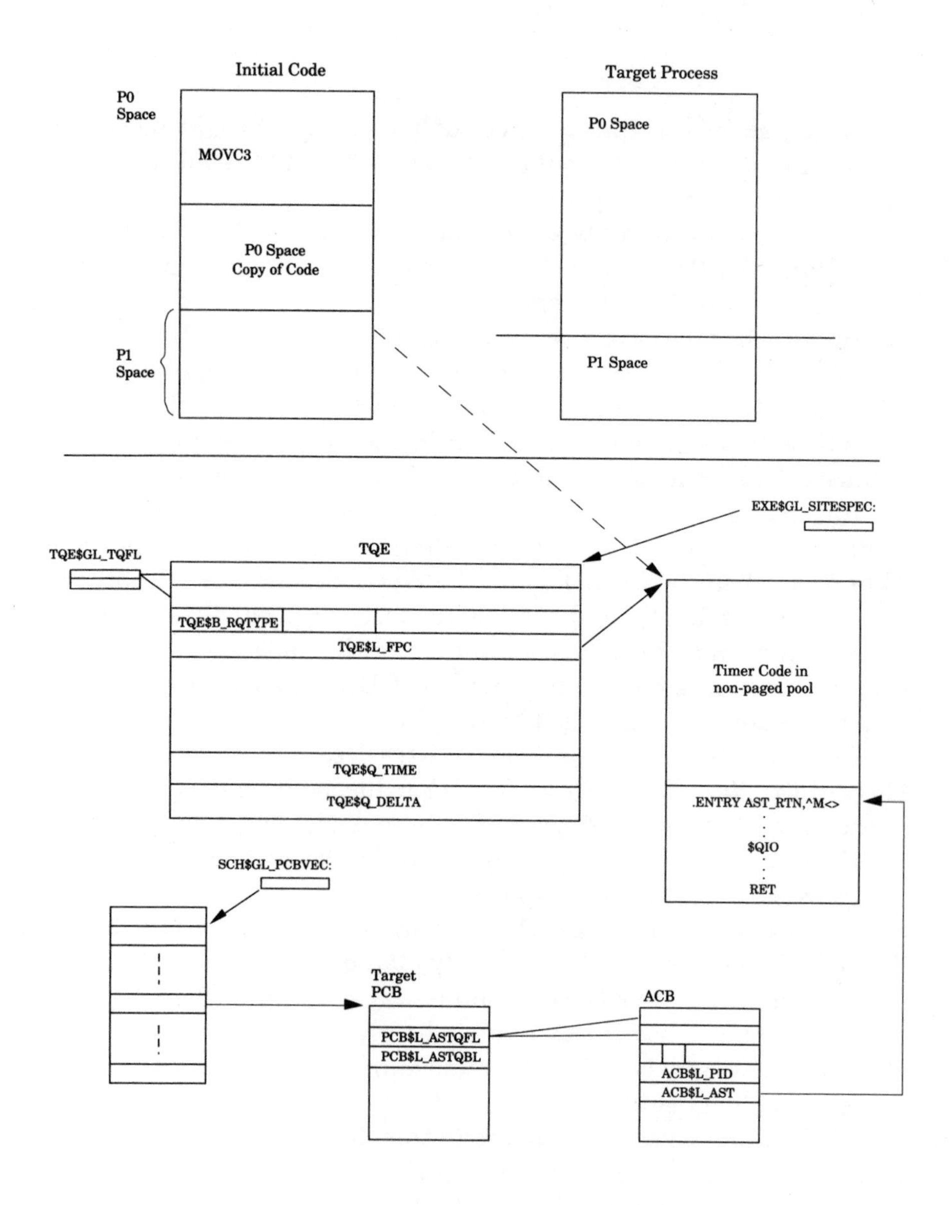

Structures used in ZAPPER.MAR

Figure 34.

```
;***************************************************************
;*      Program ZAPPER                                        **
;*                                                            **
;*      Function:       Prompts for a process name and a      **
;*                      string to be displayed at the         **
;*                      process' terminal at 10 second        **
;*                      intervals                             **
;*                                                            **
;*      Author:  Billy Bitsenbites (Bruce Ellis)              **
;*                                                            **
;*      Date written:  1/10/83                                **
;*                                                            **
;*      Revisions:  Many updates                              **
;***************************************************************
        .title  zapper
        .subtitle       User mode data for zapper
;***************************************************************
;*      System data structure definitions                     **
;***************************************************************
        .library        /sys$library:lib.mlb/
        .link           /sys$system:sys.stb/
        $ipldef
        $acbdef
        $dyndef
        $tqedef
        $pridef
        $pcbdef
;***************************************************************
;*      Data area                                             **
;***************************************************************
len:    .long   0                               ;Length of process name
prompt_name:                                    ;Prompt for process name
        .ascid  /Enter process name> /
name_in:        .long   15                      ;Descriptor used to store
        .address        name+8                  ;the process name in code area
                                                ;to be loaded into pool
str_in: .long   132                             ;descriptor for string to
        .address        msg_loc                 ;be displayed
str_prom:                                       ;prompt for input string
        .ascid  /Enter string> /
str_len:                                        ;storage for string length
        .blkl   1
zapper_begin:                                   ;Beginning of code to lock
header=12                                       ;overhead for pool header
size=8                                          ;pool size offset
type=10                                         ;pool type offset
dyn_c_ellis_type=110                            ;type of structure
delta:  .long   10*1000*1000*10                 ;10 seconds delta time
        .long   0
lock_list:                                      ;Code area to be locked down
        .address        zapper_begin            ;to prevent faults at ipl >2
        .address        zapper_end
        .subtitle       User mode zapper code
;***************************************************************
;*      Code that runs in user access mode                    **
;***************************************************************
        .entry  init_zapper,^m<>
        $lkwset_s       inadr=lock_list         ;Lock most all of program in WS
        blbs    r0,3$                           ;
        $exit_s r0                              ;if error sayonara
3$:     pushal  len                             ;Actual length of process name
        pushal  prompt_name                     ;Prompt string
        pushal  name_in                         ;Descriptor for storing proc. name
        calls   #3,g^lib$get_input              ;Go get it
        blbc    r0,3$                           ;It too long re-prompt
        movl    len,name                        ;Update length field in pool desc.
4$:     pushal  str_len                         ;Actual length of message string
        pushal  str_prom                        ;Prompt for string to be displayed
        pushal  str_in                          ;descriptor for string
        calls   #3,g^lib$get_input              ;Go get it
        blbc    r0,4$                           ;If too long re-prompt
        movl    str_len,message                 ;Update actual length of string
        $cmkrnl_s       routin=kernel_init_zapper ;Go blast him
```

Figure 34 contd.

```
        ret
        .subtitle       kernel mode initialization code

;***********************************************************
;       Kernel mode initialization code
;***********************************************************
        .entry  kernel_init_zapper,^m<r2,r3,r4,r5>
        movl    #zapper_code_len+header,r1      ;set up size of pool
        setipl  #ipl$_astdel                    ;Block process deletion
        jsb     g^exe$alononpaged               ;allocate enough pool for code
        blbs    r0,10$                          ;Not enough pool, so let's scram
        ret
10$:    movw    r1,size(r2)                     ;fill in size
        movb    #dyn_c_ellis_type,type(r2)      ;fill in type
        addl2   #header,r2                      ;point to where code will start
        pushl   r2                              ;save address of 12 bytes into pool
        movc3   #zapper_code_len,zapper_code,(r2)  ;move code to pool
        jsb     g^exe$alloctqe                  ;grab a tqe
        blbs    r0,20$                          ;If we have it, fill it in
        popl    r0                              ;else move pool+12 to r0
        subl2   #header,r0                      ;back to beginning of pool
        jsb     g^exe$deanonpaged               ;get rid of it, since we can't
                                                ; get a tqe
        setipl  #0                              ;drop ipl to normal
        movl    #ss$_insfmem,r0                 ;return error
        ret                                     ;scram
20$:    movb    #tqe$c_ssrept,-                 ;set up a system subroutine
                tqe$b_rqtype(r2)                ; with a repeat time request
        movq    delta,tqe$q_delta(r2)           ;set to go off every 10 sec
        movl    (sp)+,tqe$l_fpc(r2)             ;fill in the start of the code
        movl    r2,g^exe$gl_sitespec            ;save address for later deallocation
        movq    g^exe$gq_systime,r0             ;get the current time
        addl    delta,r0                        ;add ten seconds to expiration
        adwc    delta+4,r1                      ; bump high longword if necessary
        movl    r2,r5                           ;r5 -> tqe
        jsb     g^exe$instimq                   ;insert in timer queue
        movl    #ss$_normal,r0                  ;everything is set up, so let's
        setipl  #0                              ;scram and have fun
        ret

        .subtitle       kernel mode system subroutine code

;***********************************************************
;*      kernel mode system subroutine code                **
;***********************************************************
zapper_code:
zapper:
        tstl    name+4                          ;Have we initialized addresses so that
        bneq    data_init_done                  ;the code is pic, if so skip init
        moval   name_loc,name+4                 ;fill in address of name in descriptor
        moval   msg_loc,message+4               ;fill in address of message descriptor
        moval   term_d_loc,term_d+4             ;fill in address of terminal descriptor
data_init_done:
        pushr   #^m<r0,r1,r2,r3,r4,r5>          ;save regs and synch w/ sched db
        jsb     ellis_nampid                    ;find out if he's out there
        blbs    r0,found                        ;if he is, go get him
        brw     escape                          ; else scram
found:  movl    #acb$k_length,r1                ;Allocate an ACB
        jsb     g^exe$alononpaged               ;
        blbs    r0,got_acb                      ;if we have pool, then fill it in
        brw     escape                          ;else scram
got_acb:
        movw    r1,acb$w_size(r2)               ;fill in the size of the acb for
                                                ; deallocation
        movb    #dyn$c_acb,-                    ;The type of structure is an acb
                acb$b_type(r2)
        moval   zap_ast,acb$l_ast(r2)           ;fill in address of AST routine
        movl    pid,acb$l_pid(r2)               ;fill in the target pid
        clrb    acb$b_rmod(r2)                  ;Make it a normal kernel ast
        movl    r2,r5                           ;R5 -> acb
        movl    #pri$_ticom,r2                  ;Give him a big boost (6)
        jsb     g^sch$qast                      ;Queue the AST
escape: popr    #^m<r0,r1,r2,r3,r4,r5>
```

Figure 34 contd.

```
        rsb                                     ;go back to sleep

        .subtitle  subroutine to look up process
;***********************************************************
;*      Subroutine:     ellis_nampid                     **
;*      Inputs:         name contains ascii descriptor with  **
;*                      process name to look up          **
;*      Outputs:        pid contains target pid if found **
;*                      r4 contains pcb of target        **
;*                      r0 contains status               **
;***********************************************************
ellis_nampid:
        lock    lockname=SCHED,lockipl=#ipl$_sched  ;synch w/ sched
        moval   name+8,r3                       ;r3 -> name of target process
        movzwl  name,r2                         ;r2 contains size of name
        movzwl  g^sch$gl_maxpix,r0              ;start at the end of the list
pixloop:
        movl    g^sch$gl_pcbvec,r5              ;R5 -> the pcb vector table
        movl    (r5)[r0],r1                     ;R1 -> next PCB
        cmpb    r2,pcb$t_lname(r1)              ;Is the name the same size
        bneq    nextpix                         ;if not get next pcb
        pushr   #^m<r0,r1,r2,r3,r4,r5>          ;save regs hosed on cmpc3
        cmpc3   r2,(r3),<pcb$t_lname+1>(r1)     ;Is it him
        popr    #^m<r0,r1,r2,r3,r4,r5>          ;restore the regs
        beql    gotnam                          ;branch out if we have him
nextpix:
        sobgtr  r0,pixloop                      ;get next pcb
no_proc:
        movzwl  #ss$_nonexpr,r0                 ;If we made it here then no match
        brw     leave_nampid
gotnam: movl    pcb$l_pid(r1),pid               ;save the process id
        bbs     #pcb$v_delpen,pcb$l_sts(r1),no_proc         ;Delete pending?
        bbs     #pcb$v_suspen,pcb$l_sts(r1),no_proc         ;Suspended?
        tstb    pcb$t_terminal(r1)              ;Is terminal associated w/ process?
        beql    no_proc                         ;If not, we can't blast message
        movl    #ss$_normal,r0                  ;success
        movl    r1,r4                           ;R4 -> target pcb
leave_nampid:
        unlock  lockname=SCHED,newipl=#ipl$_timer
        rsb                                     ;scram

        .subtitle       kernel mode ast to blast message

;***********************************************************
;*      Kernel mode ast procedure to blast message
;***********************************************************
        .entry  zap_ast,^m<r2,r3,r4,r5>
        movl    g^ctl$gl_pcb,r4                         ;get his pcb
        movb    pcb$t_terminal(r4),term_d               ;Get size of terminal name
        movc3   term_d,<pcb$t_terminal+1>(r4),@<term_d+4>       ;get term name
        $assign_s       chan=tchan,devnam=term_d  ;assign a channel to
                                                  ; his terminal
        blbc    r0,leave_ast
;Blast the message
        $qiow_s efn=#7,chan=tchan,func=#io$_writelblk,-
                p1=msg_ascii,p2=message,p4=#32
        $dassgn_s       chan=tchan              ;deassign the terminal channel
leave_ast:
        ret                                     ;let him continue
        .subtitle       kernel mode "pool" data

;***********************************************************
;*      Kernel mode "pool" data                           **
;*      Note data must be at end due to tqe pc field      **
;***********************************************************
pid:    .long   0                               ;Process id
name:   .long   0                               ;descriptor for process name
        .long   0                               ;  filled in at init time
name_loc:
        .blkb   15                              ;Process name
message:                                        ;descriptor for message
        .long   0                               ; filled in at init time
        .long   0
```

Figure 34 contd.

```
msg_loc:
msg_ascii:
        .blkb   132                         ;storage for message text
term_d: .long   0                           ;descriptor for process terminal name
        .long   0
term_d_loc:                                 ;storage for terminal name
        .blkb   15                          ;
tchan:  .blkl   1                           ;channel for terminal
zapper_code_len=.-zapper_code               ;length of code to be loaded into pool
zapper_end:
        .end    init_zapper
```

Figure 35. Output from running ZAPPER.

```
$set proc/priv=cmkrnl
$
$mac zapper
$link zapper
$
$r zapper
Enter process name> DCUTLERY
Enter string> FATAL MACHINE CHECK, Please logout and use another terminal.
$
$set proc/name=DCUTLERY
FATAL MACHINE CHECK, Please logout and use another terminal.
$
FATAL MACHINE CHECK, Please logout and use another terminal.
$set proc/name=ELLISB
$
$set proc/name=DCUTLERY
$
$sh sys
FATAL MACHINE CHECK, Please logout and use another terminal.
VAX/VMS V5.3-1  on node LABDOG  25-JUN-1990 01:08:42.92   Uptime  4 10:24:19
  Pid     Process Name    State  Pri     I/O       CPU       Page flts  Ph.Mem
00000021 SWAPPER          HIB     16       0   0 00:00:03.59         0       0
00000025 ERRFMT           HIB      8    3247   0 00:00:42.18        82     116
00000026 OPCOM            HIB      8     176   0 00:00:02.14       263     140
00000027 AUDIT_SERVER     HIB     10      39   0 00:00:01.87      1328     209
00000028 JOB_CONTROL      HIB      8     216   0 00:00:01.63       175     335
00000029 CONFIGURE        HIB      8       9   0 00:00:00.31        93     135
0000002A NETACP           HIB     10     205   0 00:01:18.98       211     374
0000002B EVL              HIB      6     146   0 00:00:34.82     96990      46  N
0000002C REMACP           HIB      9      22   0 00:00:00.26        78      45
0000002D SYMBIONT_0001    HIB      4      25   0 00:00:01.00       223     113
0000002E MULTINET_SERVER  HIB      6     296   0 00:00:16.58       438     243
0000002F SMTP_SYMBIONT    HIB      4      19   0 00:00:01.20       340      42
00000030 R7_DETACHED_01   HIB      4   28158   0 00:05:51.70     16364     159
00000056 SERVER_0006      LEF      6     212   0 00:00:06.40       861     206  N
00000057 SERVER_0005      LEF      6     200   0 00:00:05.25       718     200  N
00000058 DCUTLERY         CUR      4     333   0 00:00:33.97      2344     280
FATAL MACHINE CHECK, Please logout and use another terminal.
$
```

Appendix

On VMS Kernel Mode Time

VMS supports CPU execution in one of four modes: kernel, executive, supervisor, and user. The modes allow VMS to protect the system from the user and the user from himself. To isolate bottlenecks, it's important to be able to differentiate productive CPU time and system overhead.

Running in Elevated Access Modes

User programs will move from one access mode to another to perform activities on protected data areas, such as obtaining information about a process, increasing the process working set limit, and so on. This is the technique used when calling VMS system services. The program doesn't call the service directly, but instead calls a system service vector doubly mapped to P1 space from S0 space.

To execute in a more privileged mode, the user process issues a change mode to kernel, executive or supervisor (CHMK, CHME, or CHMS) instruction. No privilege is required to issue one of these instructions. The instructions cause the CPU to trap into a routine located through the system control block (SCB). The privilege checks are performed by the system service as required.

Note that the CMKRNL privilege is not required to run in kernel mode, because you're running under the auspices of the system service code. CMKRNL is required to call one service, $CMKRNL. This service is different from the others, in that your routine is called from kernel mode so that you can do whatever you please, including crashing the system, if you're not careful.

Characteristics of Kernel Mode Time

VMS kernel mode time will occur when system services are called explicitly. This case can be common in real-time system design, and you can expect to see a larger amount of kernel mode time in real-time systems.

In typical time-share systems, kernel mode time is often activated implicitly. Page faults are activated as exceptions in the context of the process. The exceptions are processed in kernel mode. Therefore, a system with a high page fault rate can experience a high amount of time in kernel mode.

By reducing the soft page fault rate, you will decrease the kernel mode time required to resolve soft faults. This can be done by increasing the working set sizes of processes, if there is sufficient free memory. Note that it is not possible to eliminate all soft faults, as the pager is the program loader. Because of image activation, you can expect to see some demand zero, free list, and global valid faults.

Other activities that can cause additional kernel mode time include logical name translations, I/O requests, lock management requests (because of accessing shared files), and file system requests to the extended QIO procedures (XQP).

By increasing the size of transfers (one 100-block transfer instead of 10 10-block transfers), you can cut down on kernel mode time supporting $QIOs.

There is little you can do about lock management requests and kernel mode time. When concurrency of file access is required by an application, RMS must take out locks to access the records within a file. If you are accessing a file primary exclusively, you can open it privately to minimize locking activity.

You can directly track time spent in kernel mode by the XQP. The $MONITOR FCP display provides the CPU tics charged against the XQP. By decreasing file system activities, like keeping files open instead of opening, closing and later opening the same file and cutting down on window turns by keeping files as contiguous as possible, you can decrease file system tics and in turn decrease kernel mode time.

You can monitor the time spent in each mode by using $MONITOR MODES. Kernel mode time generally is considered to be overhead, taking away CPU cycles from your user programs.

How much kernel mode time is too much? This is difficult to meter. I could give you the pat answer of 20 to 25 percent, which is probably somewhat valid. However, because of file sharing requirements, you can be stuck with 30 percent kernel mode time because of locking activities.

A more valuable approach might be to address the fact that kernel mode time can be unnecessary overhead and to work on decreasing the overhead.

Where does the 20 to 25 percent number come from? The VMS performance group has given out this number in an effort to give some direction. The general philosophy is that the sum of kernel and interrupt stack time should not exceed 40 percent of the CPU time, leaving at least 60 percent of the CPU cycles to do the real work.

What can you do about too much kernel mode time? You want to isolate the activities causing the kernel mode time and determine what, if anything, you can do about reducing this overhead. This is difficult to do when you have no metrics on which to gauge how much a soft fault costs or how much it costs to serve a block in a local area VAXcluster (LAVc).

Characteristics of VMS Executive Mode Time

Executive mode time is, for the most part, dedicated to the record management services (RMS). Executive mode time is a mixed blessing. If you are spending time here, it is, to a degree, overhead, inasmuch as you need to be able to access files, and RMS provides this capability. However, if RMS is running, this could be a good sign.

When you read a record from a file, RMS reads multiple blocks into your P1 space, based on your multiblock count and bucket size. By reading more into memory, there is a chance, and a very good chance if you are accessing a sequential file, that you might be able to satisfy the read of another record adjacent or near the one last read without having to do an I/O. When the system does not have to do an I/O, performance usually improves. So executive mode time can be a blessing in disguise.

Characteristics of VMS Supervisor Mode Time

Supervisor mode time is reserved primarily for the command language interpreter (CLI). The standard CLIs include Digital command language (DCL), the monitor console routines (MCR, or more fondly the monitor confusion routines) and the Bourne (again) shell. The CLIs are responsible for reading in a command line, parsing it (i.e., figuring what you are trying to tell it), and doing it internally or activating an image to do it.

If large amounts of supervisor mode time show up on the system, it is time to explain to your users that contrary to the new if-then-else clause, DCL is not a programming language. This is not to knock command procedures as a tool. For tools that are run infrequently, command procedures provide a quick, easy-to-maintain solution.

Command procedures are not the most optimal performers for long-term solutions, because they are interpreted and most DCL commands cause images to be activated. The interpreted nature could be resolved by some type of DCL compiler, but the real slowness of command procedure execution is more tied to the image activation problem. The key is to write programs, where possible, for better performing, long-term solutions.

Characteristics of VMS User Mode Time

User mode time is set aside for execution of user-supplied programs and utilities, such as the linker and directory commands. User mode time is why you bought the CPU. There are no SYSGEN parameters that will improve the execution of user mode time.

If you are tuning for throughput and the majority of the CPU is being consumed in user mode, consider either more efficient algorithms or a faster CPU. The goal of throughput tuning is to eliminate system overhead and use the CPU as much as possible until the completion of the job.

If you are tuning for response time, the goal is to be able to respond to user requests as quickly as possible. If the CPU is being 100-percent used, there are no remaining CPU cycles available to keep up with user requests as they are being made, so the CPU has become a bottleneck.

If the CPU is a bottleneck, try forcing CPU intensive applications to run in low priority batch queues. This will allow the higher priority interactive processes to grab the CPU as they need it. This can be enforced, assuming the user does not own the application file, by the following commands:

```
$SET FILE/ACL=(IDENTIFIER=*,ACCESS=NONE) CRUNCH.EXE
$SET FILE/ACL=(IDENTIFIER=BATCH,ACCESS=EXECUTE) CRUNCH.EXE
```

Another alternative in a VAXcluster environment is to establish a batch engine, which is tuned for batch processing with less processes running concurrently on that node. When they do run, they can have larger working sets so that they can crank more quickly through the system. The QUANTUM SYSGEN parameter can be set larger, to minimize rescheduling overhead. The interactive engines would be tuned with the opposite attributes.

For response time, QUANTUM can be lowered substantially. Thinking about QUANTUM, the default setting for the parameter is 20 in units of 10 ms. This means that if everything else is equal and five processes become computable at the same time, a process might have to wait up to a second for the CPU. This kind of strategy is probably acceptable for a 750 running 25 concurrent processes but might not be on a 8810 trying to run 250 concurrent processes.

As the speed of the CPU increases, a process can get more work done in a given time slice. The overhead to reschedule a process is fairly small, roughly a few hundred microseconds on a 1 VUP (VAX unit of performance or vague unit of performance, take your pick) VAX. This means dropping QUANTUM on a 1 VUP VAX to 2 (20 ms) can cause about a one- to three-percent increase in the interrupt stack time. On a 6 VUP VAX, this would drop to less than one percent. A QUANTUM of 2 would allow 50 computable processes to share the CPU a second, at a very small hit on faster VAXs.

Characteristics of VMS Interrupt Stack Time

When interrupts occur, the system is running in system context, and there is no guarantee of a current process. This time is charged against the interrupt stack and is not charged against any process. These costs are pre-emptive, in that process priorities become totally meaningless. When the interrupt is asserted, we go to the interrupt service routine and process the interrupt, blocking process activities. In general, you should shoot for no more than 15- to 20-percent interrupt stack time. You might be stuck with 30 to 40 percent with a boot member in an LAVc.

Primary causes of large amounts of interrupt stack time include programmed I/O devices, such as DZ-11s, distributed lock management requests, and mass storage control protocol (MSCP) server requests. Programmed I/O devices can be replaced by direct memory access (DMA) devices or run at a lower baud rate to spread the I/Os over time.

Distributed locking overhead might be detected by processes being placed in RWSCS wait states. The problem tends to become prominent when a single node masters the majority of resources within a VAXcluster. The locks, which typically tend to stay around, are device locks created when disks are initially mounted. You can detect the node processing the majority of locks by issuing the $MONITOR DLOCK command on each node and determining which node has the majority of incoming locking

(ENQ) operations. This likely will be the node mastering the device resource locks. To confirm this, you can use an unsupported-undocumented-can-go-away-at-any-time feature of VMS by issuing the following commands:

```
$DEFINE/USER SHOW$DEBUG ELLIS
$SHOW DEVICE/MOUNT
```

You will see information on all the device locks in the cluster for mounted devices. In the first set of parentheses, you will see the node that is mastering the locks. If they are all being mastered by the same node, consider dismounting the drives and selectively issuing $MOUNT/CLUSTER commands on the different nodes throughout the cluster. Or, you can try the Rambo approach and reboot the node. This will cause the locks to go up for grabs during the rebuild. The nodes will compete for the locks, and they should be distributed throughout the cluster based roughly on CPU speed.

MSCP server requests are somewhat CPU intensive on the serving node. This is why the boot member of an LAVc should be chosen carefully. The faster the node, to a point, the more quickly it can process server requests. This is also a good reason to keep a local page file on satellite members of an LAVc. More memory helps only if you can minimize modified page writing and does not compensate for the current flushing of the modified page list. Even if the modified page writing becomes selective, some writes will continue to happen frequently.

Characteristics of VMS MP Synchronization Time

Multiprocessing (MP) synchronization time is new for V5 of VMS and is only meaningful on symmetric multiprocessing (SMP) systems. To support SMP, a new type of system level synchronization was required above and beyond interrupt priority level (IPL). This synchronization was implemented by creating a set of data structures, called spinlocks, and assigning them to key databases accessed by privileged code within VMS. When access to the database is required by a CPU, that CPU acquires the spinlock.

Acquiring the spinlock means that we check an in-use bit. If it's clear, we set the bit with an interlocked memory instruction. If it's set, we spin and wait for it to become clear. The time spent spinning is wasted CPU cycles and shows up as MP synchronization time.

You have little control over this time and generally write it off as overhead. However, if it's high, it could be because of high contention for the I/O fork lock for IPL8. By minimizing the I/O load on the system, the MP synchronization time also should decrease.

Characteristics of VMS Idle Time

VMS idle time is made up of unused CPU cycles. From a throughput standpoint, these are lost cycles, and I/O related activities can be blocking processes from using these cycles. When tuning for throughput, you ideally shoot for zero idle time.

From a response time viewpoint, idle time is an indicator of reserve CPU cycles that will be available when users demand them. On response time systems, shoot for some idle time. Ideally 25 to 40 percent should be a sufficient amount of idle time, depending on how responsive the requirements of the system are. This won't make the bean counters happy, but you can explain that the most costly component of a transaction processing system is people costs.

Traditionally, you could track idle CPU time by obtaining the CPU time of the null process. SMP did away with the null process. (It doesn't make sense to keep six null processes around.) VMS, now, tracks idle time on a per-CPU basis in the scheduler code.

To obtain the idle CPU time on a V5 system, you can access the per-CPU database. Each CPU (identified by a CPU/ID) has a CPU structure. The structure has a field located in it, CPU$L_NULLCPU, that contains the idle CPU time for this processor in 10 ms tics since the last boot.

To locate the CPU structures, VMS supports a table located at SMP$GL_CPU_DATA that contains 32 longwords that either contain 0 or point to the CPU structure. The valid entries can be accessed by using the CPU/ID of the valid CPUs as a longword index. The bit mask, SMP$GL_ACTIVE_CPUS has a bit set for each valid CPU/ID for this system. The program SH_IDLE.MAR illustrates accessing the CPU structures and displaying the idle time, as well as up time, and time in modes since the last boot (see Appendix Figure 1). Note: The CPU structures are user readable, so no privileged code is required here. Even if you make a mistake, the system will not crash.

Analyzing the Cost of a Soft Fault

To determine where your kernel mode time is being spent, it might be nice to know the cost of primitive system operations that are tracked in the monitor utility, such as soft faults, $QIOs, logical name translations, and so on. These numbers are not generally accessible. So I ran several studies to approximate the cost of some of these operations (see Appendix Figure 2).

The numbers presented are as accurate as I could make them based on the test limitations. Before using these numbers, you should understand the limitations of the methods used to obtain the data. These numbers are intended only to be rough approximations of these costs and should not be abused in comparison studies. The studies are CPU measures and, therefore, should roughly follow VUP rules. In other words, if a soft fault takes 520 microseconds on a MicroVAX II, it should take roughly 85 to 95 microseconds on an 8810 (6 VUPs). I welcome your studies and provide the test program for soft faults as a simple guide. SOFT.MAR (see Appendix Figure 3) runs with no privileged code.

The Test Environment

To determine the cost of a soft fault, I wrote a program that generated many soft faults. The soft faults were generated in the same way as ALL-IN-1 might generate them, by using poor locality in accessing large amounts of data. Working set limit, quota, and extent were set to 300 pages during the test.

To minimize the noise factor on the test, everything was locked into the working set of the process, except the data area that we were faulting. The process generating the faults ran at priority 31. This blocks the swapper process from writing the modified page list, assuming the process is not forced into RWMPB state in attempting to place a page on the modified page list. The RWMPB state was prevented by raising the parameter MPW_WAITLIMIT to 16000 during the test. The swapper CPU time was tracked to make sure he did not run. I also checked the number of modified page writes to make sure that the list was not written during the test. The test had a mix of roughly 4000 demand zero faults and 500,000 modified list faults. The demand zero faults should be about 50 to 55 microseconds (1 VUP) slower because of the MOVC5 instruction required to zero the page. The modified list faults should be roughly equal to the calculated values because of the number of samples. Free list faults and global valid faults should be very close to the cost of the modified list faults, based on the operations required to complete the fault.

Locking the pages had minimal effect on the runs, running slightly faster than non-locking. In fact, in non-MicroVAX II systems, the number of faults generated was the same in both cases because of the translation buffer skip working list (TBSKIPWSL) parameter.

Interpreting the Results

The only valid interpretation of the results is the following: If you are generating, say, 100 soft faults a second on a 750 running V5.0-1, you can expect that soft faulting is taking up roughly 6.5 percent of your CPU in kernel mode. Eliminating the soft faults would free up that CPU time for user programs. The same load on a 8350 would be using roughly 5.6 percent of the CPU.

In the difference between timings in V5.0 and V5.0-1, you might note that the 750 and the 8350 were faster while the MicroVAX II is slower. I can only speculate that it is somehow related to code that either performs the TBSKIPWSL check more efficiently or that somehow uses the caches on these systems more effectively.

Other Studies

A similar test was done to evaluate the CPU costs of $QIO by doing zero byte $QIOs to OPA0:. The tests were done at priority 31 with a priority 30 process looping to eat up remaining CPU cycles. These tests showed the no-op $QIO taking 1.141 ms on a MicroVAX II running V4.5 and 1.447 ms on a MicroVAX II running V5.0. Other devices should produce similar results, with the exception of the terminal driver doing formatted I/O, which scales linearly based on the size of the transfer.

More primitive tests were run using $MONITOR to track time in modes while only performing a single set of operations. These tests showed MSCP-server costs for doing three block writes in a mixed interconnect VAXcluster at 10.5 ms per transfer on a 8350 and 19 ms per transfer on a 750, both times showing up on the interrupt stack of the server node. Logical name translations of SYS$SYSTEM and SYS$LOGIN, using the default search, took roughly 1 ms of kernel mode time on a 1 VUP VAX. This set of numbers should be taken as loose approximations, because of the simplistic nature of the tests.

USE THESE NUMBERS as an aid and not a crutch, and you might be able to trim kernel mode time off your system. More important, you should be able to predict the effects of changes that you make.

—Bruce Ellis

Appendix Figure 1.

```
;^^^^^^^^^^^^^^^^^^^^^^^^^^^^^^^^^^^^^^^^^^^^^^^^^^^^^^^^^^
;       Program:        sh_idle.mar
;       Author:         Bruce Ellis
;       Function:       Formats and spills the time spent in modes
;                       and the up time for each CPU on the system
;                       using the CPU specific structures.
;^^^^^^^^^^^^^^^^^^^^^^^^^^^^^^^^^^^^^^^^^^^^^^^^^^^^^^^^^^
;macro to check status
        .macro check  ?1
        blbs   r0,1
        $exit_s         r0
1:
        .endm  check
;include system macro library
        .library        /sys$library:lib.mlb/
;link against the system system table
        .link           /sys$system:sys.stb/
        $cpudef         ;Per-CPU database offsets
        $pcbdef         ;Software process control block offsets
        $phddef         ;Process header offsets
;^^^^^^^^^^^^^^^^^^^^^^^^^^^^^^^^^^^^^^^^^^^^^^^^^^^^^^^^^^
;       Offsets from kernel mode time in cpu structure to
;       executive, supervisor, user, int stack, compatability
;       mode, and MP synchronization times
;^^^^^^^^^^^^^^^^^^^^^^^^^^^^^^^^^^^^^^^^^^^^^^^^^^^^^^^^^^
exec=4
super=8
user=12
int=16
compat=20
MPsynch=24
;^^^^^^^^^^^^^^^^^^^^^^^^^^^^^^^^^^^^^^^^^^^^^^^^^^^^^^^^^^
;       Format statements for $FAO
;^^^^^^^^^^^^^^^^^^^^^^^^^^^^^^^^^^^^^^^^^^^^^^^^^^^^^^^^^^
fmth:   .ascid $!/!/Time spent in modes, since last boot, for CPU id !UB: !/$
fmt1:   .ascid $Kernel  !10UL0ms  Exec     !10UL0ms  $-
               $!/Super   !10UL0ms  User     !10UL0ms$-
               $!/Int Stk !10UL0ms$
fmt2:   .ascid $Compat  !10UL0ms  MP synch !10UL0ms  !/Idle     !10UL0ms$-
               $!/UP time !10ULsec  Up tics  !10UL0ms$
;buffer for string storage
buf:    .long  300
        .address        10$
10$:    .blkb  300
real_int:
        .blkl  1       ;Storage for actual interrupt stack time
;^^^^^^^^^^^^^^^^^^^^^^^^^^^^^^^^^^^^^^^^^^^^^^^^^^^^^^^^^^
;       Start of main program
;       flow:
;               get CPU structure
;               dump stats
;^^^^^^^^^^^^^^^^^^^^^^^^^^^^^^^^^^^^^^^^^^^^^^^^^^^^^^^^^^
        .entry sh_idle,^m<r2,r3,r4,r5,r6>
        movl    g^smp$gl_active_cpus,r2       ;Get mask of valid cpu-ids
get_next:
        ffs     #0,#32,r2,r3                  ;locate the next cpu
        bneq    process_this_guy              ;process next cpu
        brw     got_em_all                    ;scram when no more exist
process_this_guy:
        bbcc    r3,r2,10$                     ;clear current cpu-id in saved mask
10$:
;^^^^^^^^^^^^^^^^^^^^^^^^^^^^^^^^^^^^^^^^^^^^^^^^^^^^^^^^^^
;       Format and spill the cpu id header info
;^^^^^^^^^^^^^^^^^^^^^^^^^^^^^^^^^^^^^^^^^^^^^^^^^^^^^^^^^^
        $fao_s ctrstr=fmth,outbuf=buf,outlen=buf,p1=r3
        check
        pushal buf
        calls  #1,g^lib$put_output
        movl   #300,buf                       ;Reset buffer size
        movl   smp$gl_cpu_data[r3],r4         ;locate cpu local data
        moval  cpu$l_kernel(r4),r5            ;get base of times
        subl3  cpu$l_nullcpu(r4),int(r5)-     ;factor idle time out of
               ,real_int                      ;  int. stack time
```

Appendix Figure 1 contd.

```
;^^^^^^^^^^^^^^^^^^^^^^^^^^^^^^^^^^^^^^^^^^^^^^^^^^^^^^^^^^^^^^
;       Format and spill the time in kernel, executive,
;       supervisor, user, and int. stack
;^^^^^^^^^^^^^^^^^^^^^^^^^^^^^^^^^^^^^^^^^^^^^^^^^^^^^^^^^^^^^^
        $fao_s  ctrstr=fmt1,outbuf=buf,outlen=buf,p1=(r5),-
                p2=exec(r5),-
                p3=super(r5),-
                p4=user(r5),-
                p5=real_int
        check
        pushal  buf
        calls   #1,g^lib$put_output
        movl    #300,buf                        ;reset the buffer size
;^^^^^^^^^^^^^^^^^^^^^^^^^^^^^^^^^^^^^^^^^^^^^^^^^^^^^^^^^^^^^^
;       Format and spill the time in compatability mode, MP
;       synchronization, idle, up time in seconds and up time in tics
;^^^^^^^^^^^^^^^^^^^^^^^^^^^^^^^^^^^^^^^^^^^^^^^^^^^^^^^^^^^^^^
        $fao_s  ctrstr=fmt2,outbuf=buf,outlen=buf,p1=compat(r5),-
                p2=MPsynch(r5),-
                p3=cpu$l_nullcpu(r4),-
                p4=g^exe$gl_abstim,-
                p5=g^exe$gl_abstim_tics
        check
        pushal  buf
        calls   #1,g^lib$put_output
        movl    #300,buf                        ;reset the buffer size
        brw     get_next                        ;get next cpu
got_em_all:
        movl    #ss$_normal,r0                  ;success
        ret
        .end    sh_idle
```

Appendix Figure 2. Test Results in Microseconds.

Version/ condition	CPU		
	750	MicroVAX II	8350
V4 (lock)	n/a	452 (V4.5)	488 (V4.7)
V5.0 (lock)	714	519	596
V5.0-1 (nolock)	650	546	565
V5.0-1 (lock)	652	529	554

Appendix Figure 3.

```
;^^^^^^^^^^^^^^^^^^^^^^^^^^^^^^^^^^^^^^^^^^^^^^^^^^^^^^^^^^^^^^
;       Program:        soft.mar
;       Author:         Bruce Ellis
;       Function:       Used to calculate the cost of soft
;                       faults on the system.
;       Assumptions:    To be run stand-alone, at priority 31
;                       with wsquota, wsdefault, and wsextent
;                       set to 300, MPW_WAITLIMIT should be
;                       set to 16000 to prevent modified page
;                       writing.
;^^^^^^^^^^^^^^^^^^^^^^^^^^^^^^^^^^^^^^^^^^^^^^^^^^^^^^^^^^^^^^
;macro to check status
        .macro check    ?1
        blbs    r0,1
        $exit_s         r0
1:
```

Appendix Figure 3 contd.

```
        .endm  check
 ;include system macro library
        .library        /sys$library:lib.mlb/
 ;link against the system system table
        .link           /sys$system:sys.stb/
        $cpudef         ;Per-CPU database offsets
        $pcbdef         ;Software process control block offsets
        $phddef         ;Process header offsets
 ;Large array to fault on
 big:   .blkl  512*1024
 ;Address of sections of code and data to lock
 code_lock:
        .address        c_s     ;Start address to lock
        .address        c_e     ;Ending address to lock
 c_s:
 ;^^^^^^^^^^^^^^^^^^^^^^^^^^^^^^^^^^^^^^^^^^^^^^^^^^^^^^^^^^^^^^^^
 ;      Area for system times and counters
 ;      Note:  Order and adjacency IS IMPORTANT
 ;      1) kernel time 2) write ios 3) hard faults
 ;      4) total faults 5) cpu time 6) swapper cpu time
 ;^^^^^^^^^^^^^^^^^^^^^^^^^^^^^^^^^^^^^^^^^^^^^^^^^^^^^^^^^^^^^^^^
 k_start:
        .blkl           1       ;starting system kernel time
 write_s:.blkl          1       ;starting write I/Os
 hard_s: .blkl          1       ;starting hard faults
 fault_s:.blkl          1       ;starting process faults
 cpu_s:  .blkl          1       ;starting process cpu time
 swp_s:  .blkl          1       ;starting swapper cpu time
 k_end:
        .blkl           1       ;ending system kernel time
 write_e:.blkl          1       ;ending write I/Os
 hard_e: .blkl          1       ;ending hard faults
 fault_e:.blkl          1       ;ending process faults
 cpu_e:  .blkl          1       ;ending process cpu time
 swp_e:  .blkl          1       ;ending swapper cpu time
 ;^^^^^^^^^^^^^^^^^^^^^^^^^^^^^^^^^^^^^^^^^^^^^^^^^^^^^^^^^^^^^^^^
 ;      Format statements for $FAO
 ;^^^^^^^^^^^^^^^^^^^^^^^^^^^^^^^^^^^^^^^^^^^^^^^^^^^^^^^^^^^^^^^^
 fmt1:  .ascid /kernel: !10ULOms   Process CPU: !10ULOms  swapper: !10ULOms/
 fmt2:  .ascid /total faults: !10UL  Hard faults: !10UL  Writes: !10UL/
 ;buffer for string storage
 buf:   .long  80
        .address        10$
 10$:   .blkb  80
 ;^^^^^^^^^^^^^^^^^^^^^^^^^^^^^^^^^^^^^^^^^^^^^^^^^^^^^^^^^^^^^^^^
 ;      Start of main program
 ;      flow:  lock down all but array
 ;             get start stats
 ;             generate faults
 ;             get stats end
 ;             dump stats
 ;^^^^^^^^^^^^^^^^^^^^^^^^^^^^^^^^^^^^^^^^^^^^^^^^^^^^^^^^^^^^^^^^
        .entry faulter,^m<r2,r3,r4,r5,r6>
        $lkwset_s      inadr=code_lock        ;lock everything except paged data
        check
        moval  big,r2                 ;point to array
        movl   #512,r6                ;set up outer loop counter
        clrl   r3                     ;index=0
        pushal k_start                ;pass array of stat variables
        calls  #1,get_fault           ;get stats
 out:   addl3  r3,r2,r4               ;compute address of data item
                                      ;touch every 4th page
        movl   #1024,r5               ;set inner loop counter
 in:    movl   #2,(r4)                ;touch data
        addl   #512*4,r4              ;get next data item 4 pages away
        sobgtr r5,in                  ;loop on inner till done
        addl   #4,r3                  ;point to next data item
        sobgtr r6,out                 ;loop on outer till done
 skip:
        pushal k_end                  ;pass array of ending stats
        calls  #1,get_fault           ;get ending stats
        subl2  swp_s,swp_e            ;calculate cumulative swapper cpu time
        subl2  cpu_s,cpu_e            ;calculate cumulative process cpu time
```

Appendix Figure 3 contd.

```
        subl2  write_s,write_e      ;calculate cumulative write ios
        subl2  k_start,k_end        ;calculate cumulative kernel time
        subl2  hard_s,hard_e        ;calculate cumulative hard faults
        subl2  fault_s,fault_e      ;calculate cumulative faults
;^^^^^^^^^^^^^^^^^^^^^^^^^^^^^^^^^^^^^^^^^^^^^^^^^^^^^^^^^^^
;       Format and spill the crud
;^^^^^^^^^^^^^^^^^^^^^^^^^^^^^^^^^^^^^^^^^^^^^^^^^^^^^^^^^^^
        $fao_s ctrstr=fmt1,outbuf=buf,outlen=buf,p1=k_end,p2=cpu_e-
               p3=swp_e
        check
        pushal buf
        calls  #1,g^lib$put_output
        movl   #80,buf                      ;Reset buffer size
        $fao_s ctrstr=fmt2,outbuf=buf,outlen=buf,p1=fault_e,p2=hard_e,-
               p3=write_e
        check
        pushal buf
        calls  #1,g^lib$put_output
        ret
;^^^^^^^^^^^^^^^^^^^^^^^^^^^^^^^^^^^^^^^^^^^^^^^^^^^^^^^^^^^
;       Subroutine to get stats
;       Input: 4(ap) -> Array of 6 longwords
;       Outputs:        Array will contain
;       1) kernel time 2) write ios 3) hard faults
;       4) total faults 5) cpu time 6) swapper cpu time
;^^^^^^^^^^^^^^^^^^^^^^^^^^^^^^^^^^^^^^^^^^^^^^^^^^^^^^^^^^^
        .entry get_fault,^m<r3,r5,r6,r7>
        movl   4(ap),r6                     ;Get address of buffer
        movl   g^smp$gl_active_cpus,r5      ;Get mask of valid cpu-ids
        clrl   r7                           ;clear the kernel mode accumulator
next_cpu_s:
        ffs    #0,#32,r5,r0                 ;locate the next cpu
        beql   done_s                       ;scram when no more exist
        bbcc   r0,r5,10$                    ;clear current cpu-id in saved mask
10$:    movl   smp$gl_cpu_data[r0],r0       ;locate cpu local data
        addl   cpu$l_kernel(r0),r7          ;accumulate kernel time on all cpus
        brb    next_cpu_s                   ;get next cpu
done_s:        movl    r7,(r6)+             ;return total kernel mode time
        movl   g^pms$gl_pwritio,(r6)+       ;return total write ios
        movl   g^ctl$gl_phd,r5              ;Get user-readable ptr to process hdr
        movl   phd$l_pgfltio(r5),(r6)+      ;return hard faults
        movl   phd$l_pageflts(r5),(r6)+     ;return total faults
        movl   phd$l_cputim(r5),(r6)+       ;return total cpu time
        movl   g^sch$ar_swppcb,r3           ;get swapper pcb
        movl   pcb$l_phd(r3),r3             ;get his phd
        movl   phd$l_cputim(r3),(r6)+       ;return swapper cputime
        movl   #ss$_normal,r0               ;success
        ret                                 ;beat it
c_e:
        .end   faulter
```

Bibliography

Adams, Douglas. *The Hitchhiker's Guide to the Galaxy*. New York: Pocket Books, a division of Simon & Schuster, Inc., 1981.

Adams, Douglas. *The Restaurant at the End of the Universe*. New York: Pocket Books, a division of Simon & Schuster, Inc., 1982.

Adams, Douglas. *Life, the Universe and Everything*. New York: Pocket Books, a division of Simon & Schuster, Inc., 1983.

Adams, Douglas. *So Long and Thanks For All The Fish*. New York: Harmony Books, a division of Crown Publishers, 1985.

Kenah, Lawrence J., Ruth E. Goldenberg, and Simon F. Bate. *Version 4.4 VAX/VMS Internals and Data Structures*. Bedford, Massachusetts: Digital Press Bedford, 1988.

Kenah, Lawrence J. and Ruth E. Goldenberg. *VMS Internals and Data Structures, Volume 1 Version 5 Update XPRESS*. Bedford, Massachusetts: Digital Press, 1989.

Kenah, Lawrence J. and Ruth E. Goldenberg. *VMS Internals and Data Structures, Volume 2 Version 5 Update XPRESS*. Bedford, Massachusetts: Digital Press, 1989.

Kenah, Lawrence J. and Ruth E. Goldenberg. *VMS Internals and Data Structures, Volume 3 Version 5 Update XPRESS*. Bedford, Massachusetts: Digital Press, 1989.

Kenah, Lawrence J. and Ruth E. Goldenberg. *VMS Internals and Data Structures, Volume 4 Version 5 Update XPRESS*. Bedford, Massachusetts: Digital Press, 1990.

VMS Device Support. Maynard, Massachusetts: Digital Equipment Corporation, 1988.

VMS Linker Reference Manual. Maynard, Massachusetts: Digital Equipment Corporation, 1988.

VMS Record Management Services Reference Manual. Maynard, Massachusetts: Digital Equipment Corporation, 1988.

VMS System Services Reference Manual. Maynard, Massachusetts: Digital Equipment Corporation, 1988.